Politics of Educational Innovations in Developing Countries

Reference Books in International Education
Volume 46
Garland Reference Library of Social Science
Volume 1190

Politics of Educational Innovations in Developing Countries
An Analysis of Knowledge and Power

Edited by
Nelly P. Stromquist
Michael L. Basile

Falmer Press
a member of the Taylor & Francis Group
New York and London
1999

Library of Congress Cataloging-in-Publication Data is available through the
Library of Congress.

ISBN 0-8153-3155-X

Printed on acid-free, 250-year-life paper
Manufactured in the United States of America

Contents

SERIES EDITOR'S PREFACE

This series of scholarly works in comparative and international education has grown well beyond the initial conception of a collection of reference books. Although retaining its original purpose of providing a resource to scholars, students, and a variety of other professionals who need to understand the role played by education in various societies or world regions, it also strives to provide accurate, relevant, and up-to-date information on a wide variety of selected educational issues, problems, and experiments within an international context.

Contributors to this series are well-known scholars who have devoted their professional lives to the study of their specializations. Without exception these men and women possess an intimate understanding of the subject of their research and writing. Without exception they have studied their subject not only in dusty archives, but have lived and traveled widely in their quest for knowledge. In short, they are "experts" in the best sense of that often overused word.

In our increasingly interdependent world, it is now widely understood that it is a matter of military, economic, and environmental survival that we understand better not only what makes other societies tick, but also how others, be they Japanese, Hungarian, South African, or Chilean, attempt to solve the same kinds of educational problems that we face in North America. As the late George Z. F. Bereday wrote more than three decades ago: "[E]ducation is a mirror held against the face of a people. Nations may put on blustering shows of strength to conceal public weakness, erect grand façades to conceal shabby backyards, and profess peace while secretly arming for conquest, but how they take care of their children tells unerringly who they are" (*Comparative Methods in Education*, New York: Holt, Rinehart and Winston, 1964, p. 5).

Perhaps equally important, however, is the valuable perspective that studying another education system (or its problems) provides us in understanding our own system (or its problems). When we step beyond our own limited experience and our commonly held assumptions about schools and learning in order to look back at our system in contrast to another, we see it in a very different light. To learn, for example, how China or Belgium handles the education of a multilingual society, how the French provide for the funding of public education, or how the Japanese control access to their universities enables us to better understand that there are reasonable alternatives to our own familiar way of doing things. Not that we can borrow directly from other societies. Indeed, educational arrangements are inevitably a reflection of deeply embedded political, economic, and cultural factors that are unique to a particular society. But a conscious recognition that there are other ways of doing things can serve to open our minds and provoke our imaginations in ways that can result in new experiments or approaches that we may not have otherwise considered.

Since this series is intended to be a useful research tool, the editor and contributors welcome suggestions for future volumes, as well as ways in which this series can be improved.

Edward R. Beauchamp
University of Hawaii

Preface

The set of innovation case studies presented herein was built gradually over a period of years, as instances of educational change of singular interest began to be accumulated. A special effort was made to obtain studies that would be prepared by persons who were closely involved with an educational innovation because they were associated with its evaluation or monitoring, because they played a partial role in its implementation, or because they were there to observe the innovation efforts during their years of evolution. What we obtained over this incremental process of case study collection, therefore, has been firsthand detail yet with some distance and without defensiveness of what was analyzed. While it was not possible to obtain complete parallelism in the way issues were treated in each innovation, we are confident that the main issues in each of them have been effectively addressed.

Because the contributions to this volume came at different points in time, we present cases that are drawn from different periods and philosophies of educational development. We make the argument that there is much to learn from past experiences and that sometimes the emphasis to rely only on very recent or contemporary developments prevents reflection on matters and processes that have much to teach us. It was, in fact, after reflecting on the innovations presented by several contributors that we, the editors, considered producing a final chapter re-examining the case studies from a more critical perspective. It is out of that retrospective standpoint that a singular interest in knowledge-making and its dependence on political and historical position emerged.

As editors, we are impressed with the extent to which that interest and its connections with administrative power emerged so clearly, spanning the passage of years and the different political, cultural, and historical contexts in which the innovations were first applied. Considering the absence of direct attention to this issue provided to the individual authors when the studies were commissioned originally, it surprised us that their struggles with making sense of what happened made such common ground for reflection and meta-analysis. The fact we should have been surprised at all was what prompted us to look on the studies in a new and critical light.

The intellectual trajectory that we have travelled in soliciting, finding, and editing the innovations presented here has taught us that the concept of "educational innovation" is elusive because not only does it take many forms and levels at initial moments but over time it becomes modified according to the wills of implementors, contextual forces, and dominant political forces. Innovations usually become absorbed by the prevailing features of their environment; seldom do they create radically new ways of conducting old practices or assesing them. On the other hand, innovations frequently leave their marks on organizations. They do so by affecting individuals much more than stucures or procedures. Several of those persons directly linked to the innovation or affected by it develop new mindsets or go on to new positions with the benifit of their experience in the educational innovation. In this regard, it is extremly helpful to know what occurs when innovations reach educational systems. They seldom fulfill their claimed offical intentions but do bring energy into the system, and in doing so create spaces for new insights and posibilities for some of its institutional members.

In this book, we use the term "politics" in a nonconventional sense. We apply it not to the interaction between explicit antagonistic interest groups or to the government-community nexus but to the constant subtext that characterizes modifications of ongoing organizational procedures and structures. The persons in these transactions are often far from occupying similar levels of power and distant also from emerging as explicit protagonists. Yet, their actions—political in nature because they address the direction and degree of influence—affect the shape and longevity of the innovations. The unavoidable interplay of knowledge and power is evident in the pragmatic, social status quo criteria used to assess the success of the innvoations as well as in the host of critical issues regarding the engagement and ability to shape the innovation of the intended beneficiaries that are left unexamined.

To the authors who answered our queries with patience and understanding, our thanks for their constant support. To our families, for their willingness to put up with yet more time taken away from them, our deep and public recognition. We remain appreciative of the assistance given Garland Publishing in the persons of Becca MacLaren, Marion Corkett, Chuck Bartelt, and Brian Phillips, whose different types of expertise brought this book to a happy and prompt conclusion.

Nelly P. Stromquist
University of Southern California
Los Angeles

Michael L. Basile
Murray State University
Murray

Politics of Educational Innovations in Developing Countries

1 CONCEPTUAL AND EMPIRICAL ISSUES IN EDUCATIONAL INNOVATIONS

Nelly P. Stromquist

Change does not always bring improvement, but when people feel that conditions have fallen to levels below satisfaction, there develops among some the hope that change—any change—will create a situation better than the status quo. As educational systems expand with more diversity among students, as these systems face new sets of societal demands—be it for economic competitiveness or for social solidarity, and as they run up against increasingly serious economic constraints, the search for "innovations" becomes a continuing and, at times, obsessive pursuit.

At one point in the change process, a change effort becomes an innovation, but exactly where in the process this occurs is highly variable. Complicating the definition is the observation that an innovation is simply something that is new to a given system; it does not mean that what is being attempted is new to other educational systems. Improvement to the system itself can take many forms: lower costs, greater skills within the teaching force, greater access by students to school, greater professionalism on the part of the teachers. In many respects "innovation" is in the eye of the beholder. Efforts that seem systemwide transformations to some may in fact represent merely slight reconfigurations of existing educational practices and structures. Conversely, what appears at one point to be a highly localized measure may have significant effects in other parts of the educational system. The precise amount of disturbance created by an innovation will vary from organization to organization and will most likely be connected to the particular actors involved and to their own time-space configurations. All this does not mean that one cannot define innovation; rather, definitions will be multiple and often metaphorical instead of operational in nature.

Innovations can be conceptualized as an instance of a broad phenomenon of organizational change. In this book, paraphrasing a definition first proposed by Tushman and Anderson (1986), we define innovations as the application or attempt to apply a discrete solution to a problem or process. This focused solution may be intended to affect the organizational structure, its functions, or its culture.

EDUCATIONAL SYSTEMS AND INNOVATIONS

Schools are particular organizations. They are what have been called "institutionalized organizations" (Meyer and Rowan, 1977), or entities that by virtue of functioning on the basis of a social charter are not going to suffer major questioning if they fail to deliver or are not going to disappear even in the long run because they are too much a part of the social construction of reality.

Because schools have conventional ways of operating, it is difficult and often unnecessary for them to engage in drastic changes. Their legitimacy is often based on the expectation that certain instructional processes are not going to be dramatically different from those of the past. Institutionalized organizations do not behave on the basis of feedback from users or classrooms to decision makers; rather they function on the basis of rules, routines, and scripts. In consequence, schools develop weak internal feedback mechanisms (e.g., feedback emanating from production [the teaching process in our case] to decision makers) (Morris, 1997). Often, it is easier for the educational system to change administrative features than instructional practices. Why should this be so? One explanation is that instruction is the core activity of schools, whereas administrative procedures are more generic and apply to organizations that seek to be rational, efficient, and modern.

WHEN DO EDUCATIONAL SYSTEMS INNOVATE?

Various organizational observers have noted that educational systems suffer from uncertainty: vague goals, indeterminate technology—features that create a difficult environment for identifying appropriate innovations (March and Simon, 1959; Morris, 1997). In part due to this uncertainty, many of the innovations affecting schools come from elsewhere or are top-down.

Usually government agencies push the educational system into adoption of new measures by way of legislation, court orders, and administrative incentives or restrictions. When innovations are initiated from within the system, most have been introduced by top-level administrators.

Some members of organizations, especially their leaders, are influenced by outside actors (Elkin, 1983); part of this influence includes exposure to new ideas, which may subsequently lead to the adoption of innovations. Under conditions of unclear technology and risk avoidance, the adoption of innovations through imitation offers advantages. Innovations that have been tried elsewhere reduce the amount of risk for new takers. Also, reproducing innovations tested (even if partially) in other and perhaps more prestigious settings legitimizes the adoption of innovations as being a reflection of good leadership. Social contagion travels well.

A typical occurrence in the adoption of innovations via imitation is that the new adopters will pick and choose from among its elements those judged to be the most suitable (or expedient) to the new location. While today there is little expectation that innovation adopters will engage in a completely faithful adoption of the original, it is also understood that adopters cannot merely select the features they like without a thorough understanding of how these features will represent a meaningful whole.

Innovations are attempted for a variety of reasons: Officially, they all seek to improve the efficiency and/or effectiveness of the educational system. Subrosa reasons are numerous, but they include the political expedience of endorsing a solution to the many problems of education or enhancing the replication of social norms.

Innovations sought as genuine solutions to problems constitute cases of educational exploration. They incur some risk and thus tend to be quite limited within educational systems. Since there are social expectations about how schools should behave, "legitimacy may require that instructional innovations not differ radically from those in the past" (DiMaggio and Powell, 1983, p. 150; see also Meyer and Rowan, 1977).

UNDERSTANDING INNOVATIONS

Innovation theory and research is a field that has been in existence for several decades, perhaps since Roger's (1962) work on the diffusion of innovations. According to Knapp (1997, p. 248) three main theoretical emphases have characterized the study of innovations: (1) seeing innovations as efforts to diffuse new practices. This emphasis looks primarily at the processes that facilitate diffusion. It looks also at the "change agent" and at the obstacles that may interfere with acceptance of the new messages regarding the benefits of the proposed change; (2) emphasis on the dynamics of innovation implementation. This approach highlights the way policy intentions interact with contextual forces throughout a multilevel policy system. It sees policies as sets of intentions that are constantly reinterpreted by other actors in the system and this re-reading is said to account for the variation in implementation; and (3) the view that change is the product of individual learning throughout the system and ultimately of learning by the system itself. This third perspective emphasizes organizational learning and examines the extent to which individuals and the organization to which they belong have an opportunity to learn about the innovation and thus appropriate it. Knapp (1997) distinguishes two types of organizational learning: the first concentrates on the opportunities for learning by individuals; the second would examine how institutional memory is created and how organizational routines and rituals support or hinder the exercise of the new idea. This third perspective makes clear, however, that learning is not synonymous with action. Change agents would still need to look at other structures such as incentives, environmental pressures, and the collective sense of directions to understand how to make change occur (Knapp, 1997, pp. 252–254).

In the United States there have been advances in the conceptualization of innovations, moving from faithful adoption to greater conceptual and theoretical understanding of how these reforms may actually affect classroom practices. There is great interest today in understanding how systemic (comprehensive) reform can be attained. It should be observed, however, that often the American search for system reform is based on an inward vision, focusing on the educational system and its intended clientele rather than on socioeconomic and political conditions that shape the functioning of the educational system. A problem piercing U.S. society today is the question of race, particularly the condition of its Afro-American and Hispanic populations. This problem is not explicitly addressed in educational change efforts; therefore (1) it is unresolved by the new strategies, procedures, and technologies, and (2) it underplays the crucial (dis)engagement of other societal sectors (e.g., ethnic and racial minorities).

We still have not learned much about when innovations succeed, and it is probable that such learning will be modest at best. In past studies, those conducted predominantly in the United States, much analysis took place with quantitative methods, focusing on selected variables and usually fragmenting context; they also gave more importance to the question of adoption over implementation. Studies on innovations by governmental agencies at city levels found as most important the leaders and coalitions of proponents in the adoption process. Other studies highlighted the importance of the visibility of the innovations and the degree of certainty as to their costs and effectiveness (for a fuller discussion, see Elkin, 1983). But, since organizations are sites characterized by dynamics of rich interaction between and among individuals and subunits, quantitative analyses have not provided much light on the process of adoption. Moreover, there has been a marked shift in the intellectual interest, which has moved from adoption to implementation and institutionalization. This new concern, coupled with greater acceptance of qualitative research methods, has led to the development of case studies, painting more holistic pictures of innovations by placing them in their organizational contexts. These case-study approaches permit us to capture how organizational members see and react to the proposed changes. They have also expanded our vision of intended and unexpected consequences of innovations.

The study of innovations is distant from understanding how systemic reform occurs, but it is throwing some light onto the process. The basic hope is that as significant innovative improvements are made to the educational system (be they in reducing costs, increasing instructional efficiency, enlarging the knowledge base of students, and so forth), these efforts will become institutionalized.

Such demonstrations influence policy throughout the educational field by identifying the set of requirements needed to put an innovation in place and by showing what forms and availability of support are needed for administrative and instructional experimentation. Policy can allocate resources, create appropriate materials and equipment for teachers, and provide professional development opportunities and other forms of technical assistance (Knapp, 1997, p. 234).

Building on contributions made by critical sociologists such as Habermas and Giroux, we are alert to the use of educational initiatives as a means to promote state legitimacy in an increasingly unequal world. Education as a contested terrain emerged in our reflection, especially as we observe how actors initially marginal to the innovation become essential to its functioning and continuity. We also recognize Weiler's (1981) observation, shared by others, that the motivation to engage in experimentation and pilot studies may not always be to provide scientific information but, frequently, to build legitimacy or defuse social conflict. This second standpoint, therefore, sees innovations not as solutions to educational problems but as problems in themselves, inasmuch as they avoid confronting real problems.

SOME CONTRASTS BETWEEN INDUSTRIALIZED AND DEVELOPING COUNTRIES

In several industrialized countries educational innovations today are focusing on such issues as "restructuring," "decentralization," "site-base management," new "curriculum frameworks," and "school choice." These changes for the most part emphasize new forms of management and decision making, in which teachers and parents are requiring more active roles beyond their immediate classrooms and children. Some of the changes represent strategies to reduce public financial support for education or, at least, to put a lid on expenditures. In the United States, comprehensive innovations are rather recent, dating from the mid-1980s, and involve the systemic alignment of curriculum frameworks, textbook selection, and assessment (Knapp, 1997). Being comprehensive, they attempt to align various elements into coherent unity with one another.

In developing countries, educational innovations tend to exploit more pedagogical or media technologies in order to reach more students and give teachers not new roles but more efficient and effective means so that both access and quality may be increased. In developing countries the influence of international donor agencies is fundamental and the role of these agencies in supporting adoption and experimentation with an innovation constitutes a major element in the early life of the innovation. Grants and low-interest loans lower the risks of adopting an innovation. Donor agencies play a role in the early death of the innovation as well, as processes established with insufficient local involvement are susceptible to quick demise when external funds diminish or disappear. Another feature of innovations in developing countries is that they rely on expatriates for both diffusion and adoption. This introduces another element of "otherness," since expatriates are often perceived as outsiders. Further, expatriates present varying degrees of commitment to country and change.

Initial Thoughts on a Collection of Innovation Case Studies

The idea of a collection of case studies on innovations emerged in my mind several years ago when I had become enthusiastic about the possibilities of innovations to make a significant difference in the way educational systems function to promote knowledge. My initial aim in producing this collection was to obtain a deeper understanding of why these promising programs had not been institutionalized. What, precisely, were the obstacles that prevented the generalized adoption of innovations? Why could an educational system not use something that was patently better and cheaper?

In soliciting several colleagues to provide in-depth studies of innovations with apparent great potential, my desire was to test a model of organizational and political change that would consider the proposition that the school's role of social reproduction encourages its bureaucracy to maintain ingrained definitions of "school," teacher," and "classroom" (Meyer and Rowan, 1977) undisturbed. The key assumption was that innovations that foster a redefinition of these conventional concepts would face defeat as they countered established norms in the educational system.

In this book, we examine a number of innovations that have been of substantial magnitude in terms of financial investment, duration, and scope. They are treated as case studies in that each innovation is examined as an instance of planned change in the context of a particular country. The case studies were conducted not simply to determine the effects of the innovations, but also to raise issues about the process of educational reform through the mechanism of "innovative" projects as promoted by national governments and international assistance agencies since the late 1960s. While each of the innovations has been subject to other empirical assessments sponsored by their respective donors, these case studies go beyond the scope of previously available reports to explore the influence of contextual factors on both the innovation adoption and implementation processes and the research methods used to assess impacts.

The original objective in discussing these case studies was to document the extent to which the innovations have contributed to their respective educational system by decreasing costs, increasing retention, facilitating access among marginal groups, and generating new learning.

The guidelines I gave to the contributors to this collection, beyond asking them to describe the attempted innovation, emphasized attention to the processes of innovation implementation and adaptation. Essentially, they were: to identify the elements of the innovations that became adapted or transformed; to analyze the political, cultural, economic, and geographical forces that accounted for the acceptance and, more importantly, the widespread adoption of the innovation; and to highlight the major lessons that have been gained from the experience of innovation implementation.

The case studies were selected for their representativeness of the variety of innovations presently being undertaken in developing countries. Thus, we have grouped these innovations into two main types: pedagogical innovations, or those affecting the content of what is to be learned or the methodology of instruction in a given education system; and technological innovations, or those that essentially rely on a new technology as the means of increasing access to education and improving its delivery. The innovation case studies around technologies such as self-instructional modules or the use of new modes of delivery such as radio and TV were conducted in the late 1980s. These have since been updated, with some interesting developments observed in the interim, particularly the degree to which they have become institutionalized in the respective systems that welcomed them in the pilot phase.

The newer case studies in this book concentrate on efforts to modify the curriculum either through discrete change efforts (localized in a given country at a given time) or through positions having the force of policy statements. The first set of innovations in this collection deals with modifications of the curriculum at the primary level in both Brazil and Namibia, countries facing very different historical moments. The second type of innovation focuses on the understanding of primary schooling and the multiple derived prescriptions offered by the World Bank. Although there exist innovations that seek to alter the organizational culture, this study does not include them, in part because such changes involve time horizons longer than those achieved by the innovations selected.

We, the editors, have had the time to ponder the ways in which the authors of these studies went about describing the innovations and explaining what made each function the way it did. We were struck by their use of social science research to buttress their arguments about the worth and promise of the innovation. We were able to see that ideologies regarding "equality" and "efficiency" were almost always present, and that social science research emerged as the uncontested criterion by which to judge the goodness of the innovation in terms of its ability to reach those two ideological objectives.

We realized that the case studies relied on empirical ways of conducting research almost exclusively in considering innovations worthy of continuation and expansion. Upon greater reflection, this seemed to us an intriguing fusion of knowledge and power. We argue that in applying empirical norms, the evaluations of these innovations become part of the status quo, forcing a perspective in which by definition one does not question or even consider sociopolitical contexts but rather sees innovations as aseptic interventions where the "good" is easily agreed upon and where covert and antagonistic intentions do not exist.

As a result of the editors' new approach, this book is something of a double take. At one level, it presents the case studies in the voice of their respective authors. At another level, it reflects upon what these authors have said and examines the assumptions behind the assertions they make. Our reflections on the nature of innovation assessments appear as a separate chapter at the end of the book.

In presenting these innovations to a large audience, we sought to clarify in particular the processes by which they were designed, implemented, and—especially—institutionalized or incorporated as a stable feature of the educational system. As part of the description, the case studies identify key components of the innovations, the ways in which the innovations became adapted or transformed over time, the sociopolitical contexts of the innovations and, finally, the lessons gained from their implementation.

Two common themes stand out from the diverse contexts in which the studies were conducted. First, the institutional mechanisms implementing the innovations, even in such radically variant settings, were remarkably consistent across the wide spectrum of political, social, and economic contexts. In each, for example, the state played a pivotal role in the diffusion and evaluation process, even to the extent of determining both the focus and the management arrangements necessary to conduct the evaluations. Constituting the terrain on which special interests compete, the concept of "state" used by the editors embodies the set of political relations that defined the scope and depth of the reforms. Of great interest is the authors' diversity of positions, usually implicit, on the role played by the state in its various national and international forms.

Second, most of the educational reforms were conceived through an empiricist approach to the production and legitimation of the knowledge bases that were drawn on to govern and assess the implementation process. In the extensive review of the evaluations, the editors examine the variety of methods for creating these knowledge bases in an effort to illuminate the social reproductive dimensions of empirical approaches to research. The editors investigate how empiricist approaches to knowledge creation are grounded in implicit ontological, epistemological, and methodological assumptions about the social world and how we come to know this world. The case evaluations provided the editors with concrete material in which these assumptions are brought to light. For example, the empirical research process stipulates that objectivity is necessary for the production of valid and generalizable knowledge. By focusing on specific instances in which the authors of the case studies refer to the "objectivity" of their data bases, the editors are able to bring to the surface the assumptions, constraints, and contradictions that permeated their studies. This approach is at times critical and often oriented toward the politics involved. The editors' review lays the foundation for new questions about the political effects of an empirical research process dependent on its concomitant expert-bureaucrat coalition for implementation.

The importance of this coalition for educational policy formulation and action has grown to the extent that, with the support of such international donor agencies as the World Bank and the U.S. Agency for International Development, it clearly dominates the field of innovation diffusion today. The editors thus explore several facets of the empiricist knowledge-innovation reform tandem to raise issues and questions about the effects of the empiricist approach to policy science as the mainstay of educational reform throughout the Third World. The meta-analysis undertaken by the editors to illuminate the relationships between the state agencies and the practice and assessment of the reforms is of added value to the case studies.

THE COLLECTION OF CASE STUDIES IN THIS VOLUME
This edited volume draws on evaluations of seven important educational

innovations that were undertaken in several developing countries during the past two decades. These innovations represent efforts targeting various aspects of the educational system: student-centered and multidisciplinary curricula, teacher training, use of self-instructional modules, utilization of radio and TV forms of educational delivery, and systemwide transformations of primary schooling.

In this collection the authors present different case studies of innovative projects and ideas. While the approaches followed in the development of case studies is diverse, the discussion addresses the evolution of the ideas, the forces that promoted or blocked implementation and institutionalization, the imprints that sociopolitical and economic contexts at the national level stamped on the nature of the proposed educational change.

The studies were conducted not simply to describe the attempted innovations or to characterize the processes that they unleashed, but also to raise issues about educational reforms sought primarily through the mechanism of project, a mechanism that has been promoted by national government and international donor agencies since the late 1960s. Cases in the book do not examine change from a theoretical perspective, but they do open spaces for interrogating ourselves about these processes. While each of the innovations has been subjected to a number of other empirical assessments sponsored by their respective donors in the past, the authors go beyond the scope of previously available reports to explore the influences of contextual factors on both the innovation process and the research methods used to assess impacts.

This edited volume draws on a new collection of evaluations of seven important innovations in educational reform that were undertaken in several countries during the past two decades as follows:

Mexico's experiment in the expansion of secondary education through the medium of television, known widely as Telesecondary, is reviewed by Felix Cadena. The study on Telesecondary addresses the only innovation that was institutionalized in its respective educational system. The innovation amounted primarily to a change in the delivery mechanism—using TV and classroom facilitators—rather than changing the content of the curriculum or the nature of the secondary studies. It succeeded because it proved an effective way to make secondary education accessible to rural populations and poor social sectors. Cadena focuses on the sociopolitical uses of education rather than on the skills and knowledge-production nature of the courses. He finds that the innovation reproduces ideological values of faith in the power of education as a means of social mobility. While the state and the socioeconomic structures are not likely to provide Telesecondary graduates with jobs, these forces benefit by creating a Mexican cultural identity through uniform educational programs and the expansion of an internal market.

Project IMPACT, an intentionally radical and comprehensive innovation to extend primary education, was assessed by H. Dean Nielsen and William K. Cummings. This ambitious project was attempted in six developing countries: the Philippines, Malaysia, Indonesia, Liberia, Jamaica, and Bangladesh. The innovation sought to alter the nature of primary schooling by introducing most notably self-instructional modules that enable student pacing of his/her own learning, employing facilitators rather than teachers, and using community members as educational resources. Cost reduction was a significant objective in many of the sites. Using conceptual contributions from various theoretical emphases, ranging from dependency to implementation analysis, Nielsen and Cummings explore the process of diffusion and adoption of IMPACT. Their findings, notable for their specificity, underscore the importance of external funding to support a risky innovation, the role of administrative and political forces in shaping the nature of the innovation as adopted in particular countries, and the inertia of educational systems toward retaining traditional and tried features regardless of contradictory evidence. As a set, these forces eventually solidify regular features of educational systems and prevent competing modalities from becoming accepted.

Lesotho's Distance Teaching Centre's Service Agency approach to extending nonformal education to community groups was examined by Michael L. Basile. His study documents how an institution initially designed to provide alternative forms of education to rural populations gradually— and almost inexorably—shifts objectives and procedures to fit centralized norms regarding what is essentially formal education. The possibility of having an autonomous institution design and provide alternative opportunities to compensate for the weaknesses of the formal education system proves extremely limited in a country operating with minimal economic resources and thus heavily vulnerable to influences from international donor agencies. Basile's study offers a serious reflection on how the economic forces of modernization are eroding traditional ties among the Lesotho people and introducing starker social hierarchies. In this process, the innovation to provide alternative forms of education through nonformal approaches is condemned to become a minor subset of the overarching formal education system. Likewise, the original intention to serve the needs of rural populations is replaced by prescriptions from centrally determined actors who are more interested in serving urban needs.

The study by María del Pilar O'Cadiz focuses on an innovation introduced into the educational system by a political party of progressive nature. In Sao Paulo, Brazil, the victory of the Workers' Party was instrumental in encouraging the creation of a popular democratic school characterized by participation and autonomy. Operating at the primary school level, the innovation focused on the curriculum, seeking to make it interdisciplinary. Based on the principle that the curriculum as knowledge is and should be collectively constructed and reconstructed, the innovation rested on two strategies: the creation of teams to produce the curriculum and the use of "dialogical negotiation"—both derived from philosophical principles of Paulo Freire.

O'Cadiz's examination of this innovation, the Interdisciplinary Project, is noteworthy in that it not only describes the features of the project but shows how it was experienced and perceived by the teachers who became engaged in the process of curriculum transformation. The examination of the micro-level experience of the innovation shows very differing views regarding the project and even changes over time within the same teachers as they redefine the project to fit different political moments. Moving from perceptions that the project was truly an effort to democratize knowledge to considering the project as an attempt to use teachers as political pawns, the study of the Interdisciplinary Project shows the difficulty and challenges for teachers to engage in knowledge production, and how complex the use of classroom strategies such as "generative themes" are. The project eventually lost political support, but many teachers were affected by it. The opportunity for professional reflection and concrete experience enabled these teachers to become involved for the first time in discussions about the curriculum of the classroom and in so doing introduced kernels of democratization in Brazilian schools.

Sydney R. Grant offers us substantial reflection on the educational reform efforts in newly independent Namibia. From the vantage point of an insider, Grant demonstrates how power plays up through the multiple actors and their multiple understandings of what a curriculum transformation should be. Grant focuses on one aspect of the reform: the production of K-12 curriculum, accompanied by teacher guides, and with high hopes that it would include teacher training. What at one level is defined as a curriculum-and-material-development project, at another is full of competing definitions and interests. While current reforms are based on contemporary ideas, personnel in charge of both defining and implementing the reform faced old-regime education personnel occupying key educational positions. These national actors, not totally convinced of the need to massify education, made all changes move very slowly, invoking the fear that education would have diminished standards. Donor agencies became a crucial partner in the implementation of educational reform in Namibia (via the provision of resources), yet they also introduced another set of powerful players. Grant observes that donors, by virtue of having more power, knowledge, and expertise than the national institutions they seek to support, introduce elements of power, that if unchecked, contribute to making the recipient countries "clients" rather than "partners." An important manifestation of power became reflected in Namibia when a key donor agency's demanded enforcement of "deliverables" paralyzed reform efforts for two months. At the same time, Grant's study illuminates how decreeing changes from the top is far from sufficient. Namibian educators found it very difficult to shift from teacher-focused teaching to learner-centered instruction, a move particularly difficult in countries long accustomed to rote-learning practices and with many untrained teachers.

A follow-up effort in teacher education at a distance, Logos II in Brazil, was examined by João Batista Araujo e Oliveira and François Orivel. Although the authors concentrate on the procedural aspects of implementation and an analysis of the costs and benefits of Logos II, we gain important insights of the intended consequences of this innovation. The chapter offers lessons regarding unintended outcomes, especially in terms of the types of persons who ultimately benefited from increased access to teacher training and the increased mobility of personnel that was created throughout the system. Oliveira and Orivel, unlike the other authors in this book, circumscribe their analysis of Logos II to internal problems. Thus, there are difficulties due to project design, such as having too many learning objectives, too much reliance on modules, excessive guidance. Yet the authors also show that the innovation demonstrated strong appeal, especially among poor and isolated rural teachers. Enabling these teachers to participate and progress at their own pace, and building upon their motivations to succeed in life, Logos II produced a high rate of success among its student teachers. As Oliveira and Orivel state, Logos II's success with the rural teachers created its own set of problems: retaining the trained teachers and avoiding salary increases due to an improved human capital level.

The chapter by Rosa María Torres does not address a concrete innovation but systematically probes a collection of ideas promoted by a leading international development organization and thus likely to influence many change efforts in the developing world. The chapter by Torres unpacks the concept of educational improvement by centering on World Bank's recommendations, which if followed, certainly constitute innovations in the educational systems of developing countries. She shows how ideas aimed at improving quality of schooling can be extremely influential since they are integrated into the large loans given by the World Bank. Its assumptions about how classrooms function and how they should function permeate government decisions in primary education. Thus, World Bank arguments substantially affect decisions by educational systems, and particularly the types and ranges of innovations in which these systems engage.

Torres presents a detailed analysis of the assumptions and prescriptions by the World Bank, highlighting how much certainty in its recommendations is fueled by a rather economistic perspective of education. She also identifies a number of contradictions not resolved by the literature which, in being presented without complete discussion, are likely to foster piecemeal and incomplete solutions to more endemic and pervasive problems in primary education. We consider the analysis by Torres of great importance because, while not providing examination of past actions, reflection on her arguments could avoid the implementation of innovations based along faulty conceptions. This chapter, therefore, has substantial proactive value.

SOME CONCLUDING OBSERVATIONS

Implicit in most innovation efforts is a linear process that will move the innovation from being a pilot project to becoming a demonstration project and finally to large scale via institutionalization. But reality has proven different.

A common thread among the various innovations we are reviewing in this collection is their inability to become a regular feature of the educational system. With the exception of Telesecondary—which really amounts to an alternative form of delivery—the other innovations did not take hold or were drastically modified, keeping only the most minimal set of original features.

This collection of studies does not permit us to address the point at which innovations become an integral part of the system, but it does permit us to see what mechanisms and dynamics operate to make them work the way they do. In this respect, the case studies fit with previous findings regarding the institutionalization of innovations. Alexander, Murphy, and Woods (1996) observe that educational organizations are characterized by the introduction of many innovations and, simultaneously, by the pattern that many of these innovations fade away or are later seen as far from satisfactory. In the view of these authors the current state of affairs suggests two possibilities: First, educators like to select innovations that address issues with which they are familiar and thus feel they can manage. This leads to the selection of innovations that are easy to implement rather than those most appropriate and needed. Second, educators may not accumulate knowledge of past innovations undertaken by their own organizations or they may have limited understanding of the principles that underlie such innovations (Alexander et al., 1996).

Alternative explanations for the failure to implement innovations suggested by the case studies in this collection are: (1) existing routines drive off new practices, assumptions, and values, especially when the latter are predicated on personnel and structures made possible by funds outside the regular budget; (2) school systems have weak mechanisms for organizational learning and organizational memory. Experiences from projects go into evaluations accessible to or read by few organizational actors. Turnover of personnel takes away people familiar with the purposes and practices of the innovations; and (3) resistance of a political nature (e.g., to the introduction of ideas and procedures that challenge the status quo) or a professional nature (e.g., to teachers being asked to behave in different ways in the absence of clear incentives to modify present behaviors) is an effective means of self-preservation.

While this book focuses on educational innovations, we would like to make the point that we do not see innovations as the essential managerial or administrative response to the need for the effective functioning of educational systems. On many occasions, what a system may need is not a new idea or new technology but rather a very careful understanding of how current processes are operating and what it needs to make them more effective. Replacement of procedures and adoption of new projects may be less suitable than a reexamination of the old so that its components and joining elements may be well understood. Innovations have the appeal of beginning fresh or providing a clean solution to amorphous problems. This can be disingenuous.

REFERENCES

Alexander, P., P. Murphy, and B. Woods. "Of Squalls and Fathoms: Navigating the Seas of Educational Innovation." *Educational Researcher* 25, 3 (1996): 31–36.

DiMaggio, P., and W. Powell. "The Iron Cage Revisited: Institutional Isomorphism and the Collective Rationality in Organizational Fields. *American Sociological Review* 48 (1983): 147–160.

Elkin, S. "Towards a Contextual Theory of Innovation." *Policy Sciences* 15 (1983): 367–387.

Knapp, M. "Between Systemic Reforms and the Mathematics and Science Classroom: The Dynamics of Innovation, Implementation, and Professional Learning." *Review of Educational Research* 67, 2 (1997): 227–266.

March, J., and H. Simon. *Organizations.* New York: Wiley, 1959.

Meyer, J., and B. Rowan. "Institutionalized Organizations: Formal Structure as Myth and Ceremony." *American Journal of Sociology* 83 (1977): 340–363.

Morris, D. "Adrift in the Sea of Innovations: A Response to Alexander, Murphy, and Woods." *Educational Researcher* 27, 2 (May 1997): 22–26.

Roger, E. *The Diffusion of Innovations.* New York: Free Press of Glencoe, 1962.

Tushman, M., and P. Anderson. "Technological Discontinuities and Organizational Environments." *Administrative Science Quarterly* 31 (1986): 439–465.

Weiler, H. "The Politics of Educational Reforms: Notes on the Comparative Study of Innovations in Education." Stanford: Stanford University, mimeograph, 1981.

PART 1
PEDAGOGICAL INNOVATIONS

2 KNOWLEDGE AND CURRICULUM

THE TRANSFORMATIVE POLITICS OF THE INTERDISCIPLINARY PROJECT[1]

Maria del Pilar O'Cadiz

The skewed distribution of knowledge and power perpetuated by Brazil's dual educational system—represented by the extreme inequities between the private and public sectors—has fostered a movement for the democratization of schooling in the country calling for increased access to an education of good quality for all Brazilians. Primary public schools, funded by state and municipal governments and attending to the schooling of Brazil's poor, have historically been shortchanged in favor of federally funded higher education that benefits mostly the wealthiest sectors of the population. As a consequence of such discriminatory educational politics, perpetuated by numerous historical, cultural, and economic factors, the Brazilian state has lagged in its responsibility to build an adequate public education system (Plank, 1995). A glimpse at some of the statistical data serves to highlight the extreme educational inequities that persist even as Brazil approaches the close of the twentieth century. The frightening dropout rate offers the most glaring evidence of Brazil's educational failure with 15 percent of first graders leaving school, and an additional 19 percent of fifth graders failing to go further in their education. The harsh reality is that only 32 percent of children who begin their eight years of elementary schooling finish in that time period. Limited enrollment and extensive dropout rates contribute to the country's high illiteracy rate: 19 percent among adults and 32 percent among children ages seven to fourteen (*Almanaque Brasil*, 1994, p. 79). Alarmingly, even in Sao Paulo, Brazil's largest and wealthiest municipality, nearly 18 percent of school-aged children are outside the formal school system as they enter early into the nonformal labor market or join the ranks of the thousands of children roaming the city streets (SME-SP, 1990a).

On the political forefront of the fight for a quality public education for all, the Workers' Party (*Partido dos Trabalhadores;* PT) has pursued an alternative politics of schooling in Brazil: one that seeks to transform the social, cultural, and economic inequities reproduced within the educational institutions of the country while fostering a vision of the public school as a space for the creation of a new educational paradigm. This new paradigm finds its inspiration in the politically radical tradition of "popular education" developed in Brazil and Latin America in the second half of this century and more recently resurrected and integrated into the formal school setting through the development of the notion of the *escola publica popular* (popular public school). This article discusses one of the most far-reaching organized efforts undertaken by the Workers' Party to date in advancing its political-pedagogic agenda of radically changing the politics of schooling in Brazil: the Movement for the Reorientation of the Curriculum of the Municipal Secretariat of Education of São Paulo, lead by PT-appointed Secretary of Education, Paulo Freire. Specifically the focus here is on the Freirean curriculum reform, the Interdisciplinary Project (or Inter Project), which the PT administration carried out in over two-thirds of the 678 municipal schools in the city's public educational system.

PAULO FREIRE, THE WORKERS' PARTY, AND EDUCATIONAL REFORM IN SAO PAULO

In Brazil, the Movement for Popular Culture (*Movimento de Cultura Popular; MCP*)—of which Paulo Freire stands as one of its foremost visionaries—gained momentum in the early 1960s, contributing significantly to the development of contemporary progressive pedagogic thought and the leftist politics of schooling. Like other counterhegemonic nonformal educational experiences that emerged throughout Latin America at the time, the MCP sought to shake loose from its centuries-old shackles of oppression the critical consciousness of the mass of impoverished and disenfranchised Brazilians by means of a transformative educational praxis that not only made literate those who had been kept out of the schoolhouse and forced into the slums of the country's burgeoning urban centers or the isolation of a destitute rural life, but also worked to arm them with the knowledge of how to transform that reality. Freire's role as a protagonist in the trajectory of a critical approach to popular education has significant implications for the educational reform carried out by the Workers' Party under his leadership as Secretary of Education in the Municipality of Sao Paulo. The ideal of a popular public school erected by the PT three decades after the emergence of the popular education movement in Brazil is linked both historically and theoretically to Freire's own trajectory as a revolutionary educational philosopher, activist, and visionary in Brazil and abroad.

The Interdisciplinary Project that evolved from the reform experience carried out in the municipal schools of Sao Paulo over the course of the PT's four-year administration (1989–1992) represents in some respects a unique combination of elements born of the popular educational movements that flourished decades previously and the culmination of a decade of the social democratic politics of the Workers' Party: a marriage between critical pedagogic work and the political work to construct a collective consciousness for a new democratic society. In this way, many of the educators encountered at all levels of this project, from its planners at the secretariat level to the teachers at the schools, seemed motivated by forces greater than simply a bureaucratic mandate to carry out a plan of educational action. These were individuals who had participated in the realization of an historical moment of transition from dictatorship to democracy in the 1980s and were now facing the real challenge of putting their ideals into practice, in this case, in the relm of public education and specifically primary schooling.

In 1980 the Workers' Party arrived on the Brazilian political scene, signaling the organization of significant opposition forces to the Brazilian military regime that had come into power in 1964. The bureaucratic authoritarian regime would eventually succumb to this democratization movement, in which the PT played a pivotal role, leading to the first presidential elections of 1985. Drawing from a diverse coalition of labor union leaders and workers, intellectuals, and leftist community activists, the party's political manifesto emphasized, at its onset, a commitment to the defense of universal public education at all the levels of schooling, and in its plan of action stipulated that such an education should be "oriented to the necessities of the workers" (Gadotti and Pereira, 1989, p. 61). Because education has been considered by the PT as a powerful and necessary tool in the development of a critically conscious citizenry active in the construction of a democratic socialist society, the struggle for a quality public education represents one of the fronts around which popular groups affiliated with the PT have galvanized and constitutes a major area of policy effort among the municipalities that the PT has held in recent years.

In 1988 the PT achieved one of the most significant electoral victories in the party's history, the mayorship of the city of Sao Paulo,[2] the country's largest and most economically powerful municipality, with a population of over nine million (9,626,894 according to the 1991 census) and a municipal budget of nearly four billion cruzeiros for the 1991 fiscal year (*Almanaque Brasil*, 1994). The PT municipal government under mayor Luiza Erundina de Souza—a woman from Freire's homeland of the impoverished Northeast (the origin of the great majority of Sao Paulo's working class immigrant population)—had a profound impact on the educational reality of this immense city. One of the first official appointments made by mayor

Erundina upon entering office was to name Paulo Freire to the post of secretary of education. Under Freire's initial leadership (which lasted about two years) and during the four years of its administration (1989–1992)[3] the PT's educational efforts were oriented by three principles: participation, decentralization, and autonomy (SME-SP, 1992a). These principles guided the administration in the construction of a popular public school intended to break from the tradition of a politics of grandiose campaigns, isolated pedagogic experimentalism, and formulaic solutions to the complex problems of public schooling in an urban center of the magnitude of Sao Paulo.The notion of the popular public school advanced by the PT is defined as follows:

> [It] not only is one to which all have access, but one in the construction of which every one participates. [It is a school] which truly attends to the popular interests which are of the majority; it is, therefore, a school of a new quality based on commitment and solidarity, in the formation of class consciousness. Within [the popular public school] all agents, not only teachers, take on an active and dynamic role, experimenting with new forms of learning, participating, teaching, working, playing and celebrating. (Gadotti and Pereira, 1989, p. 191)

To advance this newly fashioned vision of the public school, the PT at the onset of its administration defined four areas of action: (1) the creation of concrete proposals for the improvement of the quality of education through various programmatic and curricular changes—such as the reorganization of grade levels into three cycles and the introduction of new evaluation methods, continual evaluation and research to secure technical refinement, the provision of ongoing professional training and just remuneration for educational workers, and the establishment of a Movement for the Reorientation of the Curriculum with the implementation of the Interdisciplinary Project, as well as numerous other educational programs; (2) the advancement of the process of democratization of the administration of municipal schools through increased participation and social control of the system by creating institutional channels of communication and participatory methods of decision making as manifested in the systematic effort to make the preexisting school councils (deliberative representative bodies) legitimate; (3) the promotion of a movement for the education of youths and adults (i.e., *Movimento de Alfabetizaçâo de Jovens e Adultos;* MOVA) through the technical and financial support of existing social movements working in adult literacy training throughout the city; and (4) the democ-ratization of access through the construction of new schools and renovation and expansion of existing facilities and fulfillment of basic infrastructure necessary for adequate student performance (*Partido dos Trabalhadores,* 1992, pp. 56–57).

As such, the educational policies that emanated from Secretary Freire's administration of the Municipal Secretariat of Education of Sao Paulo (SME-SP) embodied both the transformative pedagogical premises of Freire's own philosophy and the socialist tenets of the Workers' Party's political platform, which since the party's inception have promoted a public education in the interest of the working-class sectors that make up the majority of the pub-lic school's clientele. Given the party's origins in the labor unions and grassroots movements that flourished in the 1970s in opposition to a bru-tally repressive military regime, it is not surprising that its educational vi-sion includes the association of nonformal and formal approaches to edu-cating the poor and oppressed (Gadotti and Pereira, 1989). The PT administration's effort to create a Movement for the Reorientation of the Curriculum lead to the adoption of Freire's revolutionary pedagogic ap-proach in the development of a curricular reform project for the municipal elementary schools of Sao Paulo: the Interdisciplinary Project or Inter Project.

KNOWLEDGE AND THE INTERDISCIPLINARY CURRICULUM

The literature disseminated to educators in the municipal school system by the PT municipal secretariat of education explicitly recognized knowledge as inextricably linked to relations of power inside and outside the classroom. Accordingly, Freire has identified traditional pedagogy as the "banking" method of education in which knowledge is conceived as a distinct object of linear transmission from educator to learner within the hierarchically constructed relationship between both the individuals participating in the educational act (i.e., educator and learner) and the knowledge of elite and popular sectors in society (Freire, 1970, pp. 62–63). Adopting a Freirean approach, the PT secretariat advanced the concept of knowledge as "not a simple copy or description of a static reality" but as continually evolving out of the historical context of social life of both the educator and educatee: education therefore is "a dynamic and permanent act of knowledge centered in the discovery, analysis and transformation of reality by those that live it (SME-SP, 1990a, p. 17).

The Inter Project's innovation, therefore, is its coupling of the Freirean vision of collective construction of knowledge leading to transformative con-sciousness through dialogic exchange with the idea that the comprehension of reality is best achieved through an interdisciplinary approach to the organization of knowledge in the curriculum in the context of formal schooling of elementary children. The methodological linchpin of the proposed interdisciplinary curriculum was directly gleaned from Freire's revolutionary approach to educational programming through thematic investigation of the culture and reality of the learners and the designing of a pedagogic program around generative themes discovered in a perpetual investigative process. Freire's notion of the generative theme as the basis for the development of a liberating educational praxis in the context of adult literacy training was seized on and refashioned for the schooling of elementary children: hence, the interdisciplinary curriculum via the generative theme.

One of the distinctive features of the Inter Project is that it proposes a curriculum planning process which takes the following principle as its basis: "the various sciences should contribute to the study of certain [generative] themes that orient all of the work of the school." (Delizoicov and Zanetic, 1993, p. 13). Paradoxically, however, the generative theme represents perhaps one of the more problematic and controversial elements of the PT's curriculum reform project. In fact, from the very beginning of the administration's policy planning meetings with university specialists, a fierce debate ensued and persisted throughout the reform experience—from the secretariat on down through the Nuclei of Educational Action (*Núcleos de Ação Educativa;* NAEs)[4], and to the teachers that were being guided by the NAE Interdisciplinary Teams (comprising a representative for each of the subject areas) in its implementation—regarding the feasibility of organizing an educational program for elementary students around a single generative theme.

According to project coordinators, the interdisciplinary approach signifies "an inversion of the whole mechanical process of inculcation of compartmentalized content. It presupposes a new epistemological organization of knowledge, collectively and historically constructed and reconstructed, never closed or finished (NAE-6, 1990, p. 1). The intention is to generate a curriculum that moves beyond an encyclopedic approach to the organization of knowledge as generic and discrete, divorced from human social formations, history and culture, to one that facilitates the interdisciplinary interpretation of reality in a way that more adequately addresses the "social-natural complex," working toward the "substitution of a fragmented Science by a unified Science" (Faundez, 1990). This constant striving to overcome the contradictions among the distinct areas of knowledge allows for the evolution of a macro vision of men and women in the world and ultimately points to an interdisciplinary ontological comprehension of men and women being and acting in the world (Delizoicov and Zanetic, 1993, p. 13). The theoretical undercurrent to this interdisciplinary approach stems from a new curriculum paradigm that incorporates critical theory in the development of a "critical science of the curriculum" (Silva, 1990, p. 11).

Accordingly, this particular interdisciplinary approach to curriculum building differs markedly from the standard interdisciplinary notion of simply minimizing the rigid boundaries between the disciplines; instead, it speaks from a critical perspective to the way knowledge is produced in society and how this process can contribute to either merely reproducing relations of power or to the creation of new knowledge and to the transformation of society. From such a critical perspective, the different knowledge areas serve as reference points in a continual and collaborative process of investigation around a particular theme of social-historical relevance. In this way, although the Inter Project attempted to move teachers away from the traditional practice of isolating the disciplines, it did respect the specificity of each area of knowledge. Because each subject area specialist has an important role in contributing to the curriculum planning process and to the provision of a "multifaceted" view of the totality of reality (Delizoicov and Zanetic, 1993, p. 13) the secretariat established Interdisciplinary Teams ("inter teams") at each NAE charged with developing and coordinating the Inter Project at the schools.

Interdisciplinaridade[5] refers to the notion that the curriculum should not divide knowledge into separate subject areas but that all knowledge is interrelated. However, the secretariat's literature constantly argued that such an interdisciplinary curriculum model was in the process of formulation and that the theoretical foundations of *interdisciplinaridade* would evolve based on the practical experience of the schools participating in the Inter Project and the ongoing theoretical work of secretariat personnel and collaborating university specialists. As a product of this ongoing effort to build the theoretical foundations of the project, a series of pamphlets entitled *Visão da área* (subject area perspective, i.e., mathematics, history, geography, Portuguese language, physical education, science, and the arts) was published in January 1992 . These publications included a brief history of each of the disciplines in the context of Brazilian education and guidelines for teachers on how to integrate the specific content of each area of knowledge into the interdisciplinary curriculum. Theoretical mimeographed texts and the *visão da área* pamphlets and other secretariat-produced literature served as the materials studied by teachers in what were called *grupos de formação* (continuously training groups).

Teacher training constituted an area of primary concern for the PT administration, in as much as the secretariat viewed teachers as the principal agents for the realization of its proposals for profound institutional and curriculum change in the schools. The specific nature of this administration's focus on teacher training is further elaborated as follows:

> Here, distinct from a mere educational fad or pedagogic experimentalism, it was not a matter of training teachers in a new revolutionary method, but more an effort to patiently work towards the permanent reflection of their practices, to discover alternative approaches through the exchange of experiences, to have at their disposal the assistance of conceptually sophisticated educational thinkers, to gradually elevate the level of knowledge of the teachers, to promote collective work as the privileged form of teacher formation, and to be able to afford the material conditions for all this to occur. In this manner the pedagogic innovations are appropriated, the curricular alterations are fruitful, because the principal agents [of these changes], the teachers, are considered not objects of training, but as elements that produce and re-elaborate knowledge (*Partido dos Trabalhadores,* 1992, p. 62).

Thus, the institution of *grupos de formação* was a key strategy of the SME for maintaining the process of curriculum renovation launched within the Movement for the Reorientation of the Curriculum. The *grupos de formação* gave teachers opportunities to reflect upon their pedagogic practice, explore educational theories, and develop their professional skills in a collective and permanent process. A document entitled *Em Formação* (In Formation), organized and published under the initiative of teachers of the formation groups working out of NAE-6, defines the purpose of these groups in the following terms:

> The existing power structure in schooling ends up expropriating knowledge from the educator, changing [her] into a mere executor of programs and activities. The space [created in schools by the *grupos de formação*] constitutes a political-pedagogic space in as much as the act of distancing oneself from the alienating daily reality of the school is fundamental for reflecting upon that practice, allowing [teachers] to return to that reality with *bons olhos* [fresh eyes]. (SME-SP, 1990b)

The SME was successful in instituting this professional development system on a wide scale. By 1991, 294 schools (of the approximately 662 municipal schools) had organized their own formation groups involving 4,000 teachers. Also 68 percent of school principals and 94 percent of the pedagogic coordinators in the municipal school system were involved in formation groups under the coordination of the NAEs (SME-SP, 1992b, pp. 10–11). In addition to the ongoing teacher training through formation groups, the CONAE (Coordinator of the NAEs)[6] organized workshops on numerous topics aimed at advancing the secretariat's goal of transforming the educational methods and curriculum of the schools. This was also a way to tap the knowledge resources both within and outside the municipal system as university professors, secretariat personnel, school administrators, or even teachers themselves could organize and lead workshops. Workshop topics ranged from dealing with highly charged social issues to offering practical pedagogic orientation.

THE INTER PROJECT CURRICULUM: CENTRAL CONCEPTS AND GUIDING PRINCIPLES

In order to advance their movement for the democratization of schooling in Brazil, the educators behind the PT curriculum reform project considered imperative the reconsideration of how the knowledge and culture of working-class children was to be treated within the institutional setting of the muncipal public schools, and more specifically the classroom. This meant that the Inter Project was not merely a reformulating of the technical aspects of teaching and methods of curriculum organization, but that it was directly concerned with issues of power and knowledge representation and therefore would lead to a profound reevaluation of the process of knowledge selection and construction in the curriculum. Accordingly, the project's central concepts and guiding principles included: (1) the adoption of the Freirean notion of the generative theme as the basis of the construction of an interdisciplinary curriculum; (2) the promotion of dialogue as a fundamental pedagogic method of the project; (3) the appropriation of constructivist theories of learning in the design and implementation of the project; and (4) the institution of three fundamental pedagogic moments as a methodological framework for the organization and implementation of the interdisciplinary curriculum via the generative theme.

These principles, generally speaking, signified a move away from the traditional practices of teaching from the textbook and the strict adherence to a curriculum plan formulated from outside the context of the school, which, the PT administration insisted, "is, in reality, a-historical, conformist and unrelated to daily life . . . not taking into account the 'primary culture,' and therefore unable to transmit a transformative 'elaborated culture'" (Delizoicov and Zanetic, 1993, p. 10). The proposed alternative would be an integrated curriculum developed through a dynamic participatory process which "sought to make less rigid the boundaries among the diverse areas of knowledge" (p. 10).

The project adopted Freire's methodology of thematic investigation, leading to the use of generative themes. These themes are based on real-life situations, problems, and concerns of the learners. As one of the principal theorists behind the project explains: "The generative themes, once discovered, indicate pertinent academic content. This entails a new approach to the selection of culture, dictated not by the inertia of tradition but on the basis of necessity, be it of a concrete reality or an imagined one (Delizoicov and Zanetic, 1993, p. 10). In the Inter Project, generative themes served as the building blocks for the construction of a curriculum that is more relevant to the urban poor students of the municipal schools of Sao Paulo. The objective of a curriculum based on a generative theme is to relate the students' local reality to a broad range of individual, community, and societal problems—ranging from peer-group relations in the school, to public transportation, to air and water contamination in an industrial city like Sao Paulo—and to engage students in an interdisciplinary understanding of their reality and the possibilities for its transformation, with the aim of creating a critical and participative citizenry.

"Dialogical negotiation" was the principal means to planning and implementing an interdisciplinary curriculum via the generative theme. The Inter Project struggled to establish a dialogic approach to teaching that favors active as opposed to passive learning, exemplified in the Freirean concept of education for critical consciousness or *conscientização*.[7] The act of engaging in dialogue is defined as "navigating through the sea of sufficient similarities so as to establish a communication of the sufficient differences, in order to avoid repeating one and another in a dialogue that turns into a monologue" (Pernambuco, 1993, p. 24). Dialogue as pedagogy, from this perspective, requires a predisposition on the part of the educator to relinquish his status as the sole bearer of knowledge and to recognize the validity of the positions and perceptions of the other subjects involved in a given educational context. The educator's job, therefore, is to secure an interactive space for competing discourses in the classroom to emerge and evolve. Marta Pernambuco highlights this distinctive Freirean feature of the Inter Project's dialogical approach to curriculum planning and student learning when she writes:

> Paulo Freire, in demonstrating that the student is an educatee, who
> on a par with the educator recaptures in the classroom the process

of production of knowledge, points us to dialogue as the most excellent of instruments by which that knowledge is produced. Initiated always from the universe of the student, from what for him [sic] is significant, from his manner of thinking, from the knowledge that he brings from his social group, it is in the school's capacity to make possible his overcoming that initial vision, giving him access to new forms of thinking which constitute the basis of systematized contemporary knowledge. (1993, p. 24)

On a broad level, dialogue was considered a fundamental means of developing more democratic relationships among the educational actors involved in the reform, engaging administrators, teachers, students, and community in a collective process of knowledge exchange, knowledge construction, and democratic decision making. Yet dialogue also had a specific pedagogic purpose related to the Inter Project's emphasis on the social construction of knowledge and the desired intersection of the universe of systematized knowledge and the realm of popular knowledge in that it allowed for the establishment of connections between the new knowledge that is intended to be learned and that which the educatee brings into the classrooom. A fundamental goal of the Inter Project, therefore, was to "give a voice to students, starting from their reality and bringing new possibilities into the classroom" (Pernambuco, 1993, p. 24).

Beyond the Freirean elements outlined above, many of the pedagogical tenets advanced by the secretariat were based on the constructivist theories of cognitive development (e.g., those proposed by Ferreiro and Vygotsky) which view the acquisition of language and knowledge, in general, as mediated by social and affective factors.[8] The Inter Project, therefore operated on the premise that children learn best by engaging in cooperative group activities guided by an adult educator charged with mediating the dialogic negotiation between the cognitive structure and socially acquired knowledge of the student and the accumulated historical, scientific, and artistic knowledge that is organized into the different disciplines (SME-SP, 1991, p. 30). Knowledge, from such a pedagogical approach, was not an object to be intellectually attained by individual students in varying degrees of accuracy, but instead conceived as being in a process of continual construction throughout the various pedagogical moments that constituted the learning-teaching process.

The three methodological moments that comprised the secretariat's approach to curriculum planning—(1) study of reality (*estudo da realidade;* ER); (2) organization of knowledge (*organização do conhecimento;* OC); (3)

application/assessment of knowledge (*aplicação/avaliação do conhecimento;* AC)—permeated all pedagogical instances of the Inter Project. In other words, they not only characterized the organization of the project's teacher-training sessions, but also constituted the framework for conducting the analysis of any given situation or topic in a variety of contexts, for example, in the analysis of texts in teacher formation meetings, in the discussions at school council meetings, and even in the evaluation of the project by school personnel in staff meetings. But most importantly, these moments marked the steps taken in the implementation of an interdisciplinary curriculum project on both the broad level of curriculum development and the specific context of classroom activity. In this regard, the methodological moments can be considered an overarching framework for the secretariat's intervention in the way schools functioned and the manner in which teachers taught, and students learned. Pernambuco specifies the fundamental importance of this framework for the realization of the Inter Project when she asserts that the pedagogical moments "are a means of organization used to guarantee a systematic practice of dialogue," again emphasizing dialogue as a key pedagogical feature of the project (1993, p. 33).

The implementation of the pedagogic moments as a curriculum planning and teaching methodology varied from NAE to NAE and from each school site depending on the different interpretations and applications made of the general project guidelines that emanated from the secretariat's central Directorate of Technical Orientation (DOT). These guidelines oriented but did not completely direct the work of the NAEs and the educators involved in the initial development of the project at the ten different pilot sites.[9] In general, however, the first step in implementing the project required that the school community, initially assisted by an inter team secretariat staff member from the newly formed NAEs, engage in a preliminary investigation of its reality (*levantamento preliminar*) to discern the "significant situations"—that is, social-cultural-political circumstances of the daily lives of the students which make up their "lifeworld."

Interviews of students, parents, and local residents, therefore, constituted the principal means of data collection—based on the tenets of participant action and ethnographic research[10]—which was supplemented by secondary documentation such as statistical data on the area, news articles, and other relevant literature. The SME emphasized the need to link the micro level issues relevant to a specific community as they emerge during the investigative team's preliminary analysis of the data collected with the macro issues of the broader social context in order to discern the "significant situations," which are those themes that persistently emerge in the discourse of the community and therefore represent a collective dimension as opposed to the strictly individual experience. To this end, the SME suggested that the group construct broad categories that allow for the organization of data in a way that makes evident the more significant tendencies and elements. Following these guidelines, a dialectic comprehension of reality is pursued inasmuch as the categories identified serve to orient the analysis of data at the same time that the data orients the definition of categories, which in turn signal to the investigative team those situations most significant for a given community (SME-SP, 1991, pp. 28–29).

This qualitative analytical process is central to the curriculum-building effort within the Inter Project. For example, the generative theme selected by the NAE-6 inter team at the pilot site of Sussumu was *lixo* (a word that translates literally as "trash," but connotes general conditions of sanitation and various forms of waste that contaminate the community's living space).[11] The principal socio-economic element of study became "basic sanitation" and the generative question guiding the educators' problematization of that reality was phrased as follows: "How can we interfere in the aspects of social organization that determine the location of dumping grounds (causes and solutions)?" The following comments registered from the population during the initial ER are representative of the "significant situations" facing the community at Sussumu in 1990 that pointed toward the generative theme of "trash."

COMMUNITY DISCOURSE USED IN THE DEFINITION OF SIGNIFICANT SITUATIONS (SUSSUMU, 1990)

"When they constructed the buildings they connected the sewage system with a channel that dumped out into the river of the favela."

"If people didn't throw their trash in that passageway there wouldn't be so many rats and flies about."

"The garbage truck passes up above and everyone has to take the trash up there. It's far and people prefer to throw it in the passageway or in the middle of the favela."

"The children play in the little lake of the reservoir. The sewage contaminates the reservoir. The rats attack the small children at night."

"The students bathe in the water tank of the school."

In addition, the NAE team collected statistical data that further detailed the poor conditions of basic sanitation in the community (e.g., the fact that as late as 1985 only 93 percent of the favelas in the southern zone of the city where the school is located had running water and that 70 percent of the school's student body are favela residents), confirming this theme as a significant part of daily life for most of the students attending Sussumu. From the universe of data collected the educational team inferred specific elements and conditions about the community, with relation to sanitation, that serve to orient the subsequent steps in the organization of knowledge.

Specific Socio-economic Elements That Characterize the Community

- Lack of infrastructure and planning (a complete sewage system does not exist in the area)
- Disorganization in the occupation of land
- Lack of consciousness of the utilization of public and private resources
- Lack of consciousness of the consequences of the deterioration of the environment: pollution
- Lack of rules in the organization and occupation of areas of recreation

Prior to reaching the stage of actually designing the curriculum program the qualitative and quantitative "socio-economic aspects of the theme" are identified and organized in a process called "thematic reduction" and serve as a sort of guiding framework in the selection of content for the curriculum. Schools were to organize the data collected during the preliminary ER into a school *dossiê* that would depict as closely as possible the local reality of the school and would remain open to additional contributions resulting from the continual investigations and educational work carried out within the project.

In the subsequent OC stage of curriculum construction, the team would then organize the knowledge within the interdisciplinary curriculum around the selected generative theme, connecting the different subject areas via specific "unifying concepts." The AC stage corresponded to the team's selection of learning activities (preferably offering ample opportunities for cooperative group learning to take place) aimed at building the students' critical comprehension of the generative theme at hand by addressing generative questions developed in the previous ER and OC stages of the curriculum planning process.

It is interesting to note the evolution of the interdisciplinary curriculum model at Sussumu. The previously cited program was among the first to evolve from the Inter Project effort; Sussumu was then a pilot school site receiving intensive intervention by the NAE-6 Inter Team In 1994, one year after the end of the PT administration, a small group (about 30 percent of the staff) at Sussumu was still struggling to continue their curriculum planning and classroom teaching within the pedagogic parameters the Inter Project experience. At that time, on the wall of the teachers' meeting room and under a sign which read *Interdisciplinaridade* four large charts outlined the interdisciplinary curriculum plan for the semester. As an example, the essential elements of the curricular plan for the fourth grade (the first year of the intermediate cycle) were presented as follows:

Interdisciplinary Curriculum—Outline of Program
(Intermediate Cycle/Sussumu, 1994)
   Significant Situations:
   • Lack of perspective in life
   • No political and religious conscience
   • Disillusionment with governmental bodies (corruption and dishonesty)
   Generative Theme: Constructing Citizenship
   Unifying concepts:
   • Relations × transformation × time space × subject of history × cycles × equilibrium
   Generative Question:
   • How does education contribute to the exercise of citizenship? (NAE-6, 1990).

In the Inter Project classroom, the initial pedagogic moment of ER corresponded to the introduction and "problematization" of the reality or topic to be studied aimed at relating the generative theme to the social and personal spheres of reality of the student. At this stage students were usually presented with a series of questions intended to get them to begin to analyze a specific aspect of reality as it relates to them. Ideally, the desired outcome of the first methodological step was to get students to express their opinions and experiences. Either individually or in groups they were to study materials provided by the teacher or collected from sources outside the classroom, reorganize the knowledge at hand, and raise new questions pertinent to the topic of investigation. It was recommended that the teacher, during ER, maintain more a role of questioning students and guiding the problematization process than that of providing answers and explanations. In this way the ER moment in the classroom was to offer students the opportunity to revisit knowledge previously learned in and outside the school and to express intuitive or commonsense notions (both of which may or may not correspond to the theories and facts of so—called scientific knowledge). Through the problematization of that knowledge—via dialogic classroom interaction—students were then motivated to investigate further in order to acquire new information and thus build new knowledge.

This initial dialogue between educator and educatee led to the second pedagogic moment, OC, in which the discourse of the individual or persons organizing the learning activity took precedence. At this stage in the pedagogical process the educator introduced new concepts and ways of viewing a given reality or set of problems. As such, the knowledge that the educator brought into the learning situation was essential for the educational act to take place. The reality of the learner was not the beginning and end point of this pedagogical approach. Educator and learners collectively exchanged and reorganized knowledge, ultimately resulting in the third moment, AC, the "application of knowledge," which represents the synthesis of both the discourse of the other (learner) and the organizer (teacher) without one taking precedence over the other, allowing each to perceive and recognize their differences and respective limitations (Pernambuco, 1993, p. 33). In this way, knowledge was socially constructed as the group worked to reorganize what they had learned into a collective text or group project.

The final curricular plan produced at each school varied according to different interpretations of the process to be undertaken. Some schools came up with elaborate tables and graphic representations of their analytical work. Most devised various formats or charts on which to lay out their curriculum plan for the semester. Figure 2.1 provides a graphic representation of this complex curriculum construction process and its application in the classroom as it was conceived by the NAE-6 Inter Team.

As the graphics and narrative description in Figure 2.1 attest, the Inter Project represented a theoretically sophisticated proposal that implicated a methodologically complex process of curriculum design, making it difficult for many teachers in the São Paulo schools to put into practice, given various intervening factors among which were the limited training of teachers and inconsistent technical support provided by the secretariat. But the fact that many educators continued to make an effort to work within this bold proposal for curriculum change within an innovative pedagogic paradigm of constructivist and Freirean foundations—one year after the PT's demise—speaks to the long-term impact of the Inter Project experience on the municipal schools of Sao Paulo and above all, on the teachers who most vividly lived this experience.

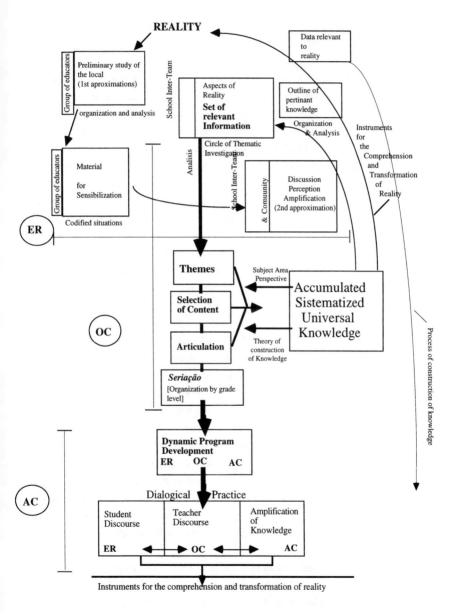

REALITY

Group of educators

Preliminary study of
the local
(1st aproximations)

organization and analysis

School Inter-Team

Data relevant
to
reality

Aspects of
Reality
**Set of
relevant
Information**

Outline of
pertinant
knowledge

Organization
& Analysis

Instruments
for
the
Comprehension
and
Transformation
of
Reality

Group of educators

Material
for
Sensibilization

Analisis

Circle of Thematic
Investigation

School Inter-Team

& Comunity

Discussion
Perception
Amplification
(2nd approximation)

ER

Codified situations

Themes

Subject Area
Perspective

**Selection
of Content**

OC

Articulation

Theory of
construction
of Knowledge

Accumulated
Sistematized
Universal
Knowledge

Seriação
[Organization by grade
level]

Process of construction of knowledge

**Dynamic Program
Development**
ER   OC   AC

AC

Dialogical   Practice

Student
Discourse

Teacher
Discourse

Amplification
of
Knowledge

ER   ← → **OC** ← →   **AC**

Instruments for the comprehension and transformation of reality

Figure 2.1.   Process of Curriculum Construction

The PT administration projected a vision of teachers as active agents of both educational and social change. In the words of a secretariat team member charged with coordinating the project, "Past administrations imposed their program and they told teachers, 'the program will be like this . . . .'" The proposal of this administration cannot be imposed, but instead depends on the adherence of the teacher. The teacher is presented with its theoretical principals, understands the approach and chooses to adhere or not to the Project. If the teacher does not willingly take an active role then the project will not work" (interview by author with CONAE team member, 1992). In this manner, the Inter Project had as its objective the transformation not only of the way knowledge is organized in the curriculum and what knowledge is considered as valid for the content and objectives of a collectively constructed interdisciplinary curriculum, but also worked at transforming the role of teachers in the classroom and in society in general; specifically, it implied a profound and continual problematization of how teachers related to each other, to their students, and to the community around the school.

The teacher profiles sketched below illustrate how teachers themselves perceived the PT's Inter Project. The selection of teachers is intended to be somewhat representative of the range of pedagogical-political positions that flourished in the context of the reform experience and in some cases continued to develop, as I was able to confirm in a follow-up field visit in 1994.

Like many of the teachers I encountered at the schools, Selma of Sussumu (one of my principal research sites) confessed to having initial doubts about the feasibility of the Inter Project but eventually became an enthusiastic advocate. Selma recalled how, for her, the Inter Project carried with it the tag of the PT and therefore at first signified a negative and definitively partisan imposition on the school and teachers. Her experience with the Inter Project changed her view of the party. According to Selma, the PT administration in Sao Paulo demonstrated an ongoing respect for the professional integrity of teachers, specifically manifested in the intensive interaction of the NAE personnel with teachers at the school site. In 1992, toward the end of the PT administration, Selma declared that she planned to continue developing her teaching practice within the framework of an interdisciplinary curriculum via the generative theme whichever the political party might be.

Selma elaborates on how the Inter Project indeed positively affected her educational thinking and practice: "Now the essence [of my teaching practice] is the formation [of the student]. I no longer have the preoccupation with finishing the book but I am concerned with forming a critical creative person." In this regard the Inter Project represented a more comprehensive educational approach for Selma than a traditional curriculum which she argued limits the role of the teacher and school to the mere transmission of predetermined knowledge:

> [That role should be] the integral formation of the citizen, starting with the daily life experience of the student and not what I [as the teacher] determine that the student needs. [The Inter Project] is a proposal that gives the student the opportunity to locate him[her]self in their reality. [The teacher] is an agent that contributes to the formation of citizens. It is not just me who is doing the teaching, it is the student who is discovering [new knowledge] by means of my mediation.

Selma concurred with other colleagues in her assessment that Inter Project at Sussumu was carried out in an uneven fashion largely because of the teachers' lack of comprehension of its theoretical basis. Despite the fact that many teachers believed in the proposal and most teachers claimed to be working within the project, in her estimation the reality was that they were not faithfully following its tenets and that it was very much up to the individual teacher as to whether or not his or her classroom was functioning under the projects' principles. Nonetheless, in 1994 she still reflected on the Inter Project experience as a positive one and in this statement reveals a very Freirean conceptualization of education: "It was a valid and enriching experience. I learned a lot; principally I learned how to learn. It showed us educators that education is not something closed: you give a course, you know, you teach . . . . No. You must learn with your student. In this way the Inter showed us that teaching and learning is an exchange [and that] there is no subject that is prohibited from being talked about [in the classroom]."

Claudio was one of the teachers at Sussumu school who was more vocal about his support of the Inter Project although he was not without his criticisms of the PT administration. Like other teachers at the school, his principal complaint was that the NAE-6 personnel "abandoned" the school once the project expanded to other sites. Theoretically he identified the Inter Project as constructivist and expressed his support for the curriculum reform proposal on that basis. In his words, "The project seeks to do away with the fragmentation of knowledge following the presuppositions of constructivism in which I believe." Claudio did not consider, however, the generative theme an essential element in the overall process of constructing an interdisciplinary curriculum: "The generative theme [he argued] is one of the means by which the process of interdisciplinariness can occur, but it is not the only one. Personally I believe that interdisciplinariness through [integration] of language arts [throughout the curriculum] would be more successful." Though he acknowledged the administration's efforts to inform teachers on the theory behind the project through its ongoing publications and teacher formation groups, like Selma, he too had reservations about how well the project was actually assimilated by teachers. In his assessment, the secretariat presented the principles of the project in a manner too theoretical for the majority of teachers to grasp, speaking to the limited professional formation that most teachers receive on the one hand, and to the fact that many of the designers of the project were university specialists accustomed to thinking in sophisticated theoretical terms on the other. Still, Claudio asserted that in general the project did impact the practice and thinking of teachers at Sussumu. He noted that as a result of the Inter Project experience teachers were now more willing to work collectively and to break away from their routine practices in the classroom: "Teachers have become more active, participative, creative, and critical." He pointed out improvements in the interpersonal relations in the school as a consequence of the project with a reduction in authoritarianism and a greater integration of the pedagogic coordinating team and teaching staff, in addition to a greater concern for the community.

Claudio did not, however, consider the changes that have occurred to be necessarily permanent ones, but in fact deemed them to be quite fragile, not only at Sussumu but throughout the municipal system. Nonetheless, in 1992, immediately following the PT defeat in the municipal elections, Claudio still held fast to the conviction that certain pockets of resistance would fight to keep the project alive at the school site level despite a political change in administration. Accordingly, a year and a half later, in 1994, he was part of precisely such a group at Sussumu, as was Selma.

Fatima, a teacher who had previously worked as part of the inter team at NAE-6 and returned to her former post as a teacher at Sussumu after the PT's demise, related to me the difficulties this group was facing:

> Last year we didn't even undergo a Preliminary Study of the Reality. The teachers just came up with a generative theme. I thought it was a contradiction to say we were doing the Inter Project in the plan submitted to the *Delegacia* [formerly what would have been the NAE] when we hadn't even done a preliminary study. The next year, some twenty-two of us went into the favela one morning in groups of three and four, to engage in a conversation with the residents. When we

returned to do the evaluation of the data it became apparent that many had never entered a favela before; the experience made them question some of their prejudices. In the end the group thought that the theme of *lixo* [sewage or trash] would come up yet again. I questioned the analysis; how can it be the same significant problem after five years? For many this meant that the model did not work and the project failed to progress. Still the experience of going into the favela was beneficial in that it ended the perception on the part of many teachers that the *favelados* are the source of problems in the community . . . . This year, there being presidential elections, [it] opened up the community discourse to include many commentaries of the political process; consequently the generative theme of "citizenship" emerged.

Fatima's narrative is emblematic of the kind of contradictions between the theory and practice of constructing an interdisciplinary curriculum via a generative theme that emerged within the groups of educators who either embraced or reluctantly joined the project, before and after the PT administration's tenure.

Among the teachers who most enthusiastically voiced their support of the Inter Project was a fourth-grade teacher, Francisco, whom I encountered at another school site, Habib (like Sussumu, also located in a poor periphery neighborhood in NAE-6). Francisco exemplified what could be called a "militant educator" in contemporary Brazil. Born and raised in the impoverished neighborhood where he teaches, he took his role as an educator as part and parcel of his political work in defense of the rights of his community. Illustrative of his educational militancy was the fact that in addition to teaching during the day at Habib, in the evenings he was an active participant in an adult literacy training group that formed part of MOVA, the literacy movement initiated by Freire's administration of the Municipal Secretariat of Education.

At twenty-two, Francisco spoke candidly of his struggle to become a teacher despite adverse conditions, which in turn had a marked effect on his political-pedagogical vision:

I live the same reality my students live, I live here in the periphery [very low-income neighborhood]. This has made me understand better my students. That experience also made me search out the reason behind the school failure of most children. School failure is related to the life conditions of the student—no food, no one to watch over them, no mother, no father. To make matters worse [at school] the child remains an outsider, receiving information that is not relevant to him.

Consequently, Francisco readily accepted the Inter Project's premise of departing from the student's local reality, especially when teaching children in a poor working-class neighborhood in a city like Sao Paulo. Along these lines, he argued, "There is no point in you talking about Paris if the student lives in Missionaria or Jardim Miriam [two low-income districts near Habib] and doesn't even know about Santo Amaro [a neighboring commercial district]." Also in accordance with the projects' pedagogical perspective, he viewed his students as "active subjects" in this learning process and conceived the role of the teacher as a catalyst to the conscientization of his students. To this end, he believed that "the teacher has to use his/her creativity to take advantage of what exists concretely in the classroom. You have to speak the language of the student, the popular language," he maintained.

Francisco considered the generative theme a vital element in the project's goal of educating for conscientization. For him the generative theme is a problem that stands out for the community, but it does not stop there. The educator's role is to problematize the significant situation for the community that is embodied in the generative theme. For example, he explained, if the generative theme is "violence" then the teacher must construct his/her curriculum around a series of "generative questions" such as, "What types of violence am I talking about?" "How do I commit violence?" "What factors make that violence intimidating for the community, for individuals?" "What other values are hiding behind the problem of violence? Because its not enough for you to just look at the problem. You have to look at the causes and what can be done to transform the process. So the generative theme signifies a challenge for revision." Apparently, Francisco directly associated the pedagogic use of a generative theme as the axis of an interdisciplinary curriculum with what he held as a political imperative to address social problems through a process of collective conscientization and transformative action. Although the greater task of galvanizing the community around a movement to build a popular public school was yet to be realized, Francisco believed that the Inter Project provided the necessary groundwork for that process to begin: "We are taking steps. We cannot say that we have effectively achieved unity [with the community] because we haven't. It's a gradual process . . . because we have had years and years of traditionalism."

In this respect, Francisco was one of the few teachers interviewed who positioned himself as strongly sympathetic to the PT and its overall project to build a popular public school aimed at the education of a critical and participative citizenry. Unlike many of his colleagues, for Francisco the PT tag gave the curriculum reform program immediate validity. He passionately articulated his position with the following words: "The PT is a government of the workers, which is precisely how it differentiates itself from previous municipal governments. The PT is a party with a very beautiful history. There were years of struggle and conquests. This is why I wear the PT star on my shirt because I believe that when something is good we must announce it." [He refers to the party's insignia—a red star with the initials PT in white—commonly worn by party supporters during the mayoral election campaign at the time of the interview in October 1992.] Like other PT supporters in the municipal schools, Francisco was very conscious of the fact that if the party lost the elections it would most surely signify a death blow to the Inter Project.

When I met up with Francisco in 1994, he was more critical in his reflections of the successes and limitations of the experience. Like others, he cited the institution of the full-time day (*Jornada de Tempo Integral*; JTI)[12] and school cycles as two factors that worked against the project's development in the final months of the PT tenure. Also, he saw the theoretical murkiness of the proposal as ultimately casting a cloud on its future. He explains: "The proposal was not clearly defined. Things often remained at the level of theory, I didn't always feel that they were being practiced, the teachers often didn't know how that theory was useful in the classroom. [In this sense], the NAE committed a sin, they should have done it in a different way. Instead of sitting us down to discuss theories they should have given us more concrete methods." Still he recognized the positive impact of the Inter Project inasmuch as "it turned teachers into researchers . . . . If they were willing, they could become active participants in the process of educational planning. The secretariat saw teachers as professionals and as professionals they had their rights as well as their obligations. [Consequently,] teachers discovered they were professionals, not babysitters." Reflecting on the general experience of the Inter Project, Francisco remained steadfast in his belief in education as a transformative tool: "As an educator I do not like to maintain a partisan outlook. I am not of the PT, I have no formal ties to the party, but I believe in some of the proposals of the PT. I believe in the public school as a space for changing society."

At thirty-six, Maribel had worked as an elementary teacher for sixteen years. Hers was a uniquely broad perspective of the Inter Project: in 1990 she had worked for brief periods at Sussumu and Habib schools at the time that the project was being initiated, and ended her experience with the project working at Marina Vieira school in 1991 and 1992, moving out of NAE-6 into the centrally located NAE-1. With the move, she immediately perceived a difference in the project's implementation. In her view, the collective effort of the teachers was ensured by the presence of the pedagogic coordinators at Marina Vieira and not so much due to the NAE-1 team intervention. Though she thought the project to have developed well at the school during its first year (1991), this progress was interrupted in 1992 due to the changes that occurred in the teacher regulations, which guaranteed extra hours even for those not working in the project (i.e., the JTI) and the introduction of the evaluation by concepts. Also, she felt that NAE activity had diminished; whereas in the project's first year they organized monthly meetings, in the second year the NAE team seemed less concerned with collaborating with teachers, and more preoccupied with finding out what was actually happening with the project in the classroom. This may have been related to the education secretariat's rush to document the outcomes of its policies at the closure of its tenure as they were facing the prospect of losing the 1992 municipal elections.

Maribel did not enter into the project voluntarily. When she arrived at Sussumu, the school had already opted for Inter. Many teachers like her entered the project due to the mere fact that the school had voted prior to their arrival. "Everyone was in the Inter and I decided to go with the majority, and try to accommodate my practice to the project." Instead of totally disregarding her previous practice—as she had been told she would have to do by other teachers—she understood the project as a "reform" offering ways to improve her teaching: in her words, "The project allowed me to add some things, and change some of my attitudes, principally my way of dealing with the student, to give the opportunity to the students to speak, to have a voice in the classroom. It was through my experience in the Inter that I began to see myself as a mediator of learning." Maribel was convinced that the project's pedagogical moments resulted in an effective means of organizing her classroom practice, as evidenced in the following statement:

> The three moments—the ER, OC, AC—are of utmost importance because from the moment that you begin with the reality of the student in order to add something else, the student has the sensation that he is learning. Even if within the project there is no programmatic, static, obligatory content matter, there exists a line of direction that orients our work. At any given grade level, there is certain content that has to be taught. But the way I work changed, because instead of arriving in class, as I did before, and writing out facts on the chalkboard

or bringing in a textbook for us to read, all the while believing that from that point on the student knew the material, that from the moment that I gave him knowledge he knew it all and that when he arrived he didn't know anything . . . so when we began to work with the ER I was surprised to see that the student arrives knowing so much and that if you start off with what he knows, then it is much easier to try to make him want to discover more.

Maribel agrees with the Inter Project's casting of the role of the teacher as a political actor; in this vein, she states that "if the teacher doesn't have an ideological position, doesn't believe in a political position, he will not understand or perceive the need to have a critical sense and no one gives that which he doesn't have." Identifying herself as a "liberal democrat" and "a political moderate that avoids extremes," despite her support for the PT's educational reform efforts she did not plan to vote for them in the upcoming elections, believing the party lacked the administrative experience to effectively and efficiently run the city. Such discord between teachers' partisan allegiances and their active endorsement of the PT administration's educational policies was common among educators encountered who fully embraced the project's general pedagogic tenets yet distanced themselves from its more radical and overtly political elements. Still, regardless of her preference at the polls, Maribel lamented the strong possibility that a change of administrations meant that the Inter Project would necessarily be dismantled as a formal educational policy effort of the SME. She emphatically stated: "Never in my sixteen years of teaching have I seen an administration so concerned with education." As such, Maribel was confident of the lasting impact of the project on the schools and teachers. To this effect she argued, "The new administration may adopt books, but teachers will not have the courage to just pass on content in a mechanistic way as they did before."

An elderly woman, Dona Teresa had been with the municipal school system in Sao Paulo since its inception over fifty years ago.[13] She is a retired principal who returned to the schools out of her devotion to the education of the less advantaged. She now taught fifth- and sixth-grade Portuguese language at Marina Vieira. In her years working in public education she has witnessed every educational reform attempted in the municipal schools and had this to say about the Inter Project:

It is a good idea, but impossible to implement in the municipal schools with the kind of clientele that we have. I know this because I have been working in the schools for five decades, first as a teacher and then as a principal. I have seen all kinds of projects come and go. This one won't work in the long run because our students need more direction. They need the text to guide them.

Her cynicism about the PT efforts to radically transform the municipal schools also stemmed from what she deemed as the limited analytical capacity of teachers in general: "The teachers simply do not have the cultural basis to discuss the theories." She further argued that its introduction into the schools was too immediate and forceful: "It was thrown upon us like a rain storm . . . there were too many meetings with highbrow philosophical discussions and teachers would get lost in the theoretical labyrinth."

For Dona Teresa, the Inter Project meant that students "learned whatever they wanted to learn." Although she recognized that students at Marina Vieira had become more "participant" in class as a result of the project, as many other teachers also argued, she believed that the project's encouragement of student participation led to a further breakdown in student discipline: "Students were left free and loose in the school." This less structured environment was further exacerbated by the institution of the three cycles and evaluation by concepts which Dona Teresa insisted resulted in her students losing their motivation to study.

Dona Teresa's Portuguese language classes followed a traditional model of teaching grammar through sentence diagramming and composition writing based on assigned topics. No vestiges of the Inter Project's methodological approach or curriculum content were evident in her classroom. She expressed her dissidence with what in her perception was one of its basic principles:

> In the Inter we are supposed to teach without a textbook. Tell me how we can teach language arts without a grammar book or workbook. I know that the people at our school, for instance, who are committed to the project are good educators, I just think that they're on the wrong track. What our students need is some good vocational training so that they can get a job once they finish their schooling.

From such a perspective, Dona Teresa maintained that the project was failing to provide students with basic academic skills. Entrenched in traditional pedagogic practices, she found it difficult to imagine the possibility of constructing the curriculum from the reality of the students, while using the text as a reference source. Instead she chose to construct a vision of the project as antitextbook and therefore irrational according to her educational paradigm in which all necessary knowledge is contained in the very textbooks that in her perception the project sought to invalidate.

In many ways, Dona Teresa represents a traditionalist-conservative educator in as much as she sought to maintain the status quo (both on a societal level and within the schools), conceptualizing her role as that of imparting basic skills and the fundamental elements of universalized knowledge, focusing on the formation of obedient and disciplined students. Accordingly, for her the Inter Project signified yet another attempt to utilize teachers as political pawns in the broader context of Brazilian society: "Teachers in the municipal system were turned into instruments of political manipulation, when our job is to teach," she chided. Ultimately Dona Teresa held the position that the PT administration had radically distorted the purpose of the public space of the municipal school, turning it into an ideological battleground essentially founded on partisan politics. Many educators such as Donna Teresa (not all necessarily from her generation) chose neither to embrace nor partially adopt the Inter Project in their daily practice, even when their schools, in majority, had opted into the project. Many such teachers (approximately 10 percent) secretly and not so secretly awaited the day that the PT would fall out of power so they could resume business as usual without wasting time with the "politics of education."

Generally speaking, the cases of Selma, Claudio, and Maribel are representative of the majority of teachers working in the Inter Project whom I identify as progressive-liberal educators. These educators, although ideologically sympathetic to the project's progressive ideals (i.e., its recognition of the important role played by teachers in the formation of critical and participant citizens), maintained a more liberal perspective focusing on the individual development of the student, adopting many of the methodological components of the interdisciplinary curriculum reform (i.e., constructivist and child-centered learning) while disregarding the more politicized or, as they sometimes perceived it, partisan implications of the PT's pedagogical-political agenda. A small yet active minority in the schools, represented here in the figure of Francisco, can be identified as critical-militant educators, engaging in what they define as pedagogic militancy through a fierce adherence to the notion of transformative politics for social change by means of a critical pedagogic praxis which they perceived as the main impetus of the Inter Project. Another somewhat larger minority maintained a conservative-traditionalist position rejecting the project on both pedagogical and political grounds. As in the case of Dona Teresa presented here, such teachers perceived their role as restricted solely to imparting basic skills and the fundamental elements of universalized knowledge, eschewing any political association to the act of educating as leftist demagoguery. Not surprisingly, these teachers expressed their resistance in a range of responses to the PT project, anywhere from apathy to fervent and vocal opposition.

The distinctly political focus of the PT's educational reform did not, however, presuppose a partisan alliance on the part of the teachers as the reforms' detractors might argue. Secretariat staff insisted that a leftist ideological position was not a requirement of the project but that it did require a certain "idealism, voluntarism, desire and need" for the kind of professional challenges the Inter Project created for teachers. Taking into account these and other factors, Secretary Cortella estimated that among the teachers actually working within the project only 40 percent fully embraced its methods while another 40 percent were in the process of being convinced and 20 percent—many due to their political opposition to the PT—were very unlikely of ever being convinced of its validity (interview with Secretary of Education Sérgio Cortella, October 1992).

CONCLUSIONS: THE POLITICS OF CURRICULUM REFORM

Among the many intervening factors in the development of the Inter Project was the varied manner in which individual teachers and whole schools deconstructed and reconstructed the project in their own vision. Divergent interpretations of the project's meaning or purpose, methods or goals, is certainly not particular to this experience in educational reform; but in this case, the fact that the reform was built on the principles of dialogic reflection and participatory action made it especially conducive to the development of a variety of interpretations of the Inter Project's objectives and the very methods applied and content matter proposed, as the previous sections attest. In effect, the education secretariat did not present teachers with a discretely packaged project, precisely formulated to carry out its political agenda of radically transforming the city's schools in the service of the working class. Instead, the project was created in broad brush strokes that outlined general principles for educators to follow in a collective effort to create the so-called popular public school . With the Inter Project, Freire's administration faced the enormous challenge of implementing an educational reform based on the philosophical principles of education as liberating praxis that had mostly evolved in nonformal educational settings by politically militant leaders of grassroots social movements in the 1960s and 1970s. It is not surprising then that in the 1990s, in an institutional setting of the proportions of the Sao Paulo municipal school system, the radical elements of Freire's proposal to educate for conscientization would necessarily meet with ideological resistance and methodological problems. Some of the most relevant issues and problems that arose during the project's implementation are summarized below.

Beyond resistance to the project on mere political grounds, several factors which worked against the project's development were consistently cited by teachers and secretariat personnel. A principal issue was the large size of the municipal school system coupled with the ambitious proportions of the project. Marta Pernambuco characterized the fact that the project was implemented on such a large scale, nearly two-thirds of the schools in the municipal system, "as unprecedented in the history of education in Brazil and certainly in the municipality of Sao Paulo" (interview by author, October 1992). This broad implementation had both its positive and negative consequences. To begin with, the project's rapid replication throughout the municipal school system, beyond the initial ten pilot sites—although aimed at fulfilling the administration's goal of creating a curriculum reform movement in the schools—logically led to a breakdown in the secretariat's ability to assist those schools that later opted into the project. Personnel at the secretariat level found themselves overwhelmed with the demands being made on them by the steadily increasing number of schools in the project. This pointed to another persistent problem which was, on the one hand, a general lack of administrative experience of NAE and CONAE personnel and, on the other hand, limited professional preparation of teachers to grasp and put into practice a theoretically complex project. Hence teachers consistently voiced their frustration at not receiving the technical support they needed from overburdened NAE personnel. For their part, the NAE staff complained that many teachers wanted the curriculum handed to them in a ready-to-teach fashion, which went against the project's very principles. The workload factor, therefore, also negatively affected teachers' reaction to the project, considering the limited monetary compensation they received (even with the extra ten JTI hours) for the intensive work it required.

According to secretariat personnel, the issue also alluded to a persistent conflict between the democratic principles they endeavored to promote and the need for a more coordinated supervision of the project (i.e., school autonomy versus accountability and supervision). This conflict was the subject of much debate at the secretariat level. Project leaders at the NAE and secretariat level were very insistent about the fact that the project was never imposed upon the teachers and/or the schools. The idea was that the school curriculum not be a predetermined package, as is traditionally the case, but that it be a continually evolving and collectively constructed product generated from within the schools. Yet many teachers who opted to join more on the basis of peer pressure than pedagogic or political conviction ultimately resented the casting of the curriculum reform in the light of a political-pedagogical movement within the schools as sheer PT demagoguery.

Another factor that was consistently cited as contributing to teacher resistance to the project was the uneven distribution of tenured and incoming teachers in the municipal system. CONAE personnel explained that in the more attractive centrally located schools where staff turnover is low there was greater resistance to the project. Teachers in those schools were often more set in their ways and less willing to adopt the sweeping changes the project entailed. At schools in the periphery, where there was greater teacher turnover, the presence of a high percentage of teachers who had recently entered the profession made them more open to the changes brought on by the project.

In addition, the ambiguity inherent in the PT proposal resulted in enormous differentiation and inconsistencies in the Inter Project interpretation among the different NAEs and schools. The Inter Project, more than a concrete curriculum proposal, represents above all, an attempt to radically rethink the whole approach to curriculum planning in the schools without adhering to a single curriculum model, but rather by promoting the proliferation of ideas and creativity on the part of educators involved. At a CONAE meeting of the project's coordinating team at the secretariat level in 1991, a discussion around the ambiguities that plagued the project ensued. At the meeting one member made this emphatic plea to establish a basic structure to the project that could be more effectively communicated to the teachers:

> We need to stop and reflect on some of the serious problems of conceptualization of the project. It is not enough to say, "'It is resistance on the part of the teacher." It isn't because he was not trained for this kind of work, and neither were we. We have to recognize that our technical support is loose. We don't have a generalized approach to the coordination of the project as a whole and each subject area is not developing in the same direction. The inter team at the NAE is being questioned at various points and moments. I feel we're in need of something more precise. We are still somewhat loosely defined in this sense and the schools that now are entering the project begin to demand more clarity. In the beginning we could say that they're resisting and don't want to join, but now this is no longer the case. We need to discuss these problems and somehow bring closure.

Addressing this issue, Secretary Sérgio Cortella identified as a primary problem of the project the need to prepare teachers better for this type of pedagogic work. He emphasized that "[The Interdisciplinary Project] demands a broad knowledge base of various elements that connect the production of knowledge . . . . It demands a knowledge of the history of science." Secretary Cortella pointed out that the teachers in Brazil are trained in a university where knowledge is compartmentalized, making it difficult for them to perceive the lines of communication between the various elements of knowledge. In addition, Secretary Cortella emphasized the persistence of the positivistic ideals in Brazilian pedagogical thinking as contributing to the difficulties teachers had in fully understanding and adopting the Freirean curriculum reform (interview by author, October 1992).

As a consequence, one of the principal difficulties which arose in the Inter Project's curriculum planning process—pointed out by many of the educators involved in the project—was the integration of all subject areas around a single generative theme. Teachers and even NAE team members were often stumped as to how to construct a curriculum that maintains continuity and coherence with the different skills of students at a given grade level. The subject areas of history and geography often became the axis point around which the whole curriculum revolved, given the facility with which teachers were able to associate the generative theme—derived from the social reality—to traditional content and skills taught in these areas. Hence, at the OC stage of program planning, problems came up with regard to the relevance of unifying concepts for all subject areas. Curriculum planning teams found that what might be conceptually important for one subject area was not of profound relevance for another; in other words, what worked for English and Portuguese did not relate to science, while they were able to unify history, geography, and mathematics more easily. One NAE-6 team member pointed out: "If it was difficult for the NAE inter team, imagine [how hard it was] for the teachers."

A subject area specialist in math, working in the CONAE, highlights this problem by posing the following questions: "How can I teach math skills without engaging in a classic explanatory format? How do you reconcile the most important math content with an interdisciplinary proposal? How to work with quadratic equations starting from situations generated in day-to-day life? Should the teacher always need to start from [real life] situations? If I want to know the general characteristics of a social group I employ the notions of 'mean' or 'median'—but if probability is not a mathematical topic taught in the fifth grade—what can a teacher do? And factoring? Should I interrupt a discussion within a generative theme in order to present some exercises for practicing skills and techniques in factoring?" (Mendonça, 1994) Interestingly, these very pragmatic uncertainties expressed by a university specialist at the core of the Inter Project's planning team reflects very accurately the concerns and doubts voiced by teachers at the schools.

Apparently, it was not clear for all teachers that the role of the generative theme was not to restrict the content matter in all subject areas to a single topic but rather to establish the interrelationship of the disciplines around a particular problem facing the community, in this way serving as a point of departure from the immediate reality of the community to the analysis and comprehension of more distant situations on a macro level of society. In this regard, many teachers possessed the erroneous perception that the generative theme was equal to reducing classroom content to talking about misery (i.e., the conditions of impoverishment of the community). In effect, some teachers argued that the generative theme was inappropriate for designing curriculum for small children in the initial cycle (first, second, and third grades).

According to various project participants, any attempt to introduce into the classroom a discussion of popular culture or contemporary issues was considered "doing the Inter Project." Rudimentary conceptions of the curriculum process under the Inter Project continually cropped up in my conversations with teachers and observations of classrooms. Piecemeal approaches to "doing Inter" might consist of writing down questions on the board as opposed to merely dictating factual statements to students or could include using the lyrics of a popular song as the content for a Portuguese class. In this way, "doing Inter" did not necessarily require working from a generative theme-based curriculum. Within such a reductionist conception of the project, the Inter Project became synonymous with the inclusion in the curriculum of any elements distinct from what would most likely be considered traditional curriculum content. Hence an anything-goes approach to content selection was adopted, leading to the disillusionment of many NAE inter team members with the path taken in the development of the project in particular classrooms at many of the schools where it was supposedly adopted.

In summary, a central problem encountered by secretariat personnel coordinating the project stemmed from the difficulty in reconciling teachers' established preconceptions of what constitutes essential content matter to be transmitted to students and the projects' insistence on linking all the subject areas represented in the curriculum to a generative theme of significance to the students. As a result of this persistent conflict between theory and practice, teachers in the project often left theory behind, falling into the above-cited practice of presenting standard exercises to cover skills they felt were not being addressed in the interdisciplinary curriculum via the generative theme. Ironically, it was precisely such reductionist interpretations and piecemeal applications of the Inter Project's principles of curriculum construction that represented a principal obstacle to the project's evolution in a positive (from the perspective of the PT administration) direction. Also, such inconsistencies in the project's implementation by school staff worked to further fuel the frustration of those who held tenaciously to the conviction that the steady transmission of traditional content matter constituted the "proper", most effective approach to educating the children of São Paulo, in contrast to what they perceived as the "watered-down" curriculum that the Inter Project produced.

Nonetheless, for many teachers the Inter Project signified a transformation of their own professional identity in that they began to see themselves and their students as active participants in the construction of knowledge not mere transmitters and recipients. In the words of a CONAE area specialist, "We know of some teachers that underwent a radical change in terms of their attitude in relation to their students. They always transmitted knowledge in a structured manner, suddenly they experienced a dismantling of that structure and perceived that this authoritarian method of simply transmitting subject matter had nothing to do with educating. [They came to realize] that it was necessary to hear the student, that the student also brought knowledge [into the classroom]." Marta Pernambuco, a principal intellectual force and key actor in the reform, also points to the creation of greater opportunities for dialogue among teachers as the key component to the secretariat's curriculum reform project:

> We were very clear on the fact that we didn't have a defined project, but that we were inaugurating a process. Nothing was resolved for anyone: we had defined the broad guidelines, but much was to be constructed along the way. For that process to continue, for the movement to happen, the most important thing was to create the mechanisms that made it possible for the project to evolve, hence the collective schedule of teachers; the meetings organized by grade level, by area; the school working as a whole was more critical than the content in and of itself. Once those foundations were established you could begin to build the rest little by little . . . . That was guaranteed through the process of expansion that made possible the mobilization of schools and the continuation of the [reform] process (interview by author, October 1992).

The overwhelming majority of teachers I spoke with in my research asserted that the one outstanding feature of the PT administration was that for the first time in their professional lives they were afforded the opportunity to have a voice. Efforts along these lines are further exemplified in the two Congresses on Municipal Education held by the SME in 1991 and 1992. At these two events—the first of their kind in the history of the municipal school system—thousands of the city's educators came together to discuss the direction of the reforms they were carrying out and to share their experiences with the Inter Project, school councils, formation groups, and other programs spearheaded under the PT administration.

Finally, it is important to point out that the underlying factor behind the idea of a multifaceted movement versus a rigidly defined reform program was a consciousness on the part of the PT educators in the secretariat that they might have only four years to carry out their efforts to impact the educational reality of the city's children and the pedagogical minds of the of teachers working in its schools. Ana Maria Saúl (director of the DOT) made the following positive reflection regarding the surge in the level of expectations on the part of teachers during the PT administration that resulted from this political mobilization strategy: "This was a very good thing, we didn't expect this, we knew they needed more resources, we were providing the necessary conditions, but we had imagined [that our mobilization efforts] would serve as mechanisms for the organization [of teachers] to pressure future administrations, but it began to happen during this administration. The schools themselves began to make demands of the administration" (interview by author, October 1992). This was precisely what the PT intended from the notion of creating a movement with the long-term effect of mobilizing teachers to continually fight to establish lasting mechanisms of change in the municipal school system.

Still, despite the limited time the PT had to advance its political-pedagogic agenda and the myriad obstacles faced, the Inter Project undoubtedly represents a landmark educational reform. Its roots in the rich tradition of a Freirean-based liberatory educational experiences that span the globe and the context of the reform in a large urban school system make the Sao Paulo curriculum reform movement one of enormous significance and far-reaching consequences. As Cortella, Freire, and Erundina proclaimed in 1992: "This experience lived by us—educators, parents, students and functionaries of the government—has demonstrated a fundamental fact to the country: that a Public Education of Quality is possible!" (*Diário Oficial*, 15 October 1992). To this effect, through its promotion of the Interdisciplinary Project throughout the municipal schools of Sao Paulo, the party laid the foundation for a new politics of education in Brazil: a politics that seeks to develop the theoretical basis and practical experience of an emancipatory educational paradigm and a new collective approach to curriculum-building that speaks to the socio-economic, cultural, and political reality of students and their community. Upon that foundation, the Sao Paulo municipal schools—and municipalities throughout the country—can begin to build their particular conceptualization of the popular public school, to investigate the reality of the school and create learning situations of greater relevance for students and opportunities for greater professional development of teachers. In effect, two years after the end of PT administration in Sao Paulo, schools revisited in 1994 continued to employ elements of a collective curriculum-planning process introduced during the Inter Project reform, and even four years later, in 1996, a school located in the former NAE-6 region reportedly *tirou o tema gerador*.[14] Moreover, other PT municipalities large and small—from Porto Alegre to Angra dos Reis—continue in the footsteps of the Sao Paulo experience recreating their own versions of popular public schooling and further building the model of an interdisciplinary curriculum via the generative theme.[15]

NOTES

1. This chapter is based on dissertation research carried out with the support of two separate grants awarded to the author by the UCLA Latin American Center in 1991 and 1992 and 1995. An ISOP Dissertation Grant supported fieldwork that took place in 1994.

2. São Paulo was among thirty-six municipalities that the PT won in the 1988 municipal elections. PT Senator Eduardo Suplicy presented himself as the PT mayoral candidate in the 1992 municipal election but lost to Paulo Maluf of the conservative right wing *Partido Democrático Social* (PDS).

3. Although Paulo Freire began his administration of the Secretariat in January of 1989, he resigned from the post of secretary of education in May of 1991, and was replaced by his former cabinet chief, Mário Sérgio Cortella. In a speech at the time of his departure from the Secretariat, Freire expressed his continuing solidarity with the PT administration and the educators in the municipal schools: "Continue counting on me in the construction of a politics of education, of a school with another 'face,' more joyful, fraternal and democratic" (Freire, 1991, p. 144).

4. The NAEs were the PT's administrative version of the former *Delegacias do Ensino* (Schooling Precincts) which in previous (and in the subsequent) administrations had carried out more of a supervisory role than one of offering ongoing pedagogical support to schools as was the case during the Inter Project. In fact, the Interdisciplinary Teams that the Secretariat instituted at the ten NAEs throughout the municipal system were responsible for the initiation and coordination of the project at the corresponding pilot sites for each NAE in 1989 and for supervising its replication at other schools that opted into the project in the three years that followed.

5. Examples of literatute by Brazilian scholars that develop the concept of *Interdisciplinaridade* include: Demétrio Delizoicov, *Concepção Problematizadora para o Ensino de Ciências na Educação Formal*, masters thesis, of São Paulo, 1982; Antonio Faundez, "Diálogo e Multidisciplinaridade" (mimeograph); Ivani Fazenda,

Integração e interdisciplinaridade no ensino brasileiro, São Paulo: Loyola, 1979; Luis Carlos de Freitas, "A questão da Interdisciplinaridade: Notas para a reformulação dos cursos de Pedagogia" (mimeograph) FE/UNICAMP, 1988; Hilton Japiassú, *Interdisciplinaridade e patologia de saber,* Rio de Janeiro: Livraria Francisco Alves, 1986; Antonio Joaquim Severino, "Subsídios para uma Reflexão sobre novos caminhos da Interdisciplinaridade," in Martins, 1989.

6. The CONAE operated out of the secretariat's Directorate of Technical Orientation (DOT), coordinating the Inter Project through the participation of two representatives from each NAE, in addition to an interdisciplinary team of subject specialists that advised the NAE teams.

7. For a complete exposition of the philosophy behind the concept of *conscientização* and the pedagogical methods implicated by Freire's proposal for a liberating pedagogy see his fundamental work, *Pedagogy of the Oppressed* (1970).

8. See also Vygotsky (1978, 1989a, and 1989b) and Ferreiro (1985 and 1988).

9. The project was first implemented at ten pilot sites (one per NAE) in the first semester of 1990 and later extended to other schools who opted into the project. The pilot sites were selected by the inter teams at the NAEs on the basis of applications submitted by schools interested in the secretariat's proposal.

10. Authors and works cited include Andre (1983 and 1989), Kosik (1972), and Lufti (1984).

11. The curriculum presented here is derived from a document, collected during my field work in 1991, which was being used to train teachers at other school sites within NAE 6 in the implementation of the Inter Project.

12. The JTI (*Jornada de Tempo Integral;* Full-Time Time Day)—a PT legislative victory in the regimentation of the municipal schools—granted teachers the right to ten hours of supplemental pay for class preparation, regardless of participation in the Inter Project, whereas initially only teachers participating in the Inter Project received such a stipend.

13. The Sao Paulo Municipal Secretariat of Education was founded on 8 July 1947.

14. *Tirou o tema gerador* implies that the school engaged in a thematic investigation of the reality and determined a generative theme for the semester's curriculum. This information was conveyed to me in a phone conversation with a key informant in April 1996.

15. A key informant of my research and a former NAE inter team member has been working since 1992 as an advisor to the Secretariat of Education of the municipalities of Porto Alegre and Angra dos Reis (both under PT governance) where they are currently implementing a curriculum reform based on the Sao Paulo Inter Project experience. In 1995, I was able to observe the initiation of this reform process during a visit to the Municipal Secretariat of Education and an elementary school in Angra dos Reis.

REFERENCES

Almanaque Braail. São Paulo: Editorial Abril, 1994.
André, M.E. D. Alfonso de. "Texto, contexto e significado: algumas questões na análise de dados qualitativos." *Cadernos de Pesquisa* 45 (1983): 66–71.
———. "A pesquisa do tipo etnológico no cotidiano escolar." In Ivani Fazenda (Ed.), *Metodologia da Pesquisa Educacional.* São Paulo: Cortez, 1989.
Delizoicov, D., and J. Zanetic. "A proposta de interdisciplinaridade e o seu impacto no ensino municipal de 1o. grau. In Nídia Pontuschka (Ed.), *Ousadia no Diálogo: Interdisciplinaridade na escola publica.* São Paulo: Loyola, 1993.
Faundez, A. "Diálogo e Multidisciplinaridade." Paper presented at the national seminar on programs for integrating the university and primary schooling, Brasilia, 1990.

Ferreiro, E. "A Representação da linguagem e o processo de Alfabetização." *Cadernos de Pesquisa* 52 (February 1985): 7–17.

———. *Reflexões sobre Alfabetização*. Trans. Horácio Gonzales et. al. São Paulo: Cortez, 1988.

Freire, P. *Pedagogy of the Oppressed*. New York: Herder and Herder, 1990.

———. *Educação na Cidade*. Sao Paulo: Cortez, 1991.

Gadotti, M., and O. Pereira. *Pra que PT: Origem, projeto e consolidação do Partido dos Trabalhadores*. São Paulo: Cortez, 1989.

Kosik, K. *Dialética do concreto*. 5th ed. Sao Paulo: Editora Paz e Terra, 1972.

Lutfi, E.P. *Ensinando Português, vamos registrando a história*. Sao Paulo: Edições Loyola, 1984.

Martins, J.L. (Ed.). *Serviço Social e Interdisciplinaridade: dos Fundamentos Filosóficos á Prática Interdisciplinar no Ensino, Pesquisa e Extensão*. São Paulo: Cortez, 1989.

Mendonça. Maria do Carmo. Curriculo de matemáticas. Campinas: Universidade Estadual de Campinas, mimeograph, 1994.

NAE-6. "Realidade e Conhecimento." Sao Paulo: NAE-6, mimeograph, 1990.

Partido dos Trabalhadores. *O Modo Petista de Governar. Cadernos de Teoria e Debate*. Sao Paulo: Partido dos Trabalhadores, 1992.

Pernambuco, M. Quando a troca se estabelece: a relação dialógica. In Nídia Pontuschka (Ed.), *Ousadia no Diálogo: Interdisciplinaridade na escola pública*. São Paulo: Loyola, 1993.

Plank, D. "Public Purpose and Private Interest in Brazilian Education." *New Education* 12, 2 (1995): 83–89.

Silva, M.N. *A Construção do Currículo na Sala de Aula: O Profesor Como Pesquisador*. São Paulo: E.P.U., 1990.

SME. *Um primeiro olhar sobre o projeto*. Cadernos de Formação Nº 1, *Série 3—Ação Pedagógica da Escola pela via da interdisciplinaridade*. São Paulo: Secretaria Municipal de Educação, February 1990, pp. 31–53.

SME-SP. *Construindo a educação pública popular. Ano. 2. 3a. Série. Vol. 2*. São Paulo: Secretaria Municipal de Educação, 1990a.

———. *Em Formação. NAE-6*. São Paulo: Secretaria Municipal de Educacao, 1990b.

———. *Estudo Preliminar da Realidade—Resgatando o Cotidiano. Caderno de Formação No. 2, 3a. Serie. Ação Pedagógica da Escola pela Via da Interdisciplinaridade*. Sao Paulo: Secretaria Municipal de Educacao, 1990c.

———. *Tema Gerador e a Construção do Programa: Uma Nova Relação entre Currículo e Realidade. Caderno de Formação No. 3, 3a. Série*. Ação Pedagogica da Escola pela Via da Interdisciplinaridade Sao Paulo: Secretaria Municipal de Educação, March 1991.

———. *Balanço Geral da SME; Projeção Trienal*. São Paulo: Secretaria Municipal de Educação, December 1992a.

———. *Diretrizes e Prioridades para 1992*. Sao Paulo: Secretaria Municipal de Educação, 1992b.

Vygotsky, L.S. *Mind in Society*. Cambridge: Harvard University Press, 1978.

———. *Pensamento e Linguagem*. 2d ed. Sao Paulo: Martins Fontes, 1989a.

———. *Formação social da Mente*. 3d ed. Sao Paulo: Martins Fontes, 1989b.

3 IMPROVING THE QUALITY OF BASIC EDUCATION? THE STRATEGIES OF THE WORLD BANK

Rosa-María Torres

INTRODUCTION

An international bank, the World Bank (WB), has in recent years become the most visible institution in the education field on an international scale, to a great extent now occupying the space traditionally assigned to UNESCO (United Nations Organization for Education, Science, and Culture).[1] Financing is not the only nor the most important role of the WB in the education sector; it has become the principal agency providing technical assistance in education in developing countries and, in league with this, a promoter of educational research at the international level. In the WB's own words "The World Bank's main contribution must be advice, designed to help governments develop education policies suitable for the circumstances of their countries" (WB, 1995, p.14). This, in turn, responds to the view that "school administrators are faced with decisions on specific cost-effectiveness quality-improving investments and various trade-offs. What they want are guides to specific investment choices" (Heyneman, 1995, p. 567).

Rather than presenting a series of isolated ideas, the WB arrives with a compact proposal—a diagnosis of problems and a package of recommendations—aimed at improving access, equity, and quality of school systems, particularly at the primary level. This reform "package" includes a broad spectrum of recommendations dealing with financial, administrative, human resources, curricular, and pedagogical issues.

This chapter analyzes and discusses the WB's proposals for the reform of primary education in developing countries. We will argue among other points that: (1) although presented as the result of scientific research and lessons drawn from international experience, the policies and strategies recommended have serious weaknesses in fundamental conceptualization, data interpretation, and analysis; (2) the strategies proposed for "developing countries" in large part take Africa (and rural realities) as a paradigm of the "developing world," specifically sub-Saharan Africa, one of the poorest regions and with one of the most problematic educational situations in the world. In fact, most of the policy recommendations that have been made in recent years and that are made today (see WB 1995 and note 1), were present in the regional study conducted by the WB in 1985 on thirty-nine sub-Saharan African countries. Ulterior information and research results have thus fundamentally served to reinforce those initial positions; and that (3) the reform package and the education model that underlies the WB's recommendations in the field of basic education, rather than contributing to changes in the said direction—improving educational quality and efficiency in the school system, and more specifically in the public school and among the poor—are contributing to reinforcing traditional tendencies in school systems. This is due not only to the nature and content of the proposals, but also to uncritical reception and application of these policies in borrowing countries.

Experience in some education reform projects financed by the WB in developing countries shows that, although originating from a homogeneous proposal, actual implementation can differ considerably from one country to another and can even "deviate" significantly from the original pattern. This is not only because each reality ends up adapting the proposal to its specific conditions, but also because there are margins in project definition and negotiation, margins that some country (and WB) officials utilize and others do not, and for which some national counterparts are capable of offering alternatives, while others are not.[2]

THE URGENCY OF EDUCATIONAL REFORM: THE WORLD BANK PERSPECTIVE

Although the visibility of the WB in the education sector is rather recent, the bank has been working in this sector for over thirty years, continuously amplifying its sphere of influence and action. Besides providing loans, WB's current activities in education include research, technical assistance to governments for the design and implementation of education policies, and mobilization and coordination of external financial resources. Since its first education project (in 1963 to Tunisia, for secondary education), total lending over the last thirty years amounts to nearly 20 billion dollars, through more than five hundred projects in more than one hundred countries (WB, 1995). The loans have covered all levels, from primary to postuniversity, in addition to vocational and nonformal education.

The WB's position with respect to education, and primary education in particular, is neither monolithic nor fixed. Within its own documents and studies (and among the personnel and spokespersons of the organization for the distinct areas, levels, and regions of the world) exist important differences in focus, divergent and even contradictory conclusions, and criticisms of conceptual frameworks, methodologies, and results of other studies published or cited by the WB. Moreover, there are changes, movement, and even significant shifts in the trajectory and policies of the WB in the education sector.

Over the last three decades, the WB has been modifying its priorities and, consequently, its investment policies in this sector. In the 1960s, WB loans favored infrastructure and secondary education and, particularly, technical and vocational education. In 1973 Robert McNamara, then president of the WB, announced a shift in the policy of the organization: the WB would focus on the poor, attending to their basic needs in housing, health, food, water, and education. In this last area such a shift translated into the prioritization of primary education as the cornerstone in the strategy to "alleviate poverty." After 1970 there was a strong and sustained increase in investment for primary education—together with an increasing role of the WB in technical assistance—and a decrease in loans for secondary education. This focus on primary education has been reinforced since the World Conference on "Education for All" (Jomtien, Thailand, March 1990) convoked jointly by UNESCO, UNICEF, the UNDP (United Nations Development Program), and the World Bank. The conference proclaimed basic education as the priority for the present decade and primary education as the "cutting edge" to achieve the basic education goal.

PROBLEMS AND SOLUTIONS FROM THE PERSPECTIVE OF THE WORLD BANK

The absolute number of children in the world who receive no education at all is likely to increase in the next twenty years.

Only two-thirds of primary school students complete the primary cycle.

Adult literacy appears likely to remain a major problem, especially for women.

In part because of past success at the primary level, the demand for secondary and tertiary education is growing faster than many education systems can accommodate.

The educational gap between the OECD countries and the transition economies of Eastern Europe and Central Asia is widening. (WB, 1995, p. 36)

Major challenges remain: to expand access in some countries and, in many others, to increase equity, improve educational quality, and speed educational reform. The current systems of finance and management are frequently not well suited to meeting these challenges. Public spending on education is too often inefficient and inequitable. In view of the competition for and pressure on public funds, new sources of financing are needed. (WB, 1995, p. 17)

Most education systems are directly managed by central or state governments, which put a great deal of effort into dealing with such issues as teacher salary negotiations, school construction programs, and curricular reform. This central management, extending even to instructional inputs and the classroom environment, allows little room or the flexibility that leads to effective learning. (WB, 1995, p. 6)

This is the vision of the WB with respect to the main problems currently affecting school systems in developing countries, the necessity of education reform, the prioritization of its components, and the definition of its strategies.

School systems in developing countries, in the WB perspective, are confronted with four fundamental challenges: (1) access, which has been achieved in most countries, in the case of primary schooling. It remains as a serious challenge principally in Africa; (2) equity, fundamentally seen among the poor in general, and among girls and ethnic minorities in particular (the segregation of girls being especially problematic in the Middle East and South Asia); (3) quality, seen as a generalized problem that affects all developing countries; and (4) the lag between the reform of economic structures and that of education systems, today most noteworthy in the transition economies of eastern and central Europe.

In the view of the WB, education reform—limited in fact to school reform—is not only unavoidable but urgent. Postponing it would have serious economic, social, and political costs. The current package of reforms proposed by the WB to developing countries is characterized by a number of features:

Priority on Basic Education

Basic education is the top priority in all countries because it provides the basic skills and knowledge necessary for civic order and full participation in society, as well as for all forms of work. (WB, 1995, p. 95)

A complete basic education is normally provided free of fees, since it is essential for the acquisition of the knowledge, skills, and attitudes needed by society. The definition of basic education is country-specific, but it typically encompasses at least primary education and often lower-secondary education as well (although not always, as the example of Korea shows). (WB, 1995, p. 103)

This basic level typically requires about eight years of schooling. (pp. 96–97)

Since 1990 the WB has encouraged countries to concentrate public resources on primary education, seen as an essential element for sustainable development and to alleviate poverty. Also, it is asserted that "in low- and middle-income countries the rates of return to investments in basic (primary and lower secondary) education are generally greater than those to higher education. Therefore basic education should usually be the priority for public spending on education in those countries that have yet to achieve near universal enrollment in basic education" (WB, 1995, p. 56), which is equivalent to saying in the majority of developing countries.[3]

It is necessary to pause and look more closely at the concept of basic education, given the variety of meanings of this term and its different uses within the WB (as also among other aid agencies and, of course, among the individual countries).

In the first regional study on the education sector conducted by the WB (*Education in Sub-Saharan Africa,* 1988), the term *basic education* was reserved for nonformal basic education for youths and adults.[4] Subsequently, basic education came to be equated with primary education. In the 1995 policy document basic education comprises primary and lower secondary education, it being estimated that the acquisition of knowledge, skills, and essential attitudes to function in an effective manner in society is achieved in school and requires about eight years of instruction. In this way, the notion of basic education, and education in general, is now firmly centered on formal education and on the education of children. Other aspects of education—and of the term basic education—such as the family, the community, the environment, work and the workplace, mass media, and so on, remain outside the margins of education policy considerations. Also outside are adult education, non-formal education, and other institutions and modalities (for example, Koranic education) not recognized within the parameters of official education. This is joined together with the emphasis placed on in-school factors (supply) to improve access, equity, and quality, while virtually excluding from the analysis and policy proposals nonschool factors (demand), which are major determinants of limited educational access, inequity, and poor quality. WB proposals thus deal with school policy rather than with education policy.

This concept of basic education diverges from the "expanded vision" of basic education that was agreed upon at the 1990 World Conference on "Education for All," one of whose supporters and organizers was the WB. This "expanded vision" of basic education includes children, youths, and adults; begins at birth and continues throughout life; is not limited to formal schooling nor to primary schooling nor to a specific number of years or levels of study; and is defined in terms of its capacity to meet the basic learning needs in each individual (see Table 3.1).

TABLE 3.1 Competing Views of Basic Education

Restricted Vision	Expanded Vision (EFA/Jomtien)
• is aimed at children	• is aimed at children, youths and adults
• takes place at school	• takes place at school, at home, through the media, etc.
• is equivalent to primary education or a specific number of years defined as compulsory	• is not measured by the number of years or certificates but by what is actually learned
• is organized around predetermined subjects	• is organized around the concept of basic learning needs
• is limited to a specific period in the life of an individual	• begins at birth and continues throughout life
• is homogeneous—the same for all	• is differentiated because social and individual basic learning needs are different
• is static, remains relatively unchanged	• is dynamic—basic learning needs change over time
• is the responsibility of the Ministry of Education	• involves all Ministries and government departments responsible for education
• is the responsibility of the State	• is the responsibility of the State and the whole society, and as such requires partnerships and consensus building

Source: Torres (1993)

Improving Quality and Efficiency as Pillars in Education Reform

The third—and probably most important—challenge [besides improving access and equity] is to improve educational quality; it is poor at all levels in low- and middle-income countries. Students in developing countries are neither acquiring the skills called for within their own countries' curricula nor are they doing as well as students in more developed countries . . . Improving quality is as important as improving access, but is even harder to achieve. (WB, 1995, p. xii)

Educational quality is equated with outcomes, and learning outcomes measured by achievement tests vis-à-vis the goals and objectives set by the school system (learning what is taught, being promoted to the next grade, completing the primary school cycle, etc). The relevance of what and how it is taught and learned are not viewed as an essential dimension of educational quality. The main indicator of educational quality is the "value added of schooling," which consists of "learning gain and the increased probability of income-earning activity" (WB, 1995, p. 46).

In the WB perspective, quality education results from the presence of specific "inputs." In the case of primary school, nine inputs are identified as determinants of effective learning. These are, in order of priority (according to the proportion of studies that would reveal a correlation of positive effect):[5] (1) libraries; (2) instructional time; (3) homework; (4) textbooks; (5) teacher subject knowledge; (6) teacher experience; (7) laboratories; (8) teacher salaries; and (9) class size (WB, 1995, p. 81). On this foundation, the WB bases its conclusions and recommendations for developing countries regarding which inputs to prioritize in terms of policy and resource allocation. While discouraging investment in the last three—laboratories, teacher salaries, and reduced class size—it encourages investment in the first ones and, specifically, in three of them: (1) increasing instructional time by lengthening the school year, increasing the flexibility of school scheduling, and assigning homework; (2) providing textbooks, seen as the materialization of the curriculum and relying on them as compensation for the low level of teacher qualification. The WB advises countries to leave the production and distribution of textbooks to the private sector, to train teachers in their use, and to develop teacher's guides for their more effective utilization; and (3) increasing teacher knowledge, especially by providing in-service training (rather than preservice training) and encouraging distance education modalities.

School infrastructure is no longer considered an important input either in terms of access or in terms of quality. In order to minimize construction costs it is recommended that: (1) education costs be shared by the family and the community, (2) school facilities be used in multiple shifts, and (3) school infrastructures be adequately maintained.

Focus on Administrative and Financial Aspects of Education Reform

Within the broader context of the administrative reform of the state, education reform tends to be seen as a primarily administrative and financial endeavor, with decentralization as a major reforming strategy. Specific measures proposed are: (1) fundamental restructuring of Ministries of Education, intermediate institutions, and individual schools; (2) strengthening information systems (especially emphasizing the collection of data in four indicators: enrollment, attendance, inputs, and costs); and (3) training of education personnel in administrative issues.

Curricular and pedagogical components of education reform are overshadowed by financial and administrative concerns. Financial resources tend to be seen as the critical factor that enables or hampers reform, while little attention is paid to the restrictions and potential of the human resources, those who ultimately conduct the reform and make it possible.

"Improving Educational Quality" as a Paradigm

WB proposals for education are fundamentally made by economists, using economic analysis.[6] Cost-benefit relationships and rates of return make up the principal categories which underlie education policy recommendations, investment priorities in this sector (for the various educational levels and the various inputs to be considered), learning outcomes, and the quality of education provided.

Economic discourse has come to dominate the education field to the point that genuine educational discourse—the dynamic of schools and the education system as a whole, the relationships and teaching-learning processes in the classroom—and its primary actors (educators, pedagogues, education specialists) are scarcely included in the discussions. At both the national and the international level, education policy formulation is generally and principally in the hands of economists or professionals associated with financial or managerial aspects of education rather than with curriculum and pedagogical issues. Many of those who advise on what should or should not be done in the education sector, and make important decisions from the local to the global level, lack the necessary knowledge and experience to deal with the fields for which they take decisions such as basic education, teaching and learning in the classroom, child learning, teacher education and training, curriculum development, linguistic policies, child and adult literacy, textbook and instructional materials development, learning evaluation, and so forth. Few of them have any actual experience in front of students in a classroom. Few have children in the public school system for which they plan and design reform measures. The virtual absence of teachers and teacher organizations in the formulation and decision-making processes contributes to further seal this discourse developed by economists to be implemented by educators.

Despite the fact that current policies are recommended and applied in the name of learning, the world of school and the classroom remains a black box, and teaching-learning issues continue to be treated as if they were "technicians" or the "details" of educational thinking, decision making, and action. From the national and international macroviews and macroproposals, top-down approaches in the formulation and application of education policies are taken for granted. It is assumed that reforms will "land" in the classroom, through declarations, decrees and normative guidelines, textbooks, curriculum, institutional reform, and teacher training, all of which would, supposedly, be accepted and adopted by school administrators and teachers, parents, and students. This "landing," however, has not occurred and remains a critical factor in the perpetual education reform movement worldwide.

Education is currently analyzed with criteria and standards of the market, the school is viewed as an enterprise (rather than a social system), and teachers are considered inputs and manual workers (Coraggio 1995; Gimeno Sacristán 1992). Teaching and teachers' role are oversimplified and misunderstood—teaching as the possession of, and capacity to select from, "a wide repertoire of teaching skills" (WB, 1995, p. 7)—and learning as a predictable result of the presence (and "proper mix") of a series of inputs. Each input is evaluated separately and is prioritized on the basis of two criteria: its influence on learning (according to selected studies which demonstrate such influence) and its cost. In the light of these parameters, a series of binary policy options are identified for primary school reforms; for example, textbooks are prioritized (strong influence and low cost) over teachers (strong influence but high cost), in-service over preservice teacher training, and textbook over school libraries.

WB documents on education show a precarious understanding of educational theory and of the accumulated research in the field. It is common to find in WB literature on education, including the 1995 policy paper, imprecision and even indistinct use of key educational concepts. These are education and training; education and schooling; teaching and learning; education and learning; education and teaching; education and instruction; schooling outputs and learning; curriculum and content; knowledge and skills; information and knowledge; pedagogy and teaching skills; pedagogy and methods; methods and techniques; textbooks and reading materials; initial education and preschool education; formal, nonformal, and informal education; adult, nonformal, and literacy education; class size and pupil/teacher ratio; and even primary education and basic education. Furthermore, there persists the association between "universal primary education" and "universal access to primary education," which ignores considerations of quality, retention, completion, and effective learning.[7]

Successive WB sectoral analyses continue to benefit little from advancement of educational research and from the contribution of related sciences (e.g., psycho- and socio-linguistics, anthropology, psychology, history) to the modern theories of learning. Education is perceived as a field that lacks specificity, antecedents, or history. It is an orphan of theoretical tradition and pedagogical discussion—a field of interaction of inputs rather than people.

It is in the curricular and pedagogical domain—the domain that essentially defines education—where the limitations of WB economists are most evident. The notion of curriculum that is used and underlies WB proposals is narrowly construed, basically understood as content (and content reduced to subjects).

The reduction of education to content (teaching as information to be transmitted and learning as information to be assimilated) underlies the traditional, transmissive, "banking" education model, and is consistent with the notion of "educational quality" reduced to "educational outcomes." This view also explains, in part, why textbooks are seen as repositories and ideal transmitters of the curriculum (the explicit content) while the central role of teachers in defining, developing, and implementing the curriculum in their interaction with students both inside and outside the classroom is ignored.

In the WB perspective, improving classroom instruction is essentially about curricular reform, not also about pedagogical reform. This responds to the traditional disassociation between content and methods, curriculum and pedagogy, and to the illusion of achieving education reform without a profound pedagogical reform and changes in the school culture as a whole.

In fact, the limitations and vices of this economics-dominated approach to education are beginning to be acknowledged and questioned by some of WB's chief staff:

> The bulk of economics research has been superfluous to making educational decisions. It has over-emphasized rates of return to expansion by level, and under-emphasized the economics of educational quality, new subjects, target groups, teaching methods, and system reforms. (Heyneman, 1995, p. 559)
>
> The field [economics of education] in general has been slow to ask the questions whose answers are necessary for educators to run

education systems better, and has been quicker to ask questions generated by concerns within the academic economics community. (p. 561)

Economics is more successful in estimating production functions when there is a single product (e.g., rice), and when the influences on productivity are physical. The difference between a classroom and a farm is that soils do not depend upon motivation. What this implies is that a tone of humility would be in order when discussing results. (p. 568)

Educational officials are held publicly accountable for error. In general, economists are not. (p. 571)

THE PRESENTATION OF PROPOSALS AS UNIVERSAL AND SUPPORTED BY SCIENTIFIC KNOWLEDGE

The WB's analyses and package of proposals for school reform appear supported by several studies—many of them promoted and financed by the WB—as well as by international experience, including the lessons drawn by the WB from its own activity in the education sector for over thirty years. Nevertheless, there are significant voids in the evidence used to support these policy recommendations, as pointed out by numerous authors (Coraggio, 1994 and 1995; Heyneman, 1995; Plank, 1994; Reimers, 1993; Samoff, 1995; Schwille, 1993; Torres, 1995b).

A Western and Anglophone Bias in Research

Most studies on which the WB bases its recommendations and which are cited in its publications (especially those dealing with basic education) refer to education in the Third World. However, the majority of such studies and publications are products of authors from the First World and from international funding agencies. There are few references to studies emanating from developing countries and/or conducted by specialists from such countries. Bibliographies that serve as a basis for policy formulation are principally anglophone, virtually ignoring important research produced in other languages. There is thus an abyss between the supposedly universal international discourse on education, and that produced at the national and regional level.[8]

On the other hand, the majority of publications cited are recent (1990s or late 1980s). This impedes a more dynamic and analytic vision of the education field and its evolution. The bibliographic selection gives priority to empirical and quantitative studies, capable of providing data and square conclusions on issues a priori identified as problematic. Conceptual or theoretical studies aimed at conceptualizing and deepening the understanding of a given subject, that pose questions and point out contradictions or dilemmas rather than providing unique and final answers, are rarely taken into account.[9]

Skirting the Difficulties That Underlie Contemporary Educational Research and Information

The "statistical problem" is widely recognized in the education sector throughout the developing world: much statistical information is not available and what is available is known not to be reliable.[10] On the other hand, educational research has arrived at a critical juncture: with the information available it is not possible to reach definitive conclusions on any specific issue. Research results exist now for practically all desires, to prove or to refute almost any thesis. However, the recognized problems of reliability and comparability that characterize current educational research and information, including that cited by the WB, is mentioned only briefly, if at all, in official WB literature. For methodological as well as ethical reasons, recognition of this fact should be clearly stated in any exposition intended to influence decision-making, priorities, and strategies in the education field.

Statements appear as monolithic and research results as conclusive, ignoring the lack of supporting evidence or, indeed, the existence of contradictory evidence demonstrated in other studies on the same research subject. Such omissions occur in numerous WB statements regarding textbooks (studies that do not find textbooks as an important input affecting the quality of learning, or that suggest a differentiated importance in different study areas, or that determine the impact of textbooks on educational quality to be a function of the presence of specific conditions); teacher training (studies that identify a positive correlation between years of teaching experience, quality of teaching, and student learning results; or studies that do not find the claimed strong comparative advantages of teacher in-service training over initial training); or instructional time (studies that find that increasing it, in and by itself, does not necessarily result in improved educational outcomes).[11]

A Strong Tendency to (Over)Generalize

A number of postulates tend to be affirmed and understood to be universally applicable, when in truth they result from only a few studies conducted in specific countries and under specific conditions. Examples here are statements about basic inputs exerting a positive influence on learning—teacher knowledge of the subject, time of instruction, and provision of textbooks. Statements about types of teacher training and teacher knowledge affecting student outcomes were initially supported by studies conducted in four countries (Brazil, India, Indonesia, and Pakistan), using different theoretical frameworks and methodologies.

A strong assertion, like the following, has no foundation: "In low- and middle-income countries school and classroom characteristics account for only about 40 percent of differences in learning achievement; the remainder is attributable to individual and family-background characteristics not typically amenable to school-level interventions" (WB, 1995, p. 81). The empirical foundations for many points are not made explicit or are extremely weak. To argue in favor of a specific policy option, the WB frequently resorts to citing one or more examples of experiences that demonstrate that such an option was adopted and had effective results, but does not describe the context—political, economic, social, historical, cultural, institutional— and the specific conditions that explain the success (or failure) of any given intervention.

In the realm of external aid agencies, it is the African (and rural) reality that, to a considerable degree, serves as the paradigm for "developing countries." In fact, the essential elements of the diagnosis and package of policy recommendations offered by the WB to developing countries in the 1990s were contained in the sub-Saharan Africa study conducted in 1985, in which thirty-nine countries were analyzed. The strategies that now constitute the heart of the WB reform package—priority on primary education, cost-recovery strategies, increasing class size, multiple shifts, central importance of textbooks, multigrade teaching, selectively recruiting teachers and reducing their salaries (or intensifying their work by organizing double shifts in schools), payment by results, in-service teacher training, among others— were recommended back then to such countries. "Strong research evidence" was already cited as the basis for these and other policy recommendations.

A Simplistic Treatment of Educational Innovations

"Success stories," "innovative programs," "best practices," or "effective schools" described in publications by the WB are often presented in boxes that are interspersed throughout the text. These boxes "bring reality" to the arguments and exemplify the strength of a specific policy recommendation. Nevertheless, the programs highlighted typically appear void of context, trajectory or movement; are described through exterior and superficial aspects; and are exempt from problems or limitations. Rarely found in such descriptions are accounts of what actually occurs in the program, or the institution in question. The dynamic in the school or classroom, even in the cases of innovations that are specifically pedagogic in nature, is not discussed. The organizational aspects of education reforms, often critical factors in the success or failure of reform attempts, are generally absent from both the diagnosis of the problem and its proposed solution.

Instead of analyzing the factors that explain the contradictory nature, the potential advantages and disadvantages of a given policy option, the path of generalization is preferred. The "Asian Tigers" are presented as ideal models—examples of the importance of will and tenacity in achieving ambitious objectives, including those for education—ignoring the specificity of these processes and their irreplicability in different historical, cultural, and socio-economic contexts. "Success" in some current education reform processes (the cases of Bolivia, the Dominican Republic, Ghana, Guinea, India, Jordan, Mauritania, Mozambique, Romania, and Thailand are mentioned in the 1995 WB report) is explained by the fact that "stakeholders have been involved in developing and implementing the reform," including teachers' unions (WB, 1995, p. 140). A direct, in-depth knowledge of any of these reform processes, each very different and complex in its own right, would call into question the simplicity of such assertions.

In the context of policy documents, "success stories" serve a clear function: rather than explaining the dynamics and the complexity of innovative interventions or education reform processes, their purpose is to convince readers and, particularly, policy makers, about the proven effectiveness and the infallibility of what is being proposed. This inevitably leads to simplification, bias, and even distortion. Innovative programs and reform processes appear without a historical context, frozen in a time period chosen as the ideal moment of their realization. Given the low survival rates of many innovations, mention of the temporal dimension (when the program was initiated, how long it has been operating, etc.) is often avoided. Because the chronic difficulties of consolidating and expanding educational innovations are known, as well as the lack of evaluation of results and impact, numbers (coverage, population affected, etc.) are rarely provided. Finally, references to costs are absent. The "innovative" tends to automatically be considered "successful" and "success" is seen as devoid of problems. Few publications opt for diffusing innovative experiences making known both their pluses and minuses "despite the cultural conventions challenged by this public presentation of 'difficulties'" (Little, Hoppers, and Gardner, 1994, p. 13).

Simplistic understandings of educational innovation and reform, and of what "works" and "does not work" in education, are not limited to the WB. This appears to be rooted deeply in the working logic of international agencies and Ministries of Education. However, such treatment by an international organization, and especially by the WB, takes on a particularly sharp profile when innovation is converted into just another marketing tool for "selling" policies and strategies to the developing world. As stated by Schiefelbein and Tedesco (1995): "A positive step in both educational reform and research would be an in-depth discussion of successful experiences" (p. 26).

A Manual Approach to Education

Despite addressing extremely complex subjects and decisions that admittedly require more information and analysis, particularly in the case of developing countries, the WB "makes few confessions of ignorance" (Schwille, 1993, p. 491) in its policy recommendations. Rather than posing questions or suggesting paths for future research, and rather than permitting a glimpse of the still fragile nature of education theory and practice, everything appears to have an answer, a precise recommendation, a clear map of options and priorities. Individuals who are not knowledgeable on education issues or do not follow education's practical and theoretical development—the usual case for a large number of policy makers in this field, and at whom WB proposals and discourse are directed—may receive the impression that everything about education has been researched, discussed, and resolved.

As will be discussed below, instead of analysis and presentation of policy options addressing a variety of objectives, situations, and contexts, WB policy options are organized according to black/white dichotomies and presented as if they were binary trade-offs: quantity versus quality, centralized versus decentralized, teachers versus textbooks, teacher training versus teacher salaries, in-service versus preservice teacher training, intended versus implemented curriculum, school breakfasts versus school lunches, and so on.

A Proposal That Dichotomizes Policy Options: Blind Alleys versus
Promising Avenues

From studies and from its own history of investment in the education sector, the WB draws a series of conclusions about what does not work ("blind alleys") and what works ("promising avenues") in primary schools in developing countries (Lockheed and Verspoor, 1991), and these are then recommended as policies.

The possibility of drawing conclusions and generalizing proposals for "the developing world" is questionable, more so given the fragile information available on education in general and for each country in particular. On the other hand, no policy decision appears in reality as a binary option, but rather as a selection from a broad menu of possibilities and shades. Educational change is systemic and does not operate on the basis of discrete, isolated elements: good textbooks without competent teachers is often a fruitless investment; teacher training, in the absence of an overall revision of the status and condition of the teaching profession, ends up increasing teacher rotation in search of better remunerated jobs; increasing instruction time does not necessarily result in improved educational outcomes if curriculum and pedagogy remain unchanged; and so on.

Curricular Reform versus School Textbooks

In light of the acknowledged weaknesses and limited results of past attempts at curricular reform, the WB now proposes to concentrate on textbooks. If the decade of the 1970s was the decade of investment in school infrastructure, the decade of the 1990s is likely to be remembered as the decade of textbooks.

The WB confronts us with a false dilemma between the prescribed curriculum (also known as the official, intended, normative, or written curriculum, and usually condensed in the syllabus) and the implemented curriculum (that which is actually realized in the classroom, also known as effective or real curriculum). Curricular reforms aimed at modifying the prescribed curriculum are being discouraged, alleging their complexity, the fact that such reform attempts generate excessively high expectations, and finally, that they have not translated into improvements in the classroom: "Most curriculum reforms attempt to modify the intended curriculum by concentrating on the courses taught and the number of hours officially allocated to them. Such changes in the intended curriculum are small, ineffective, and resisted by parents and teachers" (Lockheed and Verspoor, 1991, p. 47). Textbooks are presented as a substitute for curricular reform since they are considered in themselves the curriculum—"textbooks are the major, if not the only, definition of the curriculum in most developing countries (Lockheed and Verspoor, 1991, p. 46), that is, they condense the content and guide the activities of both teachers and students. Based on this analysis, the WB has seen an important increase in budgetary expenditures destined for textbooks within its primary education projects. In many borrowing countries, textbooks have become the first or second most important rubric of expenditure within WB-supported primary education projects, with teacher training usually ranking third or fourth in order of priorities.

The proposed dilemma between curricular reform (associated with the prescribed curriculum) and textbooks (associated with the implemented curriculum) and its underlying assumptions raises numerous questions:

1.   The curricular reform model that underlies the analysis and proposals of the WB is the centralized, partial and ineffective reform that has predominated in the past. Nevertheless, conditions currently exist to overcome that conventional, top-down reform model. There is no reason for curricular reform to be designed in a centralized and elitist manner, and for curriculum content to be prescriptive and homogeneous. The old as well as modern traditions of the reform package developed centrally by a small group of specialists have shown their weaknesses and limits, and rarely have succeeded in modifying practices and results in the classroom. But this does not refute the necessity of curricular reform in developing countries. On the contrary, accumulated experience suggests the need to revise the model and carry out reform in an alternative manner (Torres, 1993).

Indeed, renewed school systems need not only a new curriculum but, most importantly, a new manner of conceptualizing and developing the curriculum, through more participatory mechanisms and searching for social consensus, overcoming the fragmentary, partial, and short-term vision of past curricular reform efforts. These were generally focused on content, ignoring instructional methods, and on superficial addition or subtraction operations, without perceiving curriculum as a totality and without a long-term vision. Many influential educators and policy makers still understand curricular reform as a document, a decree, or an eminently intraschool intervention, rather than as a complex social process involving profound cultural change within and beyond the school system (Torres, 1993). Above all, it is urgent to understand that it is impossible to carry out curricular reform without including teachers, not only as potential trainees and change implementers, but as partners and architects of the reform process.

Renewed and participatory approaches to the curriculum and to curricular reform are, in fact, contemplated in the "Education for All" initiative. Countries were urged to organize participatory and consultative mechanisms in order to identify the basic learning needs of children, youths, and adults (WCEFA, 1990). This is neither the vision nor the proposal of the WB. In the light of pragmatism and economic analysis, school textbooks appear as an easier and faster path (a direct manipulable variable) than the sustained information, participation, discussion, and social elaboration process that is required for effective curricular reform. Indeed, the 1995 policy document recommends maintaining curriculum design and development at the central or regional level, without local participation and without forming part of the package of functions to be decentralized.

2.   The recommended prioritization of textbooks is based on two premises: (a) that textbooks themselves constitute the implemented curriculum, and (b) that textbooks are a low cost (when compared to a broad curricular reform) and a high incidence input affecting educational quality. In both cases what is in play, explicitly or implicitly, is another false option: textbooks versus teachers. From the WB economists' point of view, textbooks are a shortcut not only to curricular reform but to teacher preparation and professional competence.

The implemented curriculum is that which is effected in the classroom, with or without the mediation of textbooks, and fundamentally depends on the decisions made by the teacher (in fact, it is the teacher who decides whether, when, and how to use a textbook). Therefore, the surest and most direct manner of influencing the implemented curriculum is by addressing teachers, their motivation, preparation, and conditions. Both teachers and textbooks are fundamental for teaching, but there is no doubt that, if forced to choose, it is more important to have (good) teachers than to have (good) textbooks. Textbooks are educational tools; teachers are educational agents. It is the textbook that should serve the teacher, not vice versa.

The idea of the textbook as the implemented curriculum rests on the idea of a programmed, closed, normative, and self-contained text that orients teaching step-by-step and offers both the teacher and the students all the answers. This type of text, if highly esteemed and welcomed by the untrained or poorly qualified teacher, rather than alleviating the problem created by the continuous deterioration of teacher qualification and teaching quality, contributes to strengthen it by further disempowering teachers and perpetuating the classic (and growing) dependency of the teacher on the textbook. The need for an open and flexible curriculum, a tool of development rather than a strait jacket for teachers, is a contemporary concern, in tune with the "protagonist role," the "professional autonomy," and the "new teacher profile" proclaimed in modern educational discourse.

On the other hand, textbooks cannot be seen in isolation from the prescribed curriculum. Working on textbooks independent of the current curriculum (or that being revised) in a country implies promoting even greater internal disorder in the school system, possibly resulting in a plethora of disjointed, uncoordinated functions (e.g., a Division of Curriculum and a Division of Textbooks, each one with its own separate teacher training system), a situation which is already in operation in several developing countries. Moreover, as ratified by recent experience in many countries, this situation favors uncontrolled practices by private textbook publishers, who often end up defining the character and orientation of the reform (Coll, 1992; Ochoa, 1990; Torres, 1993).

3. While curricular reform is a complex issue, providing schools with good quality textbooks and assuring their effective use and positive impact on learning is no simple task, as acknowledged by the WB itself: "Throughout the world few individuals possess the expertise required for writing good textbooks, and most textbooks are therefore written by committees of experts" (Lockheed and Verspoor, 1991, p. 47). Therefore, the textbook option often results in contracting international experts or importing foreign texts rather than stimulating and strengthening national capacities and institutions to develop and produce quality textbooks in the medium and long term.

4. In practice, experience reveals the extremely problematic nature of projects involving school textbooks. WB lessons learned in this area include poor quality of the texts, inadequate distribution systems, the inability to sustain production, inadequate procedures for purchasing textbook inputs, lack of coordination between curriculum and textbook development, lack of synchronization between new textbook publication and teacher preparation, and the inability to establish institutions that will continue producing good quality textbooks upon finishing the project (Verspoor, 1991).

Assertions about the central importance of textbooks in the improvement of educational quality and outcomes (and, concomitantly, about the limited impact of teacher salaries and initial teacher preparation) merit additional discussion. On one hand, there are studies that refute, or at least relativize, the importance of textbooks on educational outcomes vis-à-vis teachers and teacher performance. On the other hand, several studies, including some promoted or cited by the WB, reveal that the quality of learning depends not only on accessibility but on the quality and variety of reading material in general. In spite of the fact that, according to the proposed input prioritization scheme, in which school libraries score higher than single textbooks in terms of their impact on educational quality, it is the textbook—not the library—which receives priority in WB recommendations for developing countries. To sum up, in dealing with curricular reform issues, several points need to be stressed:

1. Curricular and pedagogical reform are the very heart of education reform. Unless the what and how of teaching and learning are modi-

fied, that is, the actual practices and relations in the classroom, all other aspects—administrative, legal, institutional—are meaningless.

2. Reforming the curriculum implies working with both the prescribed and the implemented curriculum in an integrated fashion, and in a manner distinct from what has predominated in the past.

3. Modifying the implemented curriculum implies working with all elements that intervene in the teaching-learning process. The teacher occupies a central, privileged role among those factors.

4. Modifying the implemented curriculum implies working both within and outside the school system, with parents, communities and society at large.

Initial versus In-service Teacher Training[12]

In general, teachers are an issue with which the WB is uncomfortable and over which it has maintained ambiguous, inconsistent, and even contradictory positions. Teachers tend to be seen as teacher unions, and these evoke intransigence, disputes over salaries, strikes, and political maneuvering. Teachers are currently seen more as a problem than as a resource; they are seen as a costly, complex, and difficult to manage educational "input." Indeed, teachers themselves, and not only teacher training, tend to be seen as a "blind alley."

Two issues are particularly thorny: teacher salaries and teacher training. Although the WB has its views and proposals on both issues, and studies that provide a basis for minimizing the importance of both, there exist discussion, diverse opinions, and important changes in WB discourse regarding these and other subjects related to the teaching profession. For example, there is increasing recognition of the importance of teacher knowledge as a determining factor in teaching performance and learning outcomes (the 1995 policy document even acknowledges that available studies on the relationship between teacher training and student learning outcomes do not show a clear pattern). Nevertheless, teacher training continues to be relegated to low status among WB priorities and proposed strategies for developing countries, ranking behind investment in school infrastructure, institutional reform, and textbooks. Also, teacher training continues to be viewed in an isolated manner, without considering the changes needed in other spheres (e.g., salaries, professional and living conditions, and overall status) in order to make teacher training a useful investment.

In the mid-1980s, a WB study (Haddad, 1985) concluded that preservice teacher training programs financed by the WB were not cost effective.[13] In recent years, other studies have started to show that teachers with more years of study and higher qualifications do not necessarily produce better student learning outcomes. Based on this, the WB has discouraged investment in initial teacher preparation and recommended in-service training. Also recommended are distance modalities, considered more cost effective than residential modalities. Finally, it is asserted that teachers' subject knowledge impacts student achievement more than the teachers' pedagogical knowledge. As will be discussed below, these (and other) traditional "hard" WB positions are being softened in recent times.

In reality, initial and in-service teacher training are complementary and different stages of a single learning process of teachers. Both are necessary and both are currently facing problems. In-service programs—proliferating over the last few years and yet to be evaluated in terms of their impact on actual teaching performance and learning processes and outcomes—are definitely not the panacea for the school problems and much less for the broader challenge of preparing the teachers required to deal with modern, complex education goals and objectives. Subject knowledge and pedagogical knowledge are inseparable in competent teaching, as finally recognized in the 1995 policy document, although with a limited understanding of pedagogy: "The most effective teachers appear to be those with good knowledge of the subject and a wide repertoire of teaching skills" (WB, 1995, p. 7). Even more, as suggested by different studies, several of them conducted in Latin America (Filp, Cardemil, and Valdivieso, 1984), and confirmed by practical experience, teachers' attitudes and expectations can play a more important role in student learning than teacher knowledge of either subject matter or pedagogy.

Distance education is recommended as a low cost alternative for teacher training. However, experience with distance modalities for teacher training purposes in developing countries is still incipient, and there is insufficient information and evaluation to conclude that distance training modalities are in fact less costly and more effective than face-to-face, residential ones (Klees, 1994; Tatto, Nielsen, and Cummings, 1991). In fact, distance training programs promoted in the international literature in the last few years often have not achieved the same level of acceptance in their own countries.

There is growing consensus that initial teacher education is undergoing a serious crisis, and that traditional institutions offering such teacher education, whether at the secondary or tertiary level, need major reform. The heavy emphasis placed on in-service training and the open discrediting of initial teacher education over the past decade has been of course a contributing factor to this crisis. However, as in the case of curricular reform, the solution is not to eradicate what does not work properly—whether it is education reform, teacher training institutions and practices, or the school system as a whole—but to identify why it has not worked, and to change or redirect it accordingly. It is not initial teacher education but the conventional teacher education model, whether preservice or in-service, that has not worked and needs major transformation (see Table 3.2).

The importance of the school system, and of secondary education in particular, as a principal source in teacher preparation, was acknowledged in the sub-Saharan report (WB, 1988) and is further stressed in the 1995 policy document. Empirical evidence indicates that teachers tend to behave in the classroom based more on what they experienced as school students themselves than on what they learned in their formal preparation as teachers. Both initial and in-service training become merely compensatory and remedial strategies vis-à-vis a deficient general education provided by a low quality school system. A good school system constitutes indeed the best and most certain investment in teacher preparation.

Recognizing the importance of general knowledge for teacher performance and the importance of the school system in providing such knowledge, the WB's recommendations for teacher recruitment and development include: (1) ensuring quality secondary education, (2) complementing it with a short initial preparation focused on pedagogical aspects, and (3) hiring teachers based on proven knowledge and competence—national proficiency tests for teachers are suggested—with criteria and procedures similar to those utilized for hiring university professors. Points (2) and (3) were present in WB recommendations to sub-Saharan African countries in the mid-1980s. Obviously, to attract and fill this teacher profile in sufficient numbers implies a radical shift in the parameters under which both the school system and the teaching profession have been operating. Among others, such a shift supposes drastically revising teacher salaries and working conditions. On this point, the WB limits itself to insisting that teacher salaries be tied to performance and that this be measured through student learning outcomes. No analysis is provided on the viability and costs of this proposal.

Teacher salaries constitute the most slippery aspect of the entire reform package proposal. The WB's position is that increasing teacher salaries does not improve school outcomes. The argument—deceitful inasmuch as no education input, in and by itself, can affect learning outcomes—has been extended in many cases to conditioning WB loans to a nonincrease in teacher salaries.

Trapped in defense of its policy options and cost-benefit schemes, and confronted by practical developments of these policies in the borrowing countries as well as by new information and knowledge available (provid-

TABLE 3.2 The Teacher Education Model That Has Not Worked

• each new policy, plan or project starts from zero	(ignoring or disregarding previous knowledge and experience)
• considers education/training principally as a need for teachers	(and not also for principals, supervisors and human resources linked to the education system in general and at all levels)
• views education/training in isolation from other dimensions of the teaching profession	(such as salaries, working and living conditions, promotion mechanisms, organizational arrangements, etc.)
• ignores teachers' real conditions	(motivations, concerns, knowledge, available time and resources, etc.)
• adopts a top-down approach and sees teachers only in a passive role of recipients and potential trainees	(does not consult teachers or seek their participation in the definition and design of the training plan)
• has a homogeneous proposal for "teachers" in general	(instead of adjusting to the various types and levels of teachers and their specific needs)
• adopts an operational approach to teacher training	(in-service training is viewed as a tool to persuade and implement a definite policy, program, project or even a textbook)
• assumes that the need for training is inversely proportional to the level of teaching	(thus ignoring the importance and complexity of teaching young children and in the initial grades)
• resorts to external incentives and motivation mechanisms	(such as scores, promotion, certificates, rather than reinforcing the objective of learning and improving the teaching practice)
• addresses individual teachers	(rather than groups or work teams, or the school as a unified whole)
• is conducted outside the work place	(typically, teachers are brought to the training sites instead of bringing the training to them and making the school the training site)

(continued on page 82)

TABLE 3.2 *(continued from page 81)*

- is asystematic and limited to a short period of time
  (not integral to a continuing education scheme)

- is centered around the event (the course, the seminar, the workshop, etc.) as a privileged— and even unique—teaching and learning tool
  (ignoring or marginalizing other modalities such as horizontal exchange, peer group discussions, class observation, distance education, self-study, on-site visits, etc.)

- disassociates *administrative* and *pedagogical* issues as content and as learning needs
  (pedagogical issues are considered the realm of teachers, and administrative issues are consigned to others, without an integral approach to both types of knowledge and skills)

- disassociates *content* and *method* (subject matter and pedagogy, knowing the subject and knowing how to teach it) and promotes the prior over the latter
  (ignoring the inseparability and complementarity of both types of knowledge, and the need for both)

- considers education and training to be formal, stern and rigid
  (denying the educational and communicational importance of an informal environment, of play, laughter and enjoyment)

- is focused on the teaching perspective
  (rather than on the learning perspective)

- rejects teachers' previous knowledge and experience
  (instead of starting from there and building on it)

- is oriented toward correcting mistakes and highlighting weaknesses
  (rather than toward stimulating and reinforcing strengths)

- is academic and theoretical, centered around the book
  (while denying the actual teaching practice as the raw material and the most important source for learning)

- is based on the frontal and transmissive teaching model
  (teaching as the transmission of information and learning as the passive assimilation of that information)

(continued on next page)

TABLE 3.2 *(continued from previous page)*

• is essentially incoherent and contradictory to the pedagogical model that is requested of teachers in their classrooms	(teachers are expected to elicit active learning, critical thinking, creativity, etc., which they themselves do not experience in their own education and training process)

Source: Torres, 1995b

ing much more varied conclusions than the WB's package is able to accommodate), the WB has reached the critical point of being forced to review some of its positions.

It is impossible to continue asserting that in-service training is more (cost) effective than initial teacher training when, at the same time, it is recognized that in-service training is only a remedial strategy when faced with a poor quality school system or poor quality (or nonexistent) initial teacher education, and that the latter is critical in ensuring teacher knowledge of subject matter, a fundamental variable in teacher performance: "Teachers' subject knowledge, an intended outcome of pre-service training, is strongly and consistently related to student performance" (WB, 1995, p. 82). It is not possible to continue framing teacher education within the dichotomous pre/in-service scheme, while recognizing that the school system (and its improvement) is the surest source of solid general education for teachers. It is not possible to propose new parameters for teacher recruitment—the best and the most competent—while bypassing teacher salaries and professional development issues that are a condition for the adoption of such parameters in reality. Furthermore, it is impossible to continue advocating educational quality improvement without integrally addressing the teachers issue.

Reducing Class Size versus Increasing Instructional Time

Several studies quoted by the WB conclude that the number of students per class (when it is above twenty) has little impact on learning achievement. On this basis, since the 1980s, borrowing countries have been recommended not to invest resources in attempting to reduce class size—a clear tendency over the last few years, except for South Asia—and, on the contrary, to "save costs and improve learning by increasing student-teacher ratios. They would thereby use fewer teachers and would be able to allocate resources from teachers to other inputs that improve achievement such as textbooks and in-service teacher training" (WB, 1995, p. 59).

Assertions about class size and the recommendations derived from them are among the oldest and most insisted upon by the WB, and also among the most controversial and resisted in borrowing countries. Conventional wisdom (and actual standards and practice in Western industrialized countries) suggests that smaller student-teacher ratios provide better conditions for learning. The assertion that "class size makes no difference" may be true from an economist's point of view but not from a teacher's point of view, and definitely not unless fundamental curricular and pedagogical changes are introduced in the regular classroom.

It is indeed necessary to rationalize the distribution of teachers within the school system. However, a homogeneous application of this policy would also be irrational and lead to increased inequality, inequity, and poor quality of school systems. If improving educational quality is a major goal, together with drastically reducing repetition and dropout rates in primary school, developing countries should on the contrary be explicitly recommended to reduce student-teacher ratios in the first grades, typically the most overcrowded and with the worst teaching and learning conditions of the entire school system. In any case, the WB itself acknowledges that "in practice, such savings (obtained by increasing student-teacher ratios) are seldom allocated to other inputs" (WB, 1995, p. 59).

The other variable highlighted is instructional time: "The amount of actual time devoted to learning is consistently related to achievement. Students in low- and middle-income countries receive fewer hours of classroom instruction than those in OECD countries—a consequence of a shorter official school year, unscheduled school closings, teacher and student absences, and miscellaneous disruptions" (WB, 1995, p. 7). Measures recommended to increase instructional time include extending the official school year; permitting flexible scheduling to accommodate the demands of agricultural seasons, religious holidays, and children's domestic chores; and assigning homework. However, in practice, the establishment of multiple shifts and multiple use of classroom buildings, which the WB has been recommending as a means of minimizing construction costs and maximizing the labor of the teaching force, results in reducing instruction time rather than increasing it. This is a clear example of how two policy recommendations can have opposite effects and annul each other.

The subject of teacher absenteeism, as yet poorly documented and analyzed, is the expression of diverse and complex personal and work-related factors (sickness, distances and transportation difficulties, additional jobs to complement a meager salary, bureaucratic and lengthy procedures to collect salaries, training outside the workplace, and many others) that cannot be resolved simply with coercion and control by either local or central authorities, parents, or communities. The feminization of the teaching profession at the primary level, in the case of Latin America—a result of the fallen prestige and remuneration of teaching as a professional option— constitutes in itself a fundamental factor in teacher absenteeism; it implies having implicitly selected a specific teacher profile (women; low-income women; housewives; women that become pregnant, give birth, have and care for children; etc.), without having concomitantly considered the consequences of choosing such a profile and the measures necessary for combating absenteeism (child care services, emotional support services, effective mechanisms for substitution or team teaching, revising traditional masculine and feminine roles at home and in the school, etc.). In other words, the very conditions spawned in the development of the teaching profession are conducive to absenteeism.

The most expressive and devastating form of teacher absenteeism has become the strike, which is on the increase all over the world. In Latin America, teacher strikes—each time more violent and more prolonged, sometimes lasting three or four months—have become common in the majority of countries. Against this context, forcing an increase of a few hours or days of class per academic year through ways that ignore the reasons causing repeated strikes is like trying to stop a hemorrhage by applying a Band-Aid. The "savings" in teacher salaries and acceptable working conditions for teachers have a very high cost, both in terms of available time for teaching and learning and, more fundamentally, in terms of educational quality.

Concluding Thoughts

Through both conceptualization and implementation, instead of improving the quality, equity, and efficiency of the school system, the World Bank reform package is actually helping developing countries to reinforce and to invest in the wider reproduction of the existing, conventional education model, at most disguised with new clothing and modern terminology.

Some of the characteristics of the conventional education model are the following:

1. It reduces education to school. It assumes that education policies are reduced to school policies, that formal schooling is the only source of learning, and that basic education (meeting the basic learning needs of children, youths, and adults) is resolved in the classroom, thus ignoring the important educational role of the family, the environment, play, work, experience, and mass media.

2. It has an eminently sectoral vision of education, understood as a monopoly of a ministry and specialized educational institutions. Sector analyses and interventions consider health, nutrition, production, employment, the economy, and so on, as extra-educational factors. Most importantly, poverty is treated as if it were extra-sectoral.

3. It lacks a systemic vision, a vision of the education system as a system: the different levels (initial, primary, secondary, and higher) are fragmented and lack coordination; educational change is attempted by addressing discrete, isolated factors (administrative, legal, curricular, teacher training, provision of textbooks, etc) without understanding that change in education can only be systemic.

4. It is permeated by a dichotomous vision of education realities and policy options: quantity versus quality, child education versus adult education, basic education versus higher education, administrative versus pedagogical issues, contents versus methods, pre- versus in-service teacher training, supply versus demand, centralized versus decentralized, decision makers versus implementers, governmental versus nongovernmental, public versus private, teaching versus learning, teacher-centered versus learner-centered approaches, success versus failure, and so forth. Educational change and innovation are generally viewed in terms of pendular movements from one pole to the other.

5. It acts and reacts to the immediate and the short term, tied to political timing and administrative needs rather than to the needs of educational change and development, lacking a strategic and long-term vision that sees beyond particular administration periods and overcomes the "project" mind set.

6. It is vertical and authoritarian, centralized in the decision-making process, with no tradition of public information or accountability in the use of resources, and with top-down approaches to education reform and innovation. It does not promote information, communication, and social debate about the realities and prospects of education, the results of the school system, or the education policies adopted. The "failure" of a specific policy or program is attributed to lack of will or incapacity of those who implement rather than to errors in policy conceptualization and design.

7. It grants priority to quantity over quality, results over processes, how much is learned over what is learned, how it is learned, and for what it is learned. Enrollment constitutes the main, if not the only, indicator to measure educational progress (or regression), equality, and eq-

uity (and even the concept of "universal primary education" is reduced to this sole indicator), while paying little attention to retention, completion, and effective learning. Education is measured and evaluated by the number of certificates, degrees, and/or years of instruction, rather than by what is effectively learned and the usefulness of such learning.

8. It disassociates demand and supply in education. Reform and improvement strategies focus on the supply side (intraschool factors) while ignoring the demand (parents, communities, and society at large) and the importance of empowering such demand (through public information, parents' education, training at the community level, etc.) as a fundamental condition to achieve meaningful community participation, a strong school system, and quality education for all.

9. It disassociates administrative and pedagogical issues, grants priority to the former, subordinates the pedagogical model to the administrative model, and assumes that changes in the latter will inevitably bring changes in the former. Pedagogy is considered marginal in both teacher performance and policy decisions and planning.

10. It prioritizes investments in things (buildings, supplies, textbooks, laboratories, computers, etc.) over investments in people (motivation, capacity building, professional development, working conditions) involved in the education sector at the different levels (students, parents, teachers, headmasters, administrators, intermediate cadre, specialists, educational journalists, etc).

11. It is based on the supposition of homogeneity (for students as well as for teachers, for schools within a country, and for developing countries at the world level) and defines therefore homogeneous diagnostic and action frameworks for all of them. There is an inability to recognize, accept, and manage diversity, from the classroom level to the national and international policy level.

12. It does not differentiate between teaching and learning. It assumes that what is taught is learned, that modifications in teaching automatically produce modifications in learning, and that lack of learning is the fault of the student ("learning disabilities").

13. It views education as a process of transmission, assimilation, and accumulation of information, provided by teachers and textbooks, rather than as an active process of construction and appropriation of knowledge, skills, values, and attitudes that initiates well before, and goes far beyond, schooling.

14. It is based on a frontal and transmissive model of teaching, in which

teaching is equated with speaking and learning with listening. This model applies to students in the classroom and to teachers in their own preparation and training. The model is extended to the relationship between advisors and advisees.

15. It has demonstrated misunderstanding and negligence in the management of teacher-related issues: Teachers are ignored as fundamental actors in educational provision, quality, and change; they are relegated to a secondary and passive role, and their advice and participation ignored as a fundamental condition in the design, implementation, and effectiveness of education policies, and of education reform in particular.

16. It shows a marked preference for the quick and easy fix, with little attention to effectiveness and sustainability of actions over time; the decree or the formal announcement as a substitute for systematic communication, explanation, and persuasion efforts; replicating innovative experiences rather than enhancing the capacity to innovate; top-down education reform packages rather than participatory reform processes; short in-service teacher training courses rather than a comprehensive teacher education strategy; improving textbooks or adding new areas (e.g., health, peace, environment, life skills, etc.) as a substitute for a thorough revision of the curriculum; distribution of supplies rather than capacity-building efforts; consensus building understood as signatures and formal agreements rather than as an active and sustained social dialogue among stakeholders; and so on.

17. It views parental and community participation in education in a unilateral and restricted manner (e.g., limited to the school, restricted to "nontechnical" matters, etc.) and usually, and increasingly, focused on monetary aspects. Participatory rhetoric is not accompanied by measures (e.g., information, training, financial, administrative) to make it a reality.

18. Finally, it perceives education policy development as always starting from zero, without a retrospective view; discarding what was done before rather than building on it; proposing new models, policies, and strategies prior to analyzing why previous ones did not work; and giving little attention to actual implementation conditions (political, social, cultural, and organizational).

NOTES

1. In this chapter I am using as a central reference for analysis the most recent education policy document by the WB, *Priorities and Strategies for Education:*

A *World Bank Sector Review* (both the March and May 1995 preliminary drafts and the August 1995 printed draft), which will be abbreviated WB, 1995. This document synthesizes the principal studies on education published by the WB since the last documents on this sector: *Education in Sub-Saharan Africa* (1988), *Primary Education* (1990), *Vocational and Technical Education and Training* (1991), and *Higher Education* (1994). The objective of this document is "to assist policymakers in these [low- and middle-income] countries, especially those concerned with the education system as a whole and with the allocation of public resources to education" (p. xii).

2. The Bolivian education reform process offers some interesting lessons in this respect. See Anaya, 1995, for an account of such process "from within."

3. What is considered "near universal enrollment" is not specified. Latin America and the Caribbean, the developing region with the highest enrollment rates at the primary school level, admit to an official average of 15 percent of school-age children out of school.

4. Basic education generally refers to instruction in literacy and numeracy skills for out-of-school youths and adults (WB, 1988, p. x).

5. See Fuller and Clarke, 1994.

6. For a critical analysis of the economic theory underlying WB education policies, see Coraggio 1994 and 1995.

7. The assertion that "in East Asia and Latin America and the Caribbean primary education is almost universal" (WB, 1995, p. 33) refers, obviously, to primary school *enrollment*. Both Asia and Latin America are far from having achieved the goal of universal primary education, if retention and completion also are considered.

8. The 1995 policy document includes 274 bibliographic references, all of them in English. The book on primary education in developing countries by Lockheed and Verspoor (1991) includes 446 references, of which 441 are publications in English. The remaining five are in French (2), Spanish (2), and Portuguese (1).

9. An example of this is the assertion (based on a few studies) that the provision of educational inputs has a comparatively stronger impact on school outcomes in developing countries than in developed ones. From this follows the conclusion and the recommendation that justifies large investments in inputs in the Third World, and other actions—presumably more qualitative in nature—in the First World.

10. Today it is difficult to find two statistical sources that coincide over data about the same indicator or phenomenon. There are often important differences between official data provided by each country and the data provided by international agencies. There may also be significant differences in information and statistics used among international agencies.

11. A study by Harbison and Hanushek (1992) in Northeast Brazil found that textbooks had statistically insignificant or even negative effects on student achievement. However, "the authors [were] not willing to give up on textbooks (Plank, 1994) because they argued that "we know [sic] from elsewhere [that textbook use] is a powerful component of educational performance (Harbison and Hanushek, 1992, p. 161).

12. A more comprehensive analysis of teacher education issues can be found in Torres, 1995b.

13. Between 1963 and 1994 the WB was financially involved in 110 training institutions for primary school teachers (Haddad, 1985).

REFERENCES

Anaya, A. "Gestación y diseño de la efoema Educatiua Boliviana: Una visión desde adentro". La Paz: CEDES, mimeo, 1995.

Arnove, R. "Neoliberal Education Policies in Latin America: Arguments in Favor and Against." Paper presented at the CIES annual conference, Williamsburg, VA. 6–10 March 1995.

Arthur, L., and R. Preston, with C. Ngahu, S. Shoaib le Breton, and D. Theobald. *Quality in Overseas Consultancy: Understanding the Issues.* Warwick: International Centre for Educational Development, University of Warwick, March 1996.

Bacchus, K., A.A. Aziz, S.H. Ahmad, F.A. Bakar, and S. Rodwell. *Curriculum Reform.* London: Commonwealth Secretariat, 1991.

Carron, G., and R. Govinda. "Five Years After Jomtien: Where Are We"? *IIEP Newsletter* 13.3. Paris: UNESCO-IIEP, July–September 1995.

Coll, C. *Psicología y currículum.* Barcelona: Paidós, 1991.

———. *La Reforma del sistema educativo español: La calidad de la enseñanza como objetivo.* Colección Educación N° 4. Quito: Instituto FRONESIS, 1992.

Coll, C., J.I. Pozo, B. Sarabia, and E. Valls. *Los contenidos en la Reforma.* Madrid: Santillana, 1992.

Deble, I., and G. Carron (Eds.). *Jomtien, trois ans après. L'éducation pour tous dans les pays du Sahel.* Paris: UNESCO-IIEP/UNICEF, 1993.

Contreras, J. "El currículum como formación," *Cuadernos de Pedagogía* 184 (1990).

Coraggio, J.L. "Human Capital: The World Bank's Approach to Education in Latin America." In J. Cavanach (Ed.), *Beyond Bretton Woods.* Washington, D.C.: IPS/TNI, 1994.

———. "Las propuestas del Banco Mundial para la educación: ¿Sentido oculto o problemas de concepción?" *La Piragua* 11. Santiago: Consejo de Educación de Adultos de América Latina, 1995.

De Grauwe, A., and D. Bernard (Eds.). *Developments after Jomtien: EFA in the South-East Asia and the Pacific Region.* Paris: UNESCO-IIEP/UNICEF, 1995.

Espinola, V. "Los resultados del modelo económico en la enseñanza básica: La demanda tiene la palabra." In Juan Eduardo García-Huidobro (Ed.), *Escuela, calidad e igualdad.* Santiago: CIDE, 1989.

Farrell, J., and S. Heyneman (Eds.). *Textbooks in the Developing World: Economic and Educational Choices.* Washington, D.C.: Economic Development Institute, World Bank, 1989.

Filp, J., C. Cardemil, and C. Valdivieso. *Profesoras y profesores efectivos en Chile.* Santiago: CIDE, 1984.

Frigerio, G. (Ed.). *Currículo presente, ciencia ausente. Normas, teorías y críticas.* Vol. 1. Buenos Aires: Miño y Dávila Editores, 1991.

Fuller, B., and P. Clark. "Raising School Effects While Ignoring Culture? Local Conditions and the Influence of Classroom Tools, Rules, and Pedagogy." *Review of Educational Research* 64, 1 (1994): 118–158.

Gatti, B. "Avaliação educacional no Brasil: Experiencias, problemas, recomendações," *Estudos em Avaliação Educacional* 10 (July–December 1994) Sao Paulo: Fundação Carlos Chagas.

Gimeno Sacristán, J. "Investigación e innovación sobre la gestión pedagógica de los equipos de profesores." In UNESCO-OREALC (Eds.), *La gestión pedagógica de la escuela.* Santiago: UNESCO-OREALC, 1992.

Gimeno Sacristán, J., and A. Pérez Gómez. *La enseñanza: Su teoría y su práctica.* Madrid: AKAL Editor, 1985.

Haddad, W. "Teacher Training: A Review of World Bank Experience." *EDT Discussion Paper,* no. 21, Washington, D.C.: World Bank, 1985.

Harbison, R.W., and E.A. Hanushek. *Educational Performance of the Poor: Lessons from Rural Northeast Brazil.* New York: Oxford University Press, 1992.

Heneveld, W. "Effective Schools: Determining Which Factors Have the Greatest Impact." *DAE Newsletter* 7, 3 (July–September 1995).

Heyneman, S. "Economics of Education: Disappointments and Potential." *Prospects* 25, 4 (1995): 200–210.

Klees, S. "The Economics of Educational Technology." In T. Husen, and T. Neville Postlethwaite (Eds.). *The International Encyclopedia of Education,* 2d. Ed. Oxford: Pergamon, 1994, pp. 1903–1911.

Lagos, R. "Quality and Equity in Educational Decentralization: The Case of Chile." *The Forum* (May 1993).

Little, A., W. Hoppers, and R. Gardner (Eds.). *Beyond Jomtien: Implementing Primary Education for All.* London: Macmillan Press, 1994.

Lockheed, M., and A. Verspoor. *Improving Primary Education in Developing Countries.* Washington, D.C.: Oxford University Press, 1991.

Lorfing, I., and R. Govinda (Eds.). *Development Since Jomtien: EFA in the Middle East and North Africa.* Paris: UNESCO-IIEP/UNICEF, 1995.

Ochoa, J. *Textos escolares: Un saber recortado.* Santiago: CIDE, 1990.

Peru, Ministerio de Educación. "Perú: Calidad, eficiencia, equidad. Los desafíos de la educación primaria." Lima: División de Recursos Humanos del Banco Mundial, Ministerio de Educación, mimeograph, June 1994.

Plank, D. Rev. of *Educational Performance of the Poor: Lessons from Rural Northeast Brazil,* by R.W. Harbison and E.A. Hanushek. *Comparative Education Review* 38, 2 (May 1994): 284–289.

Prawda, J. "Lessons in Educational Decentralization: A Note for Policymakers." *The Forum* 2, 3 (May 1993).

Reimers, F. "Time and Opportunity to Learn in Pakistan's Schools: Some Lessons on the Links Between Research and Policy." *Comparative Education* 29, 2 (1993): 201–212.

Samoff, J. *Analysis, Agendas, and Priorities in African Education: A Review of Externally Initiated, Commissioned, and Supported Studies of Education in Africa (1990–1994).* Paris: UNESCO-DAE Working Group on Education Sector Analysis, 1995.

Schiefelbein, E., and J.C. Tedesco. *Una nueva oportunidad. El rol de la educación en el desarrollo de América Latina.* Buenos Aires: Santillana, 1995.

Schwille, J.R. Rev. of *Improving Primary Education in Developing Countries,* by M. Lockheed and A. Verspoor. *Comparative Education Review* 37, 4 (1993): 490–493.

Tatto, M.T., D. Nielsen, and W.K. Cummings. "Comparing the Effects and Costs of Different Approaches for Primary School Teachers: The Case of Sri Lanka." *BRIDGES* 10 (1991).

Tedesco, J.C. "Estrategias de desarrollo y educación: El desafío de la gestión pública." *Boletín del Proyecto Principal en América Latina y el Caribe* 25 (1991).

———. *El nuevo pacto educativo: Educación, competitividad y ciudadanía en la sociedad moderna.* Madrid: Grupo Anaya, 1995.

Torres, R.M. "¿Qué (y cómo) es necesario aprender? Necesidades básicas de aprendizaje y contenidos curriculares," In *Necesidades básicas de aprendizaje. Estrategias de acción.* Santiago: UNESCO-OREALC/IDRC, 1993.

———. *Los achaques de la educación.* Quito: Instituto FRONESIS-LIBRESA, 1995a.

———. "Teacher Education: From Rhetoric to Action." Paper presented at the UNESCO/UNICEF International Conference on "Partnerships in Teacher Development for a New Asia," Bangkok, 6–8 December 1995b.

UNESCO-OREALC. *Situación educativa de América Latina y el Caribe 1980–1989.* Santiago: UNESCO-OREALC, 1993.

Verspoor, A. "Veinte años de ayuda del Banco Mundial a la educación básica." *Perspectivas* 21, 3 (1991).

WCEFA. *World Declaration on "Education for All" and Framework of Action to Meet the Basic Learning Needs.* New York: WCEFA, 1990.

World Bank. *Education in Sub-Saharan Africa: Policies for Adjustment, Revitalization, and Expansion, A World Bank Policy Study.* Washington, D.C.: World Bank, 1988.

———. *Priorities and Strategies for Education: A World Bank Sector Review.* Washington D.C.: World Bank, 1995.

4 POWER, CULTURE, AND TRANSFORMATION

EDUCATIONAL REFORM IN NAMIBIA

Sydney R. Grant

INTRODUCTION

In this case study of educational reform in Namibia, the former South-West Africa, which became independent from South Africa in 1990, I will show how knowledge and power affected those who planned and participated in the reform efforts. The participants in the reform belonged to three major groups: educators of the former colonial regime, educators from the newly independent majority, and the international advisors assigned to the Ministry of Education and Culture (MEC). They were all deeply involved in an historic transition between a past colonial era and a new, emerging, independent one.

The reform efforts described here cover the period between 1991 and 1994, when the Namibian government began to implement its reform in education. The author was a participant, and served from October 1991 until November 1993 as the director of the Florida State University (FSU) twelve-person technical assistance team, assigned by the Minister of Education to work directly in the MEC on the reform. I had been seconded from my regular work as a professor in the department of educational foundations and policy studies in the college of education at FSU in Tallahassee.

When I started my assignment in Namibia, I had not planned to do a study of the situation, because I did not have the time to keep a log or collect materials and was too busy to carry out a formal research project. The reform itself was a full-time job. However, as a habitual note taker, I kept notebooks of daily activities. Also, I became secretary to one of the major committees of the reform, the Technical Coordinating Committee (TCC), and this helped me to maintain a more organized perspective.

It was only after the gyrations of the local USAID mission became evident that the political aspects of the reform became increasingly apparent. Even so, the work of the reform itself was so pressing, that one was

consumed with daily tasks, making political analysis a subconscious enter-
tainment rather than a purposeful undertaking. Thus, the political analysis
presented here was developed after leaving Namibia when there was more
time to reflect on the experience.

When the team was given the assignment, team members were advised that it would be a curriculum-and-materials-development project, and
that there might be political undertones in the situation. Most team members had worked in other overseas development projects in education and
accepted the situation as a customary one. As FSU team leader, I had worked
in a similar project in Peru in 1964–1968, and had some idea of what the
work might entail, but the situation turned out to be quite different, and it
came to me as a big surprise to see, in Namibia, how deeply race, history,
and considerations of power would affect the personnel and decisions made
in planning and carrying out the reform.

A major difference between the reform in Namibia and the one in Peru
was that in Peru the Ministry of Education seemed eager to make progress,
and resistance was not intentional, but rather grew out of the normal leth-
argy and lack of expertise in the client system. There was no entrenched
political opposition. Furthermore, in Peru there was only one technical assistance group, whereas in Namibia there were many (Grant, 1992).

The relationships and rivalry among the donor agencies were an
added power-politics dimension. The uncertain policy and changing signals
of the U.S. Agency for International Development (USAID), the largest donor, toward its Namibian client and towards the FSU team was completely
unanticipated, and came as a surprise, since team members had worked on
many USAID-related projects in the past, and had been usually favorably
impressed with USAID's approach and programs.

The activities and the interplay of factions within the reform in
Namibia presented a panorama that was replete with considerations of how
knowledge is perceived and how the strains and stresses of power permeated the whole reform process. However, because such forces are often covert and dimly perceived, it is doubtful that the participants at the time fully
realized the extent to which they were playing out a deeper and more subtle
process as they earnestly went about their daily work.

Turning to the case study of Namibia, and considering Namibia in a
worldwide context, the Namibian educational reform is unique in several
respects. First, Namibia achieved independence from a neighboring African
state (South Africa), and not from a remote European power. Furthermore,
South Africa was itself in transition to a black majority government, but at
the time of Namibia's independence, South Africa was still under white mi-

nority rule, and had not yet held a general national election with the participation of its black population. (This election took place later, in April 1995.)

Secondly, Namibia was a latecomer to the education-for-development process worldwide, which had started in the late 1950s (Spaulding and Singleton, 1968). Lastly, representatives of the previous regime, in the person of Namibian Afrikaners of South African descent, had remained in Namibia and in the new Namibian civil service, and so were still players in Namibian education, and active in the reform.

The presence of the Namibian Afrikaners was the result of an agreement at independence between Namibia and South Africa which guaranteed the continuance of a certain percentage of civil servants from the previous regime in the new civil service. It was also part of the Namibian government's policy of reconciliation and continuity. (Reconciliation meant that no reprisals would be taken against members of the previous regime, and continuity meant that laws and procedures of the old order would continue, except apartheid, until such time that they would be specifically derogated or changed by subsequent legal procedure.)

The Context of Educational Reform in Namibia: Historical and Political Background

As is the case in other countries (see Hanson and Brembeck, 1966), the reform of education in Namibia closely followed political developments. There was a close parallel between what was constitutionally mandated, and the official policies of the democratically elected regime. These policies were based on the notions of "continuity" and "reconciliation," and so there was an officially recognized political linkage to the past.

Namibia became an officially recognized independent nation in March 1990 through its own liberation struggle and the good offices of the United Nations. Previously, Namibia, known as South-West Africa, had been a German Colony from the 1880s until taken over by British and South African forces in 1915 during World War I. In 1920, South-West Africa became a League of Nations mandate under the control of South Africa. South Africa treated Namibia like a colony, and at the end of World War II in 1945 Namibia—still known as South-West Africa—became a United Nations trusteeship under South African control, and subject to all South African laws, including apartheid. In 1966 the UN General Assembly recognized the area's indigenous name, Namibia. However, the question of independence remained uncertain (Katjavivi, 1988).

The Namibian people quickly realized that South Africa had no intention of giving them independence, and in 1966, following the example of other African nations that had already gained independence during the previous three decades, the Namibians formed their own resistance movement, calling it SWAPO, the South West African Peoples Organization. SWAPO worked both within Namibia and in exile to achieve independence. The struggle was both political and military, for though the UN had called for an end to the trusteeship status, South Africa had refused to relinquish its control, and so SWAPO took to the field and waged guerrilla war, chiefly from Angola and from within Namibia itself (SWAPO, 1987).

After complicated negotiations, including brokering by the UN involving Cuba (whose troops were then in Angola) and South Africa (whose troops were in Namibia on the northern border facing Angola), an agreement was reached whereby Cuba withdrew from Angola, and South Africa withdrew from Namibia. With assistance from other nations, elections were held in Namibia under UN auspices. A new, popularly elected, independent government was formed under SWAPO political leadership, and Namibia became independent in March 1990.

Like all new nations, Namibia was faced with the task of "nation building," and, following accepted wisdom in the rest of Africa and elsewhere in the Third World, one of the major instruments selected to achieve national growth and development was education (Fagerlind and Saha, 1989). Namibia's new government was based on a well planned and forward looking constitution with a structural balance of power in three branches of government: executive, legislative, and judicial (Government of Namibia, 1991).

Under South African rule prior to independence, Namibia, an area about twice the size of California, had consisted of eleven ethnically defined areas, each with one or more different languages. South Africa took advantage of these language and ethnic divisions by establishing and maintaining separate "authorities." South Africa governed the one-and-a-half million people using the Bantustans model similar to its divide-and-conquer "homelands" policy within South Africa itself (Ellis, 1984).

South Africa had occupied Namibia for approximately seventy years, and in order to have some administrative community—if not a united social, ethnic, or political community, which South Africa wished to avoid, the South Africans promoted one of their own languages, Afrikaans, as an official language throughout Namibia (Amukugo, 1993).

When the newly independent government came to power, it eschewed earlier Marxist SWAPO rhetoric and opted for a free enterprise capitalist economy. It took decisive action in all sectors of national life to reshape former South-West Africa into a new Namibia. Nowhere was this so evident as in the field of education. However, the task in education was in many ways more complex than in other sectors, because the entire school program had to be changed, and it was a change in the way of thinking as well as a change of command. Furthermore, English had been mandated as the official language of Namibia, and this required a special effort by the MEC to introduce English as the eventual language of instruction.

Regarding the policy of "continuity," at independence Namibia's constitution allowed for the continuation of all laws, rules, and regulations of the past regime except those like apartheid that were ipso facto unconstitutional. However, other South African laws and procedures were still in place, including the administrative and educational procedures in the Ministry of Education and Culture, although it was assumed that these might be changed in the future.

The policy of "continuity" was shown in programmatic ways as well as in personnel matters, especially in the MEC's reluctance to break off too severely from past programs or to innovate too boldly. Thus, the administrative knowledge and know-how of the former administrators, many of whom were still in place, guaranteed them power and influence, and they were able to play active roles in the reform. With the advantage of years of experience as leaders in the previous education regime, the Afrikaners exercised power and influence that greatly exceeded their numbers.

The new Ministry of Education, Culture and Sport—later changed to the Ministry of Education and Culture (MEC)—under its Minister, Mr. Nahas Angula, a black Namibian who had been with SWAPO in exile, quickly moved to abolish the previous eleven administrative "authorities," and to create a single, national education system, organized into six regions. Another major priority was a curriculum development effort to build a new national curriculum from grades 1 through 10, and the introduction of the new language policy (Angula, 1991).

At the suggestion of USAID, the MEC created a new administrative unit to coordinate the reform, and called it NIED (National Institute for Educational Development) (Namibia Ministry of Education and Culture). NIED was created to plan and design the curriculum and to produce the content and syllabi for the subjects, grades 1–10. A parallel function of NIED was to provide for in-service education and training for MEC teachers and administrators, and to provide the materials for instruction. A third, less prominent task was to set up a way to evaluate the reform. NIED was deemed so important and central to the MEC's plans, that a special complex of buildings was constructed for it, located in Okahandja, an hour's drive north of Windhoek. The facility was occupied in July 1995.

NIED's personnel consisted of specialists in the various subject matter fields: that is, math, science, languages, and others. However, many of the positions in NIED remained vacant during the first three years of the reform process, because there were not enough funds to appoint people to the openings, and also because the MEC had been unable to identify persons with the appropriate experience, expertise, and political acceptability to staff the vacant posts.

In order to coordinate the reform activities throughout the MEC, and with the educational regions, a special group of approximately twenty persons, called the Technical Coordinating Committee (TCC), was appointed by the minister. The TCC was composed of representatives from most of the major units in the MEC, and they met weekly or every other week—depending on the press of business—to consider reports of progress and other issues that needed to be attended to. The TCC was meant to be an advisory committee to the minister, but in reality many of the discussions and recommendations of the TCC were actually operational. The establishment of the TCC was one of the original "conditions" set by USAID, but it is likely it would have been created anyhow.

In 1994, after three years, the TCC ceased to function because some of its members thought it had become bogged down and unwieldy. The TCC had kept development activities on the agenda before the group, and this became a bother to those who preferred a quicker and less public discussion of issues, even hoping that some of them would go away, and be forgotten. The TCC was replaced by a much smaller three-person "executive management committee." In the meanwhile, USAID's original mandate and program had expired and were not renewed by the MEC. This may have made members of the TCC feel that, with USAID's original program gone, they were no longer obliged to maintain the TCC. However, the FSU team continued, because it was not officially dependent on USAID but on the MEC itself.

The goals of the reform were designed to fulfill the mandates of Namibia's constitution and to fulfill the policies of the SWAPO-led government. Essentially, the reform aimed to achieve four major objectives: to introduce English as the official language of the country, to provide nonracial, nondiscriminatory educational opportunity for all children, to develop a learner-centered program, and to create a relevant educational program benefiting an independent African nation at the end of the twentieth century.

Prior to the reform, under South African rule, Namibians followed the South African "Cape Curriculum." The school system was racially segregated, and full access to educational activity was not guaranteed. The schools for the white population were markedly better provisioned than all other schools. Afrikaans was the language of instruction in the majority of cases. One of the major goals of the previous, South African system, was to ensure that secondary school graduates in Namibia could qualify for admission to South African or European universities.

CURRICULUM DEVELOPMENT

NIED began its curriculum reform thrust in 1991 in secondary education. A new curriculum was developed and implemented during 1991 and 1992, and because NIED did not have the luxury of time, the implementation itself served as a field evaluation of the new program. In any case, there were so many changes taking place simultaneously in Namibian education that a formal evaluation of the secondary reform (grades 7–10) would have been impossible.

Aware of the improvised and pragmatic nature of the reform at the secondary level, the acting director of NIED decided to develop a document outlining the philosophical basis for the reform. He also developed a set of guidelines to undergird the reform at the primary school level. However, the document was really meant for the full gamut, grades 1–10. It contained the new philosophy of education in Namibia, a brief explanation of an evaluation system, the subjects to be included in the program and the amount of time to be assigned to the various subjects grade by grade, as well as statements regarding methodology, especially a definition of the learner-centered curriculum, which was a major innovation of the new program (Namibia Ministry of Education and Culture, 1992).

TECHNICAL ASISTANCE AND EXTERNAL INFLUENCES: ANOTHER POWER ARENA

There were many foreign advisors in the MEC from the United Kingdom, the European Community, Sweden, Denmark, Germany, and the United States. The United States team had the greatest number of advisors, twelve (nine from the U.S., three from the UK, and one from Kenya), followed by Sweden and the UK which had about five or six each. These advisors were supported through donations from the various donor countries. As was common in other African countries, some European advisors served in "line" positions as the actual directors of units, and not just as advisors. In the FSU team, all were advisors and did not serve as directors or unit heads (King, 1991).

In an unusual departure from its custom, the local USAID mission experimented with the innovation of funding technical assistance through a bloc grant to the government of Namibia (GON) rather than by contracting directly with any U.S. technical assistance entity. This experimental approach by the local USAID group did not permit direct payment of funds to the advisory body (which turned out to be Florida State University), but instead provided funds directly to the Namibian finance ministry. In turn, drawing on these U.S. funds, the MEC contracted directly with the American technical assistance institution, and paid it monthly on a cost-reimbursable basis.

Although USAID insisted it was not paying the money directly into the Namibian reform, it nevertheless held the MEC to absolute compliance with the education reform targets specified in the original U.S.-Namibian project agreement, and with the minister's "letter of intent," which was a letter required by USAID prior to an agreement. Both the project agreement and the letter of intent had the force of law for USAID; however, MEC leadership personnel did not appreciate the legality of these two documents. A few months after the agreement was implemented, an outside evaluation team was brought in from the United States by USAID to measure compliance by the MEC on the original agreement. At the end of its one-week review, the evaluation team declared, to the dismay of the MEC, that forty-two stipulations in the MEC-USAID agreement had not yet been met by the MEC.

There was great anger and consternation, and the entire MEC geared up to implement a crash program to prove on paper that the MEC had indeed met the forty-two stipulations. USAID gave the MEC sixty days in which to do this. MEC personnel, assisted by all the foreign advisors, were able to meet the sixty-day deadline, showing progress on all points. (These stipulations had to be met by the MEC before USAID could release a scheduled several million dollar tranche to Namibia.)

However, all was not well. The submission of the documentation to USAID in Namibia was subject to further review by the USAID legal staff located in USAID's regional African office in Nairobi. The legal staff there found two of the forty-two documents unsatisfactory, and since it was an all-or-nothing agreement, the Nairobi legal office vetoed the scheduled release of the money.

The MEC personnel, from top to bottom, along with the foreign advisors were deeply angered. It seemed to them an inexplicable lack of understanding and a show of power and disregard for the amity usually found between nations who had good relations. Officially, the MEC said nothing, but there was a great deal of resentment against USAID. MEC personnel returned to the work on the reform, which had been set aside during the sixty days required to document progress on the forty-two stipulations.

The use of quid pro quo agreements between USAID and its client countries and their ministries and agencies is not unusual. It is viewed by USAID as a guarantee that donor money will not be subverted or squandered. It is also considered part of the system that one country with money and power may use "leverage" over a recipient country to achieve foreign policy and specific local objectives. It is essentially the same system used by the International Monetary Fund to force client nations to accept structural adjustments and other aversive measures (Berman, 1992).

It was fortunate that the American technical assistance team (FSU) had been held at distance by USAID as part of USAID's experiment. USAID's view was that the American technical assistance team belonged to Namibia and not the United States. This helped the mostly American FSU team avoid most of the backlash in the MEC from USAID's rejection of the MEC's submission.

For Namibia, USAID's "experiment," or innovation, in technical assistance, meant that relatively large sums of money (US$35 million) would be given to Namibia over a five-year period as a good will gesture upon independence. The only official quid pro quo was that the money could not be used for the armed forces or for police, and that there be a reform in the education sector. The reform goals were spelled out in the project agreement and minister's letter of intent, mentioned previously. The money was channeled directly into the treasury of the government of Namibia. USAID would not contract any technical assistance team. This was to be done (and was done) by Namibia itself. The team was explicitly informed by the USAID representative that it was not part of the U.S. "official family," and was to maintain itself apart and independent of USAID, not even reporting unofficially to it. (Eventually, this procedure, which was so unusual by USAID standards, resulted in an audit of the local USAID mission by Washington.)

The Curriculum Development Process

The curriculum development process was complex and time consuming. Subject matter panels designed and produced the course syllabi. The panels were chaired by experienced classroom teachers or subject supervisors. Each panel was advised by a foreign advisor. The work was painstaking and plodding. None of the panel members, except the advisors, had done this sort of work previously. NIED officials led and coordinated the work to guarantee integrity and uniformity in the products. NIED was also responsible for in-service training and for evaluating the new program. The FSU and other foreign advisors helped with this work, but the lack of Namibian specialists was a stumbling block to the rapid and smooth program development.

The process was very slow, but by the end of 1993, the secondary school curriculum was operational in its first stage (prior to formal evaluation), and the subject panels for grades 1–6 were just finishing their syllabi. Math, English, and science syllabi were complete as were the courses of study in draft, for English (grades 1–6), math for grades 4 and 5, and for science in grade 4. A special feature of this work was the development of teachers' guides to help teachers in using the syllabi in their classrooms, and accompanying English language guides to assist the teachers in teaching the subject in English. At the same time, plans were being developed for the inservice training programs that would accompany the implementation of math and science.

Simultaneously, the MEC undertook a carefully planned evaluation program to measure progress in math, science, English, and Oshindonga, one of the local languages. The evaluation measured achievement at grades 4 and 7 with an eye toward establishing baseline data from which future progress could be gauged. The evaluation was undertaken by a MEC team working in collaboration with technical advisors from the FSU team, which had a subcontract with SIAPAC, a social science research group located in Namibia.

POLICY AND POLITICS: A CRITIQUE AND COMMENTARY

This critique is organized into three sections: consideration of the reform process itself, an account of the internal political and psychological forces affecting the reform, and a discussion of related external forces that were both institutional and political.

CONSIDERATION OF THE REFORM PROCESS

In Namibia the reform process was driven especially by the need for the MEC to develop quickly a new approach to education that would be free from the previous dependence on the South African educational program. This included the absolute undoing of the apartheid system and its concomitant segregation and discrimination against blacks and people of mixed race. A major feature of this struggle against apartheid was the need to guarantee access to schooling for black Namibians.

A second motivating force was the need to rid Namibian education of the favored prominence of the Afrikaans language. Since English had been selected and specified in the constitution as Namibia's official language, this was a mandate, as well as an important resolve on the part of the MEC's leadership (Angula, 1991). It would be a powerful blow to the Afrikaners and against the former regime.

A further rationale favoring English was its utility as the language of science, technology, and commerce, and its universality in terms of the number and distribution of its speakers worldwide compared with Afrikaans. Afrikaans was the lingua franca, along with various indigenous African languages, in much of Namibia except in the far north. The plan was to make English the language that Namibians themselves would use in communication with one another, from region to region. Besides, for many black Namibians and Namibians of mixed race, Afrikaans was considered the language of the oppressors.

The introduction of English was a major undertaking, for it is one thing to make such a decision and quite another to implement it, especially in the face of an entrenched status quo, and with a severe lack of strong English speakers nationwide. Furthermore, a strong language policy was a way to advance the power of the state as had been done in other developing countries such as India, and in Israel where a selected language was utilized to bolster the power of the state, unite, and forge a new nation.

A third factor motivating the reform was the need for the government to fulfill its election promises and show forward movement in the education sector as part of the overall achievement of national independence. For the education sector, this was a daunting challenge since the deficits in education were so severe. Namibia not only had to launch a new program, but had to do so with increased enrollments resulting from greater access to education. Furthermore, educational progress had to be carried out simultaneously with the introduction of a new language of instruction, a language not yet widely used nor spoken nationwide.

A fourth factor was the need to develop a program that would be free from the rote, "banking concept" of instruction (Freire, 1970) by shifting to an individualized, learner-centered program. There were two aspects in this shift that were formidable. First was the concept itself which put an emphasis on learning rather than on teaching, and the second was the need to use different methodologies to bring this practice about. Most teachers in Namibia were used to the traditional teacher-as-the-source-of-knowledge approach, and to teaching the class as a group, relying primarily on the lecture method, or by group oral repetition of the lesson, or by writing the lesson on the chalkboard for the children to copy into their notebooks. For Namibian teachers—as for teachers everywhere—the introduction of a radically different methodology was a major shift.

OTHER INTERNAL POLITICAL AND PSYCHOLOGICAL FORCES AFFECTING THE REFORM
Within the MEC itself, and out in the regions, there were people who did not favor the reform, or who viewed it with distrust and trepidation. True, many understood that a reform was necessary because Namibia was a new,

independent country, and the past programs had been directly linked to South Africa, the old colonial regime. But their agreement stopped there. There was a legacy of racial paternalism: some of the Afrikaners thought the reform was too ambitious for the majority of Namibians and, in the beginning, there was no consensus on what a new program should be, nor on how to achieve it.

Regarding consultation on the reform, teachers and administrators in the field had never been consulted previously on instructional matters, and expected that directives would be forthcoming from Windhoek (Snyder, 1991). The minister and the MEC leadership had to spell out what they wanted to achieve in the reform by means of public statements, in-house meetings, and through circulars and articles from the central office in Windhoek about the reform. Many people in the field did not understand some of the circulars and they were used to being told what to do (Fair, 1994). For many, it was very hard to accept the idea of consultation, where they would be expected to give feedback.

There was also a power-politics dimension. Within the central office of the MEC, there were groups with different viewpoints and varying degrees of enthusiasm for change. There were, for example, the SWAPO educators who were the new wave, represented by the minister and most of the leadership personnel in the MEC headquarters. They supported the reform and pushed strongly for it. They were the "true believers."

Next, at the other extreme, was the most conservative group: the Namibian Afrikaners. They were the white Afrikaans-speaking educators (who, by the way, spoke fluent English, too) who had held important posts under the previous regime and who, because of the policy of reconciliation, were still present in leadership or in midlevel technical positions. They obeyed the wishes of the minister, but were so imbued with their own tradition that they did not give their full support, and even opposed many of the reform efforts. (Before independence, it had been anticipated that many of the Namibian Afrikaners would emigrate to South Africa when independence was declared, but this did not occur.)

They liked to term themselves "realists," and were eager to point out why some or all of the reform could not, or should not, be carried out. Their approach was a go-slow, critical approach, and their general outlook was one of plodding "progress" toward any goal. They feared that the extension of educational opportunity to the newly empowered masses would weaken past and present educational standards. They looked upon the new language policy as a kind of linguistic and cultural genocide aimed at Afrikaans and at Namibian Afrikaners.

They feared that the previous state support for the formerly all-white schools would be diminished and that these schools (formerly *their* schools) would go into decline, and spoil Namibia's "reputation." (Some people in the MEC looked upon South African education as a guarantee of quality and as a link to the rest of the world. Even after independence, the external examinations system run from Cape Town and the UK were still considered important and essential to maintain.) Despite the fact that this group was now a political minority, the Afrikaners still exercised considerable power because they had the knowledge and experience in the system, and the system was being largely run under the rules, regulations, and procedures of the previous regime. Furthermore, many of them still held important positions in the chain of command.

A third group were the white German-speaking and English-speaking Namibians who were few in number, but who seemed much more open to the reform and its vision, and who worked hard to assist the MEC in carrying it out. Their approach was to offer their support, knowledge, and expertise in the reform process. Like the Afrikaners, they had considerable knowledge and expertise. On the whole, they were much more sympathetic to the reform.

A fourth group were the experienced black and "colored" (mixed race) educators who had had years of service in the schools of the previous regime and who now, through independence, for the first time finally had gained access to positions of influence and responsibility. For the most part, these persons were avid supporters of the reform, and their experience and know-how served as a counterbalance to the views and opinions of the Afrikaner conservative group who were at best reluctant participants.

(The terms "colored," and "Afrikaner," are designations that follow the linguistic reality left behind in Namibia by South African *apartheid* racial laws and system. These designations are common terms still used openly in Namibia. Their use here follows that common usage. The use of these terms, borrowed from one context to another, is an example of how "terms of reference" can frame the debate, and even determine how one may think about certain issues.)

A fifth group were the "expatriate" (foreign) advisors who held both advisory as well as (in some cases) line positions in the MEC. As would be expected, the foreign advisors were strongly aligned with the minister and with the leadership group. The differences of opinion among them were usually slight, or suppressed in the interest of overall harmony. The advisors supported the reform and in many cases were meant to be the "engines" of the reform in providing money, materials, know-how, advisement, and facilitation for MEC activities.

In addition to these internal groups, there were administrative differences between the central MEC and the outlying nine regional offices. Administratively, the reform strategy envisioned eventual decentralization in the relationship between the central MEC in Windhoek and the regional offices, but in the beginning, the reform required a large degree of centralized decision making, and, as mentioned, the mindset of the personnel in the regions was not yet open to accepting and exercising the authority that MEC headquarters seemed eager for them to share. The minister was insistent that the people in the regions be participants as much as possible, but everybody realized how difficult this would be, because of communications and tradition.

MONEY, KNOWLEDGE, AND POWER: RELATED EXTERNAL FORCES AFFECTING THE REFORM

Several external agencies exercised influence on the MEC and the reform. The influence of some of the donor agencies was great. SIDA, the Swedish International Development Authority, especially was an influential player in the MEC through carefully targeted inputs and a Swedish technical assistance team of advisory personnel from the University of Umea to assist in the reform of pre-service teacher education.

The influence of the United States, another influential donor, was exercised through USAID, which at independence had made a pledge of some U.S. $35 million to be disbursed over a period of five years. Its approach was a generalized one which it called nonproject assistance.

One important additional aspect regarding the MEC-USAID relationship was that during the early days, in 1990 and 1991, most of the MEC specialists and leaders claimed not to know anything about the specific details of the USAID agreement. They did not know that the MEC was legally obliged to achieve or make specific changes, meet conditions, and produce "deliverables," to be approved by USAID so that U.S. funds could be released to the Namibian government's Ministry of Finance. Further, USAID, as the donor, was the sole judge of the MEC's "compliance" with USAID's "conditionalities."

The reform in education in Namibia continues. The MEC anticipates that the curriculum effort will produce a new, independent, and improved program. However, follow-up studies suggest that teachers and administrators in the regions and in the schools do not fully understand the new initiatives in reform, and that much greater in-service training for the rank and file teachers and administrators in the field is needed (Fair, 1994).

DIMENSIONS OF POWER

From the perspective of power, it is clear that most external assistance is based on inequality: the donor has superior resources of money, knowledge, and expertise. It extends these—or not—depending on the context of the times and on the basic foreign policy relations between the donor and the recipient. Namibia, as a "client" of the donors, was at a disadvantage, and the degree to which it expressed its sovereignty had to be a matter of prudence.

The Namibian educational reform has made moderate progress in phasing out the old and bringing in the new. The most remarkable characteristic of the reform has been its embodiment of continuity and reconciliation. It had to take into account the past and the traditions of the administrators, officials, teachers, and the children, and their parents, but also meet their aspirations and rising expectations. It had to break new ground—within stringent financial constraints. In this sense, it is like other African nations facing educational change within awful restraints and a neocolonial heritage (Samoff, 1993). As in all reforms, we must wait for a decade at least to know what results have been truly meaningful and significant, and if they meet the real and implied promises of this newly emerging nation.

Regarding an overall evaluation of any reform, reforms are only linear in a chronological sense. They have a beginning and perhaps an eventual end, but events do not always follow the plan, and objectives may be dropped or added as a reform unfolds. A reform is not just a set of documents: it is a framework within which real people act out their perceptions and perspectives, and satisfy their individual, social, and political needs. Their acts are not only individual, but are embedded also in a social, institutional, political, and historical context that in itself is also interactive and emergent, and which basically represents a struggle for power. There are many agendas (Amukugo, 1993). Nowhere is this so clear as in Namibia with its rich ethnic mix and in a reform that straddles two eras, aiming to amalgamate them through some new alchemy.

In this chapter, I have described the basic outline of the Namibian reform in education, and have shown how it is embedded in a social, cultural, political, and historical context. The struggle for power has been implicit at almost every turn: among the ethnic groups, among the international donor agencies, between the MEC and the donor agencies, and between those who would prefer to live in the past and those who are striving for a more equitable and promising future.

REFERENCES

Amukugo, E. *Education and Politics in Namibia: Past Trends and Future Prospects.* Windhoek: New Namibia Books, 1993.

Angula, N. *Language Policy for Schools 1992–96: Explanatory and Information Statement by the Ministry of Education and Culture.* Windhoek: Ministry of Education and Culture, November 1991.

———. *Language Policy and Implementation: Choices and Limitations.* Ongwediva: Contribution to the Proceedings of the National Conference on the Implementation of the New Language Policy, Ongwediva Teacher Training College, 21–26 June 1992.

Berman, E. "Donor Agencies and Third World Educational Development, 1945–1985." In Robert Arnove, Phillip Altbach, and Gail Kelly (Eds.), *Emergent Issues in Education: Comparative Perspectives.* Albany: State University of New York Press, 1992.

Ellis, J. *Education, Repression and Liberation: Namibia.* London: World University Service and the Catholic Institute for International Relations, 1984.

Fagerlind, I., and L. Saha. *Education and National Development: A Comparative Perspective.* 2d Edition. Oxford: Pergamon Press, 1989.

Fair, K. *Passing and Failing Learners: Policies and Practices in Ondangwa and Rundu in Grades 1 to 3.* Vols. 1 and 2. Windhoek: Namibia Ministry of Education and Culture and UNICEF-FSU, September 1994.

Freire, P. *The Pedagogy of the Oppressed.* New York: Continuum, 1970.

Government of Namibia. *Constitution: Republic of Namibia.* Windhoek: The Directorate of Production and Publicity, The Ministry of Information and Broadcasting, 1991.

Grant, S.R. "Peru" in P.W. Cookson Jr., A.R. Sadovnik, and S.F. Semel (Eds.), *International Handbook of Educational Reform.* New York: Greenwood Press, 1992.

Hanson, J., and C. Brembeck, *Education and the Development of Nations.* New York: Holt, Rinehart and Winston, 1966.

Katjavivi, P. *A History of Resistance in Namibia.* London: James Curry, 1988.

King, K. *Aid and Education in the Developing World: The Role of the Donor Agencies in Educational Analysis.* Hong Kong: Longman Group, 1991.

Namibia Ministry of Education and Culture. *The National Institute for Educational Development at Okahandja.* Windhoek: Namibia Ministry of Education and Culture, 1993.

Namibia Ministry of Education and Culture. *Curriculum Guide for Formal Basic Education.* Windhoek: Namibia Ministry of Education and Culture, 1992.

Samoff, J. "The Reconstruction of Schooling in Africa," *Comparative Education Review* 37, 2 (1993): 181–222.

Snyder Jr., C. (Ed.). *Consultation on Change: Proceedings of the Etosha Conference—First National Consultative Conference on Basic Education Reform.* Tallahassee: Learning Systems Institute, Florida State University, 1991.

Spaulding, S., and J. Singleton. "International Development Education." *Review of Educational Research* 38, 3 (1968): 197–304.

SWAPO. *To Be Born a Nation: The Liberation Struggle in Namibia.* London: Zed Press, Department of Information and Publicity, SWAPO of Namibia, 1987.

PART 2
TECHNOLOGICAL INNOVATIONS

5 THE IMPACT OF IMPACT

A STUDY OF THE DISSEMINATION OF AN EDUCATIONAL INNOVATION IN SIX COUNTRIES[1]

H. Dean Nielsen and William K. Cummings

IMPACT, Instruction Managed by Parents, Community and Teachers, was one of the developing world's most revolutionary educational experiments of the 1970s and 1980s. Originally conceived in 1973 by a small group of pioneering educators who established and staffed an intergovernmental organization in Southeast Asia known as INNOTECH, IMPACT was designed as an economic and effective system of providing mass primary education in low-income countries.

This was a particular challenge at the time, given steadily increasing unit costs of conventional schools and new attempts to extend basic education to isolated rural areas and underserved youth. Moreover, as countries pressed toward universal primary education, problems with declining achievement levels and increasing dropout rates also became commonplace. Thus, unlike other sectors of national growth and development such as agriculture, in which expanded output was accompanied by increased productivity, education was actually becoming less productive.

Many, in fact, felt that what this sector needed was a major revolution, similar to the "green revolution," led by the development of a "hybrid strain of education." And this is essentially what the INNOTECH innovators proposed, devising an entirely new approach to rural education which, in its original conception, contrasted in almost every fundamental respect with the conventional school.

THE IMPACT CONCEPT

Drawing from the revolutionary "deschooling" notions of Ivan Illich (1970), the mastery learning concepts of Benjamin Bloom (Bloom, 1975), and the emerging field of educational technology, the IMPACT designers conceived a delivery system in which the school would be replaced by a "community learning center," the classroom teacher by a roving instructional supervisor capable of managing 100–200 students simultaneously, textbooks by "programmed" self-instructional or peer-mediated modules, and classroom lessons by small group exercises guided by peer or cross-age tutors (often called programmed instruction). Communities would also have a larger stake in this system than in the conventional school as the name community learning center implies. Parents and community leaders would provide additional learning facilities in the form of community or neighborhood learning centers (or kiosks), parents and older siblings would act as tutors or monitors, and craftsmen or specialists would provide training in practical subjects on a volunteer basis. In sum, through its flexibility and community outreach the system would be extended to disadvantaged and hard-to-reach learners, through its high student-teacher ratios and use of voluntary labor it would greatly economize resources, and through its active learning processes it would enhance learner motivation, achievement levels, and retention rates.

Experiments to Develop National Prototypes

Beginning in 1974 the INNOTECH group began experimenting in the Philippines with the new concept where it retained the name of IMPACT and in Indonesia, where it was modified and given the localized name of PAMONG.[2] Perhaps because of its proximity to the INNOTECH Center, which eventually came to rest in the Philippines, the system pioneered in Cebu in that country developed an operational "prototype" which was very close to the conceptual model. In more remote central Java the Indonesian model shed some of its more controversial "deschooling" features (e.g., its learning centers were called PAMONG schools) and developed a more elaborate system of community outreach in which out-of-school youth could earn a primary school certificate through self-instruction at community learning posts operated by village leaders with the help of an itinerant teacher.

After a few years of operation the innovation in the two countries began to demonstrate its viability and effectiveness. Older students proved they could learn effectively through self- and peer-mediated instruction and could become competent cross-age tutors. Volunteers could be found to teach practical skills. Perhaps most importantly in the Philippines, the system proved capable of operating with one-half to one-third the number of professionals employed in conventional schools at seemingly little or no loss in student achievement.

These apparent successes naturally drew the attention of local educators who flocked to the experimental sites to observe the revolutionary system in operation. However, perhaps even more enthusiastic was the donor agency community which was keen to find and disseminate educational innovations that really seemed capable of addressing the intractable problems mentioned above. It was not long before new varieties of the IMPACT system sprouted in other countries, in Malaysia and Jamaica through the support of the International Development Research Centre (IDRC) which had supported INNOTECH's original efforts, in Liberia through the support of USAID which was also cofinancing PAMONG development, and in Bangladesh through World Bank support.

In each new country the system was scrutinized and modified in order to adapt to local conditions. In Malaysia, the main feature that was adopted by Project InSPIRE was that of programmed instruction, thought to be needed in rural classrooms where teacher preparation was relatively weak and instructional aids limited. The emphasis was on providing the classroom teachers with neatly packaged programmed lessons which could increase their effectiveness. Peer-mediated instruction and self-instruction were also included but as vehicles for *improved student performance* in rural schools. The economizing and community involvement features of IMPACT did not enter into this model.

In Liberia the model called Improved Efficiency of Learning (IEL) was similar to that in Malaysia in its emphasis on structuring the classroom behavior of the teacher. However, it also placed much emphasis on the overall organization of the village school and efficient use of existing resources. Thus, individual teachers were assigned to carry out programmed instruction in the first three grades while a single teacher supervised a mixture of conventional and programmed self-instruction in the upper grades. This system sought to reduce unit costs by increasing school attendance and reducing dropout rates while preserving the same level of staffing. Programmed materials (modules) were expected to be less expensive than the imported texts used in conventional schools as well as more relevant to local conditions.

In Jamaica, the experiment known as PRIMER decided to rely on the existing textbooks, but to supplement these with instructional guides and innovative instructional aids. Cross-age tutoring or programmed instruction was used in the first three grades with self-instruction using self-contained modules being introduced only in grade four, the first grade in which reading skills were considered adequate. The concern was with improving the quality of education through more individual attention as well as community involvement, and not with reducing costs.

Bangladesh followed the IMPACT model developed in the Philippines in most respects and kept the original name. However, rather than relying completely on modules, it developed adjunct modules to supplement the official texts. Also as school buildings tended to be overcrowded, double sessions were sometimes held: the lower grades were led by a shift of peer teachers in the mornings with the upper grades meeting in the afternoons. As in the Philippines, the basic student unit was called a family, a multiclass unit consisting of as many as 150 students supervised by two adult teachers with the help of student tutors. With this form of organization it was expected that substantial savings could be realized. Table 5.1 provides a summary of the features of IMPACT projects in the six implementing countries.

OBSTACLES TO NATIONAL-LEVEL DISSEMINATION

As impressive as this phenomenon of intercontinental diffusion was, once the prototype developers attempted to persuade local authorities to adopt their prototypes for wide-scale dissemination, many obstacles and disappointments were encountered. In the Philippines a series of national dissemination meetings eventually resulted in the system's being transplanted to only five new locations. In Indonesia project developers, having met a deadline for the preparation of "dissemination packages," discovered that the Directorate of Primary Education had never been prepared to receive them. When the developers and ministry officials finally got together it was clear that the ministry only needed certain components of the system to help them in their march, financed by new windfall oil revenues, toward universal primary education. By the late 1980s variants of the system were in place in approximately three hundred small schools in Kalimantan, Sulawasi, and east Java, and there were about one-third that number of full schools in east Java. The system had virtually disappeared at its original experimentation sites in central Java and Bali.

In Malaysia programmed materials had already been developed for several grades, capturing the interests of teachers and their national association, when the government promulgated a new primary school curriculum which urged the classroom teacher to exercise more individual initiative in lesson design and structure. InSPIRE with its highly structured programs thus fell out of favor with the school authorities (though not with teachers) of peninsular Malaysia and project developers were banned from further developing the system there. Before its project activity came to a halt, Sabah, one of the two Malaysian provinces on the island of Borneo, discovered the system and requested that it be used in its remote country schools. Eventually on peninsula Malaysia, central authorities, responding to pressure from teachers who appreciated the high quality and usefulness of InSPIRE materials, asked project developers to provide enrichment and remediation modules for use with the new curriculum. Thus the system began to serve two purposes: mainstream instruction in at least thirty schools

Table 5.1 Comparing the Initial National Prototypes

Characteristics	Philippines	Indonesia	Malaysia	Jamaica	Liberia	Bangladesh
Objectives:						
Lower Unit Costs	Y	N	N	N	Y	Y
Improve Education Quality	Y	Y	Y	Y	Y	Y
Reach Dropouts	N	Y	N	N	N	N
Personnel:						
Instructional Supervisors						
Replace Teachers	Y	Y	N	N	Y	Y
Community Volunteers Welcome	Y	Y	N	Y	N	Y
Adolescents Tutor Pupils	Y	N	N	Y	N	Y
Specialist Teachers	Y	Y	Y	?	N	Y
Instructional Materials:						
Self-Instructional Modules	Y	Y	N	N	Y	N
Instructional Guides and Instructional Aides	Y	Y	Y	Y	Y	Y
Pupil Worksheets	Y	N	Y	Y	Y	N
Radios to Supplement Written Materials	Y	N	N	N	N	N
Instructional Organization:						
Integrated Instruction of Several Subjects	Y	N	N	N	N	N
Periods Longer than in Conventional Schools	Y	N	N	N	N	?
Classes Divided into Smaller Groups	Y	Y	Y	Y	Y	Y
Older Pupils Assist in Instructing Younger	Y	Y	N	Y	N	Y

(continued on page 116)

TABLE 5.1 (continued from page 115)

Characteristics	Philippines	Indonesia	Malaysia	Jamaica	Liberia	Bangladesh
Instructional Organization: *(continued)*						
Peer Tutoring	Y	Y	?	?	Y	Y
Programmed Learning in Grades 4–6	Y	Y	N	N	Y	Y
Differential Pacing Allowed	Y	N	N	N	N	Y
Other Features:	Kiosks for group study; Multigrade classes or "families"	Movable flat desk combined for group study; All in a group must need 90 percent on post-test to finish a module; Several variants noted in text.	Weekly instructional guide can be held in hand; Small school variant developed for Sabah.		Quality materials developed despite lack of official curriculum; High-tech for editing, printing, and distributing materials.	Morning session for grades 1–3; Afternoon for grades 4–6; "Family" as in Philippines; Use adjunct modules.

Note: Y = Yes   N = No   ? = Unclear

in remote areas of Sabah and enrichment/remediation throughout peninsular Malaysia.

In Jamaica the system seems to have disappeared. This was not because of problems in system dissemination but because of failure in establishing a workable prototype, due to the collapse of the experimental project.

Dissemination prospects in the other two countries seemed more positive but, as of the late 1980s, were far from clear. In Liberia the system survived the 1980 coup d'etat but later got into difficulty over a less than laudatory evaluation report (Galda, 1982, 1983). A second evaluation (Kelley, 1984a, 1984b) reversed the conclusions of the first and by the mid-1980s a tentative decision was reached to make IEL an integral part of the national system of education. In Bangladesh the national dissemination situation was slow in developing. By the mid-1980s there had been no clear national policy statement on IMPACT dissemination and no evaluation of the system's effectiveness. Nevertheless, the World Bank second-phase project (1985) included a phased expansion of IMPACT from eighteen to three hundred schools.

This checkered record of national level dissemination is far from what was expected when INNOTECH embarked on its revolutionary experiment. It has also been a disappointment to the national developers and donor agency supporters. It leads one to question why an innovation, which has such intuitive appeal and such a reputation for success has fallen so short of expectations. Beyond that, why has it thrived in some places and not in others, including the places it was originally designed for? And why were some components adopted more readily than others? In the ensuing pages we shall try to address these questions by drawing on various theories of organizational development and dissemination. Although no clear-cut answers are given, the exercise may be of use to those in the future who are naive or courageous enough to attempt a major educational innovation.

ANALYTICAL FRAMEWORK

As Havelock and Huberman observed in *Solving Educational Problems* (1977), "a complete analysis of barriers to innovation requires an integration of understandings from the perspective of practically every discipline, in particular economics, history, geography, political science, anthropology, psychology and sociology" (p. 120). They continue as follows: "To a large extent, each country and each innovative situation represents a unique configuration of elements related to each of these disciplines" (p. 120).

In trying to isolate an adequate framework for analyzing our multicountry case studies, we surveyed the literature from many fields and

perspectives including that from classical administrative theory, the diffusion of innovations (Rogers, 1962), organizational change (Daft and Becker,
1978), social networks (Flores, 1981), implementation analysis (Pressman
and Wildavsky, 1984; Warwick, 1983), social reproduction (Bourdieu and
Passeron, 1977; Giroux, 1983), and dependency theory (Berman, 1982;
Arnove, 1980). We found elements from most of these perspectives which
related to the problems which we observed. However, since as Havelock and
Huberman stated "each innovative situation represents a unique configuration of elements," we decided to construct our own framework of explanatory factors, as shown in Table 5.2, drawing both from the literature we reviewed and the phenomena we observed.

TABLE 5.2 Analytical Framework

1. Strength of the Innovation's Prototype
   (a) conceptual soundness
   (b) acceptability
   (c) documented success of prototype
2. Availability of Resources for Dissemination
   (a) local funding takes over from outside agencies
   (b) national economic situation
3. Administrative Context
   (a) readiness for reform
   (b) effectiveness and flexibility of the bureaucratic infrastructure
   (c) number and strength of competing systems
4. Project Organization
   (a) locus of project office
   (b) foreign expert involvement
   (c) open-endedness
5. Consistency and Skillfulness of Leadership
   (a) consistency
   (b) gamesmanship

In this section each of the elements of our framework will be explained and
then in the following section applied in analyzing the problem of national-
level dissemination.

STRENGTH OF THE INNOVATION'S PROTOTYPE

To be even considered for dissemination, innovations need to have established at least the reputation for being sound and realizable. Proponents of

implementation analysis maintain that first among the conditions that effect program implementation is the soundness or validity of the concepts on which the project is based. Diffusion theorists on the other hand stress the appeal or acceptability of innovations to potential adopters, especially opinion leaders. Both subjective and objective elements enter the related persuasion process, as potential adopters are influenced by both effective communication of objective information and the spread of rumors and gossip. Beyond that, there is the premise in all projects involving a pilot-testing phase, a feature of all IMPACT projects, that wider dissemination depends upon or is even driven by successfulness of the prototype model. A corollary to this premise is that such success will be determined through the vehicle of evaluation research and communicated through dissemination of the research findings.

Availability of Resources for Dissemination

This feature is basically a matter of finance and human resource: once the externally funded pilot phase is over are there local or alternative funds available to cover the start-up and recurrent costs of wider operations and are there enough trained persons available to keep the system going and growing? Availability of resources overlaps with questions of financial and manpower planning, government priorities, and overall economic conditions, which in least developed countries are subject to wide fluctuations.

Administrative Context

This is the most complex feature of our framework. It begins with the premise that all wide-scale disseminations are controlled by national bureaucracies which have their own priorities and mandates, their rules and regulations, their capacities for responding to and processing change, and their ways of coping with the pressures of competing groups and programs. For the sake of simplicity we have broken this feature of our framework into three components, the first related to organizational policy ("readiness for reform"), the second to bureaucratic processes ("effectiveness and flexibility of bureaucratic infrastructure") and the third to the management of competing systems ("number and strength of competing systems"). Special attention will be placed on the second component, the effectiveness and flexibility of the bureaucratic infrastructure, since this is where dissemination management must take place. As Havelock and Huberman (1977) observe, existing administrative and technical structures are often unable to cope with the complex demands of new projects. As a result, "demands are held up or transformed in such a way as to be more compatible with existing rules, norms and rules. In doing so, the infrastructure is acting to reduce drastically the rate and magnitude of change which had been the principal goals of the project" (p. 72).

PROJECT ORGANIZATION

Among the many aspects of project organization those which seem to be particularly relevant to dissemination are the locus of the project office, the foreign expert involvement, and the degree of open-endedness or operational flexibility in the project. With respect to the locus of the project, implementation analysis has emphasized the effect of the number of organizational actors or bodies on the proliferation of communication problems during implementation, while diffusion theory notes the difficulties of persuasion with increasing physical distance. Extent of foreign involvement seems to be related to the project country's sense of ownership of or commitment to the project and the prospects for widespread diffusion. The issue here is not only the proportion of expatriates on the project staff but also their positions and the aspects of the project cycle (planning, execution, evaluation, training) they are involved in. The degree of open-endedness refers both to explicit conditions of contracts between project personnel and their donor agency funders—the degree to which the project is obliged to meet specific contractually binding goals, and less formal conditions—and the degree to which the management allows for "creative adaptations" during the predissemination period.

CONSISTENCY AND SKILLFULNESS OF LEADERSHIP

Clear support of a project at the highest levels of the relevant administrative structures contributes to its prospects for institutionalization, especially in countries where decision making is relatively personalistic. Dissemination efforts are often subverted when the original patrons of a project are replaced by new leaders who have less understanding and psychological investment in the project. However, even stability of leadership is not sufficient for an effective dissemination strategy. Implementation theorists highlight the importance of manipulative skills in making negotiations and trade-offs and decisions about timing and staffing. This is often referred to as "gamesmanship" and the arena, the "implementation game."

ACCOUNTING FOR PROBLEMS IN IMPACT DISSEMINATION

In this section we will apply our framework in accounting for problems in IMPACT project dissemination at the national level. Since the projects and their national contexts varied widely some aspects of our framework will be more salient in some countries than in others. When appropriate we will attempt to explain why some explanations fit some countries better than others. In the end we will attempt to extract some common features across the six countries and some general lessons about the dissemination of educational innovations.

1. Strength of the Innovation's Prototype

CONCEPTUAL SOUNDNESS

In each country where a version of IMPACT was tried out, the original proponents enthusiastically endorsed most of the system's basic concepts and assumptions: that rural education could be extended and improved through the use of programmed instruction, that students could act as tutors and communities could provide support services and resources, that teachers roles could be radically redefined, and that changes in student-teacher ratios could substantially reduce costs.

As these concepts were operationalized and field-tested in the respective countries, however, the validity of some of them began to be challenged. Two key concepts which eventually revealed serious flaws were that programmed instruction could become a substitute for the classroom teacher and that the community could make substantial voluntary contributions to the operation of rural schools.

In the early IMPACT projects, those in the Philippines and Indonesia, where the substitution of teachers was initially a prominent feature, two main obstacles emerged. The first was bureaucratic rigidity. For example, in the Philippines, despite the very large potential savings in teachers' salaries afforded by raising the student teacher ratio to nearly 100 to 1, budgeting systems made it almost impossible to transfer the funds allocated to teacher salaries for the purchase of the essential programmed materials or modules. Also, development funds allocated for textbook production could not be shifted into module or programmed text production. The second was an underestimation of the power and importance of the teacher in rural communities. In the Philippines, teachers even at one point organized against IMPACT because of its potential threat to teacher positions. In Indonesia policymakers never abandoned their emphasis on new teacher recruitment and upgrading, the teaching profession being seen as a crucial instrument of national integration and socialization and a means of upward mobility for rural talent. In Jamaica, from the very beginning, teachers made sure there would be no teacher reductions. Most of the more recent IMPACT projects have, in fact, avoided this goal of radically increasing the student-teacher ratio (e.g., the projects in Malaysia and Liberia were developed to enhance the instructional role of the teacher), and Indonesia has backed away from it almost completely.[3] In contrast, in the Philippines where there was already an overabundance of teachers, IMPACT maintained its emphasis on reducing the numbers of teachers in school, a factor which seems to have weakened its potential for widespread adoption there.

The concept of voluntary community participation in IMPACT—the PA (parent) and the C (community) factors in its acronym—has not held up well either. The early projects discovered that parents were neither willing nor, in many cases, able to help their children with schoolwork, due to their own low level of education.

Sustained voluntary community support in the form of tutors, aides, and skill instructors was also difficult if not impossible to generate. It was apparent that the opportunity costs of such involvement had not been taken into account, especially among those in disadvantaged areas where the press of making a living left very little time for sustained voluntary assistance by parents and paraprofessionals. In addition, planners had not considered the fact that requiring such a contribution from poor communities and not from relatively affluent ones was a form of regressive taxation. Such community factors did not appear in the later versions of IMPACT (except in Bangladesh) and have been de-emphasized in Indonesia, where PAMONG schools are no longer called community learning centers. Once again, and ironically, it is in the country where these features of IMPACT were the most fully developed, the Philippines, that dissemination has been among the least successful. This recurrent finding suggests a hypothesis which we will elaborate more fully in subsequent sections, namely, to the extent that more controversial features of IMPACT were abandoned or modified, the system more easily gained acceptance for dissemination.

ACCEPTANCE

According to the diffusion framework acceptance or adoption is at least a two-step process, involving opinion leaders (decision makers; senior bureaucrats; village leaders) and end users (teachers; parents). The acceptance of the system in various countries was not always the same at all levels. In Indonesia the system seems to have enjoyed widespread acceptance at regional offices of education, among community leaders, and among teachers (at least initially). This is one explanation for its successful diffusion in east Java. There was some evidence of teacher disaffection over time, however, especially at the predissemination site (Bali) where increased workloads were not met with increased benefits. At the central ministry, however, there has been an ambivalence toward PAMONG, some features (like peer-mediated and self-instruction) gaining acceptance but with relatively low levels of financial support.

In Malaysia the system became popular among teachers but lost support among crucial central bureaucrats who saw it as antithetical to the country's new curriculum. Ironically, as the new curriculum was diffused, the popularity of InSPIRE increased, not only among teachers, who felt it helped them deal with the lesson preparation requirements of the new curriculum, but among administrators in marginal areas (e.g., Sabah) who doubted the applicability of the new curriculum to their circumstances. The popularity of InSPIRE among the blocks of supporters seems to have kept it alive despite central office opposition and eventually opened up new, although limited, avenues for its expansion.

In the Philippines, officials at INNOTECH have maintained their enthusiasm for IMPACT, as have numerous educators who helped pioneer the concept. However, central ministry officials remain lukewarm to the concept as do (or have) parents and teachers who have sometimes voted with their feet (or their children's feet in the case of the parents) against the project because of a widespread, through probably misguided, feeling that the project was an esoteric experiment for elites, and thus not appropriate for "regular" children.

Documented Prototype Success

It seems reasonable to assume that documented successfulness of an innovation prototype would be strongly related to dissemination success. Indeed, the main purpose of prototype development and testing during a pilot project phase is to provide policymakers a firm basis for moving ahead with dissemination. To provide some sense of how this logic applied to IMPACT we have summarized the success of the various prototypes in Table 5.3.

The hypothesis linking prototype success and dissemination seems to be clearly confirmed in the case of two countries: Jamaica, where dissemination was nil, showed lack of success on all criteria; and Liberia, where dissemination was planned to be extensive, showed high success on three of five criteria, including the documentation of project results through research.

In three other countries the results are equivocal. In Indonesia where dissemination has been moderately successful, the prototype has also shown moderate success, except on the criterion of reaching new groups of learners where it has been highly successful—perhaps the critical factor in its dissemination success. In Malaysia, where dissemination success has been low to moderate, success on the criteria has also been low to moderate, except in the case of reaching new groups of learners, where it was also high. Fi-

TABLE 5.3 Successfulness of IMPACT Prototypes

Criterion	Country					
	Philippines	Indonesia	Malaysia	Jamaica	Liberia	Bangladesh
1. Reached new group learners	Mod	Hi	Hi	Lo	Mod	Mod
2. Student achievement equivalent or superior to that in regular schools	Hi	Mod	Mod	Lo	Hi	?
3. Demonstrated cost-saving potential	Hi	Mod	Lo	Lo	Mod	Mod
4. Documented results through evaluation research	Hi	Mod	Mod	Lo	Hi	Lo
5. Level of innovation	Hi	Mod	Lo	Lo	Hi	Mod

nally, in Bangladesh, where dissemination efforts showed signs of at least limited success, the prototype criteria were moderately successful but with no documentation of results and uncertainty about student performance, indicating perhaps that decision makers there were taking their signals from the positive outcomes obtained in other countries.

The hypothesis takes a resounding blow in the case of the Philippines. In that country, where dissemination has been limited, high levels of success have been attained on four of five prototype success criteria, and they have been well documented. Experience in that country clearly shows that it takes more than a successful prototype to guarantee success in dissemination. Earlier we proposed that IMPACT's very success in being highly innovative eventually became an obstacle to its dissemination. But it may also be the case that the project's poor record in reaching new groups had something to do with it. Beyond these there are still many other complex factors to consider, not the least being the resources available for dissemination, to be discussed next.

2. Resources Available for Dissemination
LOCAL AND OUTSIDE FUNDING FOR DISSEMINATION
In all countries, outside agencies (IDRC; USAID; World Bank) provided

funds for the pilot phase. Beyond that, the success of dissemination depended, at least in part, on the availability of funds for expansion. The assumption in most cases was that such funds would come from local sources.

In the two cases where dissemination was the slightest, Jamaica and the Philippines, there were no national government funds committed beyond the end of the experimental phase, and external funding ceased as well. In contrast, in the four countries where better progress was made toward national dissemination, new funding was obtained. For example, in Indonesia two new donors provided funds for the predissemination stages of PAMONG and its small-schools variant. In addition, the national government provided support for module production and regional staff training. In Malaysia InSPIRE received funds for dissemination in Sabah from the Sabah Foundation and for the production of enrichment/remediation modules from the Ministry of Education. In addition, the project has been exploring self-financing schemes through the direct marketing in InSPIRE modules. In Liberia and Bangladesh the financing of further expansion is being written into large World Bank loan programs.

Trained Persons Available to Carry the Project

Human resources have also been a factor. While Jamaica is a highly literate society, the project experienced difficulty in recruiting and maintaining a qualified staff—educated people preferred to work in the cities or even overseas rather than take up the insecure and modestly rewarded positions offered by the project. In contrast to Jamaica, the general level of education in Liberia is much lower, but the project was able to recruit and retain qualified staff thanks to the combination of a depressed national economy with much educated unemployment and the attractive monetary incentives offered to project managers. Liberia's staffing problem lay primarily in the retention of capable foreign advisors. In the other projects, staffing did not pose a major problem.

National Economic Situation

Shortage of funds is only a sign of deeper economic problems. Funds were cut off in the least successful case, Jamaica, partly because of untimely reverses in the national economies. While the national economy of Liberia faced a similar economic reverse, the project continued to receive the portion of funds committed by USAID and ultimately the Liberian government renewed its commitments. Only in Indonesia and Malaysia were the projects blessed with a reasonable level of financial support, but even this showed fluctuations and changing conditions based on the national economic situation. For example, in Indonesia windfall oil profits in the midseventies enabled the central government to plow enormous resources into expanding the conventional school, such that the cost saving factors of PAMONG appeared less important than they did early in the decade. Emphasis thus shifted to using PAMONG as one of the means to attaining universal primary education, irrespective of costs. By the time PAMONG was ready for widespread dissemination in the early 1980s, oil revenues had fallen and ambitious plans were scaled back. By the mid-1980s policymakers began to consider PAMONG's cost-saving potential again.

3. Administrative Context

READINESS FOR REFORM

The objective diversity of the six countries and their educational systems cannot be overemphasized. They range from Indonesia, the world's fourth most populous nation, to Jamaica, with only two million people; from Bangladesh, characterized by a high density of population, to Liberia and major parts of Malaysia and Indonesia which are sparsely populated. Per capita GNP in the mid-1980s ranged from threee thousand dollars in Malaysia to below one hundred dollars in Bangladesh. Monthly teacher salaries ranged from twenty-five to five hundred dollars, and average student-teacher ratios from 25:1 in Malaysia to up to 60:1 in Liberia.

Despite this diversity, common to all six countries was the recent completion of a major educational review or sector report which emphasized the inadequacy of primary education, especially in rural areas. The Liberian and Bangladesh reviews were most explicit in stressing the likelihood of mounting quantitative problems in view of demographic projections for a rapid increase in the size of the primary school cohort. In the other countries, the reports placed at least as much stress on issues of quality. Malaysia's Drop-Out Survey (Murad, 1973), the Philippines Soutele (EDPITAF, 1977), and Indonesia's Educational Assessment (Office of Educational and Cultural Research and Development, 1972) had all highlighted rural-urban differences in educational achievement; such that in these countries there was also considerable interest in upgrading the quality of rural education. In Jamaica, the progressive Manley government, having just been reelected, was determined to extend its reform program to new areas, and among these primary education, which had long been neglected relative to secondary and tertiary education, was accorded high priority.

In each of the countries, the search for reforms in primary education led to contact with members of the international network of individuals who had some experience with the IMPACT concept. Trips were arranged for key educators from each of the latter countries to visit ongoing IMPACT schools in the Philippines and Indonesia. Thus the IMPACT idea was communicated in a timely fashion.

Effectiveness and Flexibility of the Bureaucratic Infrastructure
This element of our model applies particularly in the cases where a prototype is sufficiently developed to be ready for insertion into the mainstream of national educational programming. Thus it applies more in the case of the earlier projects (Philippines, Indonesia, and Malaysia) than the later ones.

The issue here is the extent to which a new system can be inserted into the routine system of educational management. In Indonesia this issue itself became the object of experimentation during the predissemination phase, with some mixed results. For example, it appeared to be almost impossible for the ministry to reduce the number of teachers assigned to a school once that number had been set, a factor which made changing student-teacher ratios difficult. In addition, the project was unsuccessful in getting the ministry to substitute modules for conventional textbooks. The result was that PAMONG classrooms got both modules and textbooks, a situation which undermined another cost-saving feature of the system. Moreover, the project was unable to alter the rhythm and content of the regular testing cycle. Although PAMONG had established a self- or group-paced system, pilot school students still had to participate in standardized trimester and end-of-year achievement tests. Finally, students from the out-of-school component of PAMONG were required to take exactly the same school leaving exam as regular students, even though their self-instructional program did not include such tested subjects as music and physical education.

In the realm of school supervision, the school supervisors for PAMONG schools were at somewhat of a loss concerning procedures for gauging student and teacher performance in the schools. New PAMONG supervision systems were designed but they were difficult for supervisors, accustomed to a standard routine, to implement.

These examples illustrate problems which confronted the other systems as well. In the Philippines, the enormous cost-saving potential of the full IMPACT model has never been realized partly because the government has not been willing to allow funds for textbooks to be used for producing modules and the savings implicit in increased student-teacher ratios to be used to hire tutors, to provide incentive pay to staff, and to buy supplementary materials.

These points of resistance do not appear to be a part of a grand scheme to repel innovation and change. They simply illustrate the inertia inherent in large, centrally run systems. To make an exception to the general rule, even when justifiable, adds to the administrative burden of operatives whose main goal is to avoid hassles and minimize paperwork. The better organized, the more institutionalized, and the more centralized the bureaucracy, the greater the resistance to such innovations. That is perhaps another reason that the potential for dissemination appears greatest in Liberia and Bangladesh, countries where the administrative machinery is less entrenched. It may also help to explain why dissemination within the administratively more advanced countries is more promising in the periphery (Sabah in Malaysia; Outer Islands in Indonesia) than in the mainstream.

NUMBER AND STRENGTH OF COMPETING SYSTEMS

This element is closely related to the bureaucratic considerations mentioned above. The IMPACT system did not appear in an organizational vacuum in any of the countries, for in all but Liberia and Bangladesh there were already strong systems in place or competing systems being nurtured, systems which had created their own constituencies and beneficiaries ready and willing to defend them against "intrusions." Malaysia and the Philippines had already attained near universal primary education through conventional schools and a strong teacher force. In rural areas such schools were both expensive and poor in quality, but changing them meant undoing something that already existed. Besides, powerful groups were already developing their own reform programs in the form of new curricula (Malaysia) and decentralized planning and upgrading (Philippines).

In Indonesia huge sums of money were being spent on expanding and improving the conventional school while a development school concept was being piloted by the nation's educational research and development center with the help of external funds and a raft of foreign advisers. Entering the mainstream under such circumstances, was like trying to introduce a new brand of soap into a saturated market.

In Malaysia and Indonesia, however, there were still gaps in the "market," spaces where the conventional school and existing alternatives appeared to be inappropriate and into which existing IMPACT models were sufficiently flexible to fit. In Malaysia this meant developing InSPIRE to cater to rural schools in relatively underdeveloped Sabah and to complement the new curriculum through the development of enrichment and remediation packages. In Indonesia this meant the adaptation of PAMONG to the needs of small schools on outer islands, where teachers were already trying (generally ineffectively) to implement multigrade classroom management, and to the needs of school dropouts throughout the country who were seeking a second chance for a primary certificate. In all of these cases of "gap filling," the system was inserted into a situation where no adequate programs had been developed yet. Thus there was no need to undo or reform an existing program. To fill these gaps, the project managers had to leave behind some features of their original models, often their most innovative or elegant features. However, being able to do so allowed them to open up new "markets" and provided them the space to evolve new models and dissemination strategies.

The situation in Liberia and Bangladesh was quite different: in these countries there were still large gaps in the mainstream, gaps which IMPACT, with its foreign funding and reputation for success was in a good position to fill. For example, in Liberia most schools were exceptionally small and located in rural areas where there were virtually no facilities nor trained teachers. Into such gaps the IEL system fit comfortably. In Bangladesh the educational system had only recently been organized on a nationwide basis and was extremely short on all kinds of resources, including an official apparatus for developing experimental projects. These conditions coupled with the objective characteristics of high population density and relative underdevelopment of the conventional system provided the original IMPACT model space to prosper.

4. Project Organization

Locus of Project Office

Another important factor influencing progress toward dissemination was the set of relations that evolved between the project leaders and the relevant authorities. As a background for discussing these relations, it will be helpful to study the different structural linkages of the six cases. As illustrated in Table 5.4, one dimension along which projects varied was the number of bureaucratic levels standing between project directors and the Minister of Education. A second dimension was the physical location of the project office: at a university campus, in a ministry office, or at some other kind of location.

TABLE 5.4 Structure and Physical Location of Project

Bureaucratic Levels Between Project Director and Minister	Location of Project Office		
	University	Government	Other
Few		Jamaica	
	Indonesia		Liberia
	Malaysia		
		Bangladesh	
Many	Philippines		

The locus of the office was a critical factor in what Pressman and Wildavsky (1984) have referred to as the complexity of joint action. Project officers who were outside of government had more channels to work through in order to get things done than did those with formal authority. For example, in the Philippines where the project director even lacked the formal authority to discipline teachers in the project schools (who were public officials), this lack of authority posed a problem. Also, as the Philippines had the most decentralized government among the six cases, the complexity of joint action was greatest. The full chain of command included the project director, the local education supervisor, the governor, the central government's office of primary education, and finally the minister of education. The chain of command was nearly as complex in Malaysia and Indonesia; while the bureaucratic chain was not as long, the priorities of foreign donors in the case of Indonesia and the Sabah Foundation in the case of Malaysia added a different dimension to the complexity. In contrast, in Jamaica, Liberia, and even Bangladesh, the project director had direct access to the head of primary education and through that office to the minister. To the extent this chain of command was abbreviated, the projects found it easier to maintain high-level support, which in at least the case of Liberia has seemed to contribute to positive decisions about dissemination.

FOREIGN TECHNICAL ASSISTANCE

Needless to say, in most developing countries, there is considerable resistance to proposals for carrying out a multiyear project to develop a plan of action. Experimental work is viewed as risky and wasteful of scarce human and financial resources. To minimize the risks involved, grants from foreign donors were secured to subsidize all of the experiments, except in Bangladesh where the experiment was authorized as one component of a large World Bank project in universal primary education. Included in the contracts of several of the external grants were provisions concerning the attainment of specific quantifiable goals and the participation of foreign advisors. Table 5.5 provides a summary of the arrangements made between the respective governments and outside donors with respect to these dimensions. The dimension of foreign advisors will be discussed in this section; that related to project goals (open-ended versus closed) will be discussed in the next.

A look at Table 5.5 reveals that there were three countries, Indonesia, Philippines, and Liberia, in which the number of foreign advisors were many, and two, Malaysia and Jamaica, in which there were few. Bangladesh is in an intermediate position—there were only one or two foreign advisors at a time in that country but the overall staff was always small and one of the foreign advisors was always the project director.

TABLE 5.5 Foreign Technical Assistance

Project Goals	Foreign Advisers	
	Many	*Few*
Open-ended	Indonesia	Malaysia
		Jamaica
	Philippines	
		Bangladesh
Closed	Liberia	

In general there appears to be no consistent relationship between degree of national level dissemination and number of foreign advisors. Of the four countries where national dissemination looks relatively promising, two have had many foreign advisors, one few, and one an intermediate number. Of the two countries where dissemination is relatively unpromising, one has had many advisors, the other few.

It does seem likely, however, that number of foreign advisors inter-acts with other factors including some which have been described above, among which are administrative environment and innovativeness. For example, it appears that a high or intermediate number of foreign advisors is conducive to dissemination in countries where the organizational environment is relatively sparse (Liberia, Bangladesh). In countries in which the organizational environment is dense, the situation is ambiguous. In Jamaica, where the project never gained national stature, the project could have perhaps been saved from marginalization by more foreign participation. However, in Malaysia, where the project developed a sound product, InSPIRE was saved by the adroit maneuverings of a politically savvy and entirely local staff. In the Philippines many advisors were available to help in the development of product of demonstrated quality, but they were unable to help project staff overcome its image of being disconnected with the educational realities of the country. Finally, in Indonesia where many advisors also worked in technical fields the project maintained the reputation of being a nationally controlled experiment and was steered in its political maneuverings by some skillful national leaders. (See "gamesmanship" below.)

Foreign advisors, coming from the outside and connected with a community of reform-minded educators, are likely to press for high innovation. This was certainly true in the case of the Philippines, Liberia, and Bangladesh, in which they were given free reign over project substance. As we have demonstrated above, this quality of innovativeness proved to be conducive to project dissemination in the institutionally sparse environments of Liberia and Bangladesh, but caused negative reactions and dissemination obstacles in the institutionally dense environment of the Philippines.

In sum, we can say that the use of foreign advisors in a project does not seem to have any clear and direct relationship to project dissemination. However, there is a sense that too strong a foreign advisor role in a project can disassociate it from national political realities especially in a dense organizational environment, and too little a role can lead to its marginalization and neglect.

OPEN-ENDEDNESS OF PROJECT GOALS

Contracts between donor agencies and recipient country institutions often spell out in rather specific terms what the expected outcomes of the assisted project will be. These terms often specify such details as the number of children to be served, the numbers of teachers to be trained, the numbers of modules to be produced and the percent of improvement on indicators of achievement and student dropout to be expected. Beyond the formalities there are differing degrees of actual adherence to such terms, some project managers paying strict heed to the goals and plans in contractual documents and some paying less attention to such things and more attention to changing conditions—adapting goals and plans according to experience. By open-endedness, we refer to the extent to which the project is administered in a way which allows for changing goals and plans, either because contracts have provided such flexibility or because managers act despite formal terms and agreements.

Table 5.5 (see previous section) provides an impressionistic view of the open-endedness of the projects in the various countries. In general there appears to be an inverse association between the number of foreign advisors and the degree of open-endedness of the projects. Indonesia is an exception to this rule, a reflection of the fact that the project's main decisions were always taken by the Indonesian director, a proponent of "creative adaptation," who did not consider the terms of the foreign contracts to be binding on his decision making.

Just as with the number of foreign advisors, the relationship between open-endedness and dissemination is not clear-cut and linear. There are good dissemination prospects for two countries at the high end of the open-endedness scale and for two countries at the low end of the scale. Once again the concept of density of the organizational environment seems to be an important interactive factor. Of those countries with dense organizational environments, those at the high end of the spectrum (with the exception of Jamaica) were the ones with the best prospects of dissemination. On the other hand, in the low organizational density countries dissemination seems related to a relative tightness in project goals and plans.

This seems to reflect a need for flexibility in the high density countries—a need for political maneuvering and project adaptation. Two examples illustrate this point. In Indonesia, when it became apparent that the director of primary education was not going to adopt the full PAMONG model (in-school plus out-of-school), the staff began successfully "marketing" various versions of the outreach component of the system. In Malaysia, when it became apparent that InSPIRE wouldn't be taken into the mainstream, project managers agreed to concentrate on enrichment and remediation modules using InSPIRE techniques.

The Philippine project did adjust and improve its delivery system over time but at the time of dissemination only had one integrated system to offer. Prospective adopters of the system were faced with taking all or nothing, and since start-up costs were high and staffing factors controversial most ended up taking nothing.

Such flexibility did not seem to be a factor in the countries of low organization density. Since there were fewer competing projects in those countries, prowess in marketing, including the development of alternative packaging strategies, did not seem to be a concern. If the project seemed to attain its goals, it was brought into the incompletely developed mainstream.

5. Consistency and Skillfulness of Leadership

The foregoing discussion on technical assistance highlights the importance of consistent and skillful leadership in the host country. Respected leaders, who stay with projects and skillfully lead them through changes in external conditions and internal politics, are presumably capable of dealing with the competing agendas and pressures and maneuvering projects into a position for widespread dissemination.

CONSISTENCY

The facts concerning consistency of leadership in the respective projects are summarized in Table 5.6. The table shows the number of times a particular leader changed during the project from the beginning to late 1984. Since a project's "staff" (last row) consists of many individuals the table merely indicates whether its composition significantly changed or remained the same during the period.

TABLE 5.6 Consistency of Leadership (Number of Changes)

Office	Philippines	Indonesia	Malaysia	Jamaica	Liberia	Bangladesh
Prime Minister	0	0	2	2	2	2
Minister of Education	3	3	2	3	2	2
Center Liaison Officer	2	0	2	3+	0	2
Project Director	0	3	2	0	0	0
Staff	Some	None	None	Some	None	None

It is difficult to specify which leader is the most critical to dissemination success. Since the minister is usually the one who sets general policy, he/she might be considered to be particularly critical. In addition, the person who is the project's broker or advocate in the ministry's central office, the "central liaison officer" (our term) would be expected to be a crucial negotiator for project adoption. The prime minister would probably be less critical since he/she would be involved with more global issues and the project director less so since he/she is more concerned with technical matters.

When we examine the table it is apparent that the countries in which there was the most instability in the two critical positions, minister of education and central liaison officer, were the countries in which the dissemination prospects were the least promising. The extreme case is Jamaica, where there were more than three changes in the project's center liaison officer even though the project ran for a shorter time than the others. In Indonesia there were also many changes in one critical officer, the minister of education, but this seems to have been compensated for by no change in the center liaison officer.

An interesting feature appears in the consistency of the project leader. There is a tendency for project leader consistency to be negatively correlated with project dissemination. For example, the director did not change in the Philippines and Jamaica where dissemination was limited, but changed several times in Indonesia and Malaysia where the dissemination picture was positive and based on technical flexibility. It seems that such flexibility may require a change in field management once in a while.

SKILLFULNESS OR "GAMESMANSHIP"
Skillfulness in this context is defined as "gamesmanship," or winning others over in the face of delays or unanticipated opposition to the implemen-

tation of a program. Gamesmanship is essentially a spontaneous skill mobilized in reaction to unanticipated situations.

The original INNOTECH group devoted little thought to external reactions, assuming that the merits of a well-researched experiment would speak for themselves. But the naïveté of this thinking was quickly exposed. In the early experiments, some of the most threatening early problems stemmed from adverse community reaction. Especially in the Philippines a rumor spread that the new school was elitist and neglected the ordinary student; many children left the experimental school to join an ordinary school. While the project members were able to overcome this temporary setback, they quickly realized the need of maintaining close contact with the local community. Thereafter, they exerted a special effort to establish rich communication with parents. And as quickly as they could they prepared data to refute the local rumors.

This first shot across IMPACT's bow proved a useful warning to later projects with the result that most devoted extra attention to anticipating community moods. One important tactic evident especially in Indonesia and Bangladesh was the early provision to the community of valuable goods, respectively a grant to start a community savings and loan association and the construction of new school buildings; these acts, by immediately signifying the project's intent to benefit the community, established a favorable attitude for the time-consuming process of introducing the new prototype. The need to develop approaches to reassure recipients and counter potentially destructive rumors is surprisingly neglected in much of the available implementation literature.

Toward the end of the experimental stage all of the projects faced the challenge of convincing those higher in the government that the experimental prototypes should be introduced to an expanded and regionally more diverse set of schools. For success in the drive for dissemination, a different form of gamesmanship was crucial. Seemingly attractive approaches were developed in several of the countries: for example, in the Philippines, key national education officials were invited along with the chief educational officers of each province to a multiday workshop. Similarly, in Indonesia several national workshops were convened, and in addition key central government officials who favored the project made a number of visits to the offices of interested governors. But in only four countries did these approaches lead to some level of success. Given the numerous other factors involved, it would be imprudent to attribute the successes only to skillful gamesmanship or the failures to poor gamesmanship. But clearly there are differences that deserve mention.

In the Philippines, the project's achievements in bringing together important national and local educational leaders was impressive, but the project leaders failed to appreciate that the key problem lay elsewhere. Without basic changes in the regulations affecting funding, IMPACT had little chance for wider dissemination. These regulations were the province of the Ministry of Finance. Thus prior to persuading educational leaders, the project needed to address the Ministry of Finance. The Philippines' gamesmanship was directed to the wrong target.

Malaysia's InSPIRE certainly encountered the most complicated local situation, and the project was ultimately able to prevail. One critical factor was appearance of favorable articles about InSPIRE in the popular press which helped to galvanize public opinion in support of the project. A second factor was the supporting university's skill in bringing about overt changes in project strategy at crucial points. Especially significant were the two instances of replacing project leaders who had run into conflict with central government officers with new faces that sought amends for the prevailing tensions. In this way, the project managed to move forward.

In Indonesia the project's center liaison officer skillfully structured the project to suit Indonesian conditions and then won the support of local educational and political leaders (sometimes through providing the community with a "valuable good" as mentioned above). Once a relatively successful prototype was available, he sold the idea of further developing and disseminating it to numerous donor agencies, including IDRC, USAID, and UNICEF. With the help of these three donor agencies the program managers were able to develop a number of different variations or subsystems of PAMONG and served them up in different dissemination packages, some of which were eventually taken up by the Ministry of Education.

The gamesmanship in Indonesia was not so strong when it came to selling the full PAMONG system to the ministry. The center liaison officer adopted a policy of keeping director generals of executing departments "out of the kitchen while the soup was being cooked." As a result they were not ready to receive PAMONG's main course when it was served to them. In retrospect, a more astute policy might have been to involve and consult with them at various points along the way.

In both Liberia and Bangladesh, the crucial factor in the progress of the projects was, most probably, the keen interest and gamesmanship of donor agencies. In Liberia, this motivation led the donor, when confronted with a potentially damaging initial evaluation, to commission a second one. Based on the favorable results of the second evaluation, the donor then persuaded the government of Liberia to apply for additional assistance to expand the project. While the actions of the donor were less visible in the Bangladesh case, the donor's known preference for the project certainly had an important influence.

In sum, after all other factors are considered, it finally is necessary to accord due importance to the particular tactics used by projects to advance their positions.

CONCLUSION

The innovation called IMPACT, implemented in various ways across the developing world, stands as a fascinating chapter in the history of dissemination of educational innovations. At its peak this innovation attracted the attention and praise of educators and donor agencies around the world; its widespread dissemination seemed assured. Contrary to predictions, however, this did not occur. A complex array of political, organizational, and technical factors conspired to limit dissimination within each of the countries to not far beyod their project's original (and mostly successful) experimental sites. Today there is very little left of the IMPACT experiment. Nevertheless, its innovative—almost revolutionary—features and accomplishments remain as vivid lessons on how quality basic education can be delivered to rural communities at a reasonable cost. Perhaps even more helpful in the context of widening concern for universal access to basic education are the lessons about the dissemination of innovations that these six sister projects can contribute. We conclude by summarizing six such lessons.

INNOVATION VERSUS IMPLEMENTATION

The original INNOTECH group developed a new concept that radically departed from norms of conventional education and sought to introduce it in its original form at two diverse experimental sites, one in the Philippines and one in Indonesia. Their efforts soon met with stubborn opposition from local educators and parents who worried about the soundness of such revolutionary systems. In the subsequent experiments, the original concept was modified to take account of local circumstances and preferences. In general, the less innovative the experiment appeared, the greater its chance of adoption.

COST REDUCTION VERSUS CONTEXT

Reduction in unit costs and the development of a delivery system appropriate for isolated rural areas were two of the original goals of IMPACT that proved somewhat contradictory. In most of the countries where IMPACT was introduced, it was more costly to provide the same service to an isolated rural area than to a more accessible area due to poor roads, communication, and the difficulty of attracting qualified personnel unless incentive pay was provided. Under the circumstances, providing the same service at the same cost is already an impressive achievement. Failing to recognize the realities of poor rural communities, the IMPACT innovators made unrealistic promises.

RATIONAL IDEAS VERSUS PERSISTENT PEOPLE

One of our concerns in reviewing the IMPACT experience was to determine the role of educational research in expediting the process of implementation. It was disturbing to find that the projects that had best documented their achievements were not necessarily those that gained the best acceptance. In some cases, this was because the research took too long and thus was not available at the time the big decisions were being made; in others it was because the research reinforced the notion that the system must be taken as an integrated whole. However, even when the research was available, its impact was dependent on forceful advocacy by project leaders. This advocacy usually had to continue over a protracted period until a wide audience was familiar with the innovation's promise, or to put it differently the opponents were worn down. Just as potent as advocacy based on research was the assertion, however, thinly based on fact, that the experiment had already proved successful in a number of other countries. Thus, persistence and international reputation served to complement or even overshadow the value of research in the advocacy process.

REPLACING SCHOOLS VERSUS OCCUPYING NEW SPACE

The early thinking of the IMPACT innovators was directed toward developing a model that could replace the existing schools. Instead, IMPACT's major successes turned out to be in filling gaps—in serving isolated and thinly populated geographic areas where traditional schools were few and inadequate, or in serving educational groups such as dropouts that were not being served by the regular school system. Thus educational reform has proved easiest in those situations where there is "policy" space. IMPACT's main contribution to traditional schools has been the addition of adjunct modules, the enrichment of teaching guides and instructional aids, and the incorporation of group learning or peer tutoring strategies. The established educational bureaucracies have been reluctant to allow IMPACT to replace the traditional school and central financial authorities have resisted proposals that funding allocations be made flexible.

INDIGENOUS VERSUS FOREIGN STAFF

In reaction to the *often* inappropriate technologies proposed by foreign donors and the high costs associated with foreign staff, self-management and national staffing is increasingly advocated by Third World leaders. In two of the IMPACT-related projects, virtually all of the staff were local. While recognizing the liabilities associated with a strong foreign presence, the IMPACT experience also suggest some advantages: foreign specialists bring in new perspectives, a network of connections, and a quality of commitment and drive that may be less forthcoming from overloaded local staff. The IMPACT experience suggests that foreign technical assistance may sometimes contribute to the success of a new venture.

POLITICAL WILL VERSUS VESTED INTERESTS

Innovations, even those as attractive as IMPACT, do not sell themselves but must be inserted into the existing system through skillful political maneuvering or gamesmanship. The brick wall of vested interest which IMPACT innovators have come up against has not been weakened by direct frontal attacks, but through the creative and persistent search for holes, weak spots, ways of going through, around, or above existing obstacles. For this reason those innovations which have maintained maximum flexibility have been those which have achieved the highest degree of penetration.

NOTES

1. This account is based on an international evaluation of IMPACT sponsored by the International Development Research Centre (IDRC) of Canada in 1985–1986. The evaluation was planned by H. Dean Nielsen, then IDRC regional program officer in Singapore. William K. Cummings was the chief consultant for the project. See Cummings (1986). Other important accounts include Flores (1981) and Socrates (1983).

2. The meaning in Indonesian is <u>P</u>endidikan <u>A</u>nak oleh <u>M</u>asyrakat, <u>O</u>rang Tua da<u>N</u> <u>G</u>uru.

3. In densely populated areas PAMONG schools kept their full complement of teachers but covered community-learning-center students in addition to their regular students; in sparsely populated areas PAMONG procedures were used in "small schools" which only had one to three teachers in the first place.

REFERENCES

Arnove, R.F. "Comparative Education and World-Systems Analysis." *Comparative Education Review* 24, 1 (1980): 48–62.

Berman, E. "The Extension of Ideology. Foundation Support for Intermediate Organization," *Comparative Education Review* 26, 1 (1982): 68.

Blooom, B. *Evaluation, Instruction and Policy Making.* Paris: International Institute for Educational Planning, 1975.

Bourdieu, P., and J.C. Passeron. *Reproduction in Education, Society and Culture.* Beverly Hills, Calif.: Sage, 1977.

Cummings, W.K. "Low-Cost Primary Education Implementation and Innovation in the Nations." Ottawa: International Development Research Centre, 1986.

Daft, R.L., and S. Becker. *The Innovation Organization.* New York: Elsevier, 1978.

Educational Development Projects Implementating Task Force (EDPITAF). "The Outcome of the Philippine Elementary Education: A Report of the Major Findings of Project SOUTELE." Manila: EDPITAF, 1977.

Flores, P. *Educational Innovation in the Philippines: A Case Study of Project IMPACT.* Ottawa: International Development Research Centre, 1981.

Galda, M. *Analysis of 1982 Achievement Results.* Monrovia: USAID, 1982.

———. "Trip Report on IEL Project." Monrovia, USAID mimeograph, March 1983.

Giroux, H.A. "Theories of Reproduction and Resistance in the New Sociology of Education: A Critical Analysis." *Harvard Educational Review* 53, 3 (1983): 257–293.

Havelock, R.G., and A.M. Huberman. *Solving Educational Problems: The Theory and Reality of Innovation in Developing Countries.* Paris: UNESCO, 1977.

Ilich, I. *Deschooling Society.* New York: Harper and Row, 1970.

Kelley, E. *Horse Races, Time Trials, and Evaluation Designs: Implications for Future Evaluations of the Improved Efficiency of Learning Project.* Albany: Center for Educational Evaluation, SUNY-Albany, 1984a.

Kelley, E. *Preliminary Report No. I-Overall Test Results.* Albany: Center for Educational Evaluation, SUNY-Albany, 1984b.

Murad, M.N. *Study of Opinion about Education and Society.* Kuala Lumpur: Malaysian Ministry of Education, 1973.

Office of Educational and Cultural Research and Development. *Educational Assessment of PAMONG.* Jakarta: Ministry of Education, 1972.

Pressman, J.L., and A. Wildavsky. *Implementation.* 3rd ed. Berkeley: University of California Press, 1984.

Rogers, E.M. *Diffusion of Innovations.* New York: Free Press, 1962.

Socrates, J.B. *The IMPACT System of Mass Primary Education.* Manila: INNOTECH, 1983.

Warwick, D. *Bitter Pills.* New York: Cambridge University Press, 1983.

6 THE ADOPTION OF THE NATIONAL SYSTEM OF TELESECONDARY IN MEXICO

Félix Cadena

On March 21, 1968, Channel 5 of Mexico City and Channel 6, the retransmitting station in Las Lajas, Veracruz, broadcast the first program of the National System of Telesecondary. The Mexican state thus launched a new model of educational services.

During the second half of the 1970s, Mexico suffered a breakdown in its economic history. Still resounding at the time were the echoes of statements made four and five years previously asserting that Mexico had "taken off" in its development path. The sustained growth shown by the GNP, which during several years attained rates that surpassed 5 percent, had been the basis for the myth of the Mexican "miracle." However, in recent years the first cracks could be observed in the structure of the model of capitalist industrial growth that the ruling class had adopted in its entirety. In particular, the relative food self-sufficiency of the nation was being quickly lost.

For over one hundred years the Mexican countryside had produced agricultural and animal products in percentages greater than the rate of growth of the population, which permitted a relative food self-sufficiency,[1] and even the export of various products. The foreign income generated from these exports was a fundamental pillar in this model of dependent capitalism. The model had assigned the peasantry four main functions: to contribute raw materials and food at low prices, to make an inexpensive labor force available to urban industry, to depress urban-industrial wages by serving as a reserve labor army, and to contribute through its work to the production of agricultural products for export—thus generating the foreign revenues needed for the development of the industrial firms, depending mainly on the technology of the United States.

These functions were accompanied by an almost total lack of attention to the peasantry, except for the survival of the process of agrarian reform, which was being implemented more for the purposes of political cooptation and economic return than for social justice. Moreover, the existence of a series of mechanisms ensured a great inequality in the economic exchange between the peasants and the rest of society, which produced consequences that are well known: the decapitalization of the countryside, the abandonment of lands, massive migration toward the poles of industrial development, and the fall of agricultural production. These manifestations of the structural crisis of the peasantry and the increased lack of legitimacy of the ruling class, as well as its incapacity to satisfy the expectations of the middle class (which had shown impressive growth in the last twenty years) ended ultimately in the violence of the student movement of 1968.

THE NATIONAL EDUCATION SYSTEM

Background

Among the main banners of the 1910 revolutionary movement was the democratization of education. In the case of Mexico, democratization meant more than access by the great majority to educational services. The political-ideological battle between liberals and conservatives during the nineteenth century led to significant differences on issues of educational philosophy and the teacher's role. In consequence, a basic objective of the alternative project sought by the leaders and organic intellectuals of the revolution was to promote a secular, nationalistic, and popular education. The weight of this demand made it become a social guarantee in the text of the constitution of 1917, which opened the new postrevolutionary order. It is in Article 3 that the rights and principles concerning education are set. This article has led to important national debates and to various interpretations that have improved its text.

The key pieces in the political plan of the new classes were: the advisability of satisfying educational demands that, ultimately, did not question the hegemony of the ruling class in the short term; the need to consolidate the nation-state in such a vast territory, inhabited by numerous ethnic groups; the need to address the extremely high level of illiteracy[2] (derived from the fact that only 3 percent of the school-age children were attending schools); and the country's modernization process.

These considerations led the Mexican state to promote education at all levels. The expansion was remarkable in the creation of services, the building of classrooms, and the preparation of teachers, which ever since has meant a high percentage of the national budget going to education. In its qualitative aspect, the efforts in the first years generated experiences of substantial importance, known as the Mexican "rural schools." Programs such as the "community brigades," the "people's houses," and the rural normal schools—which involved youths, the majority from rural areas, with limited training but with a strong sense of solidarity and commitment—produced experiences of great pedagogical quality.

In the past fifty years, the expansion of these services has maintained a significant pace. However, quality has been on the decline and the innovativeness of the 1920s and 1930s has given way to the adoption of U.S. and French models with little relevance and efficiency.

Current Structure of the System

According to the Federal Law of Education, the national education system is composed of three levels: elementary education, comprising preschool and primary education (six years); secondary education, comprising junior high school (three years) and senior high school (two to three years); and higher education, leading to the B.A., M.A., and doctoral degrees.

In recent years, it has been constantly proposed that a basic level of education, to include the current primary level plus three years of high school, be instituted. It should be noted that, formally speaking, the state has developed an infrastructure that enables the entire population between six and fourteen years of age to have primary education, with the exception of remote communities, children of migrant laborers, and similar cases.

Secondary education, in its current form, was created in 1925. It was conceived mainly to lead to university studies. Since the 1930s, the high school has provided technological and agricultural knowledge, which share two fundamental functions: to facilitate admission to higher education and to facilitate access to the labor market. The increased access to primary education generated an increasing demand for high school education. However, the supply of secondary schools has always lagged significantly until the 1950s, when high school enrollment tripled. From 1958 to 1976 the rate of growth averaged 12 percent per year. Since that time, this growth has been surpassed by increases in university enrollment. High school education is provided in various forms and approaches, each placing a high value on the continuation of studies at subsequent levels. The types of basic secondary education are: general secondary, technical secondary, telesecondary, open secondary, and workers' secondary.

CONDITIONS LEADING TO THE ADOPTION OF THE TELESECONDARY SYSTEM

THE EXPANSION OF PRIMARY SCHOOLING

By 1964 the number of youths completing elementary schooling reached almost 6.5 million, of which a large proportion sought to continue in high school. However, there was insufficient capacity to accommodate the demand at that level, and a little more than 3 million youths between fifteen and nineteen years old could not enroll. The educational projections at that time predicted that toward the end of the 1970s, of every 100 children admitted into primary schooling in the countryside, only 10 would complete primary and only 1.2 would enter secondary, in part because in communities having fewer than 2,500 inhabitants there were practically no high schools. In this regard, one must realize that in 1964 Mexico had over 90,000 rural communities with populations less than 2,500.

In 1979 the government decided to strengthen its efforts in education: it created the Technical Council on Education and undertook financial commitments to implement the eleven-year plan. One of the elements of this plan was a "national plan for the improvement and expansion of primary education," which was implemented via heavy investment in classroom construction, teacher training, and production of textbooks for free distribution, among other efforts.

DEMAND FOR HIGHER LEVELS OF SCHOOLING IN THE LABOR MARKET

Also during the decade of the 1970s, a large number of peasant families, pushed by the lack of food in the countryside and pulled by the false promises of the industrialization process in the cities, migrated massively to urban areas, subsequently creating the slums known as the "lost cities" and "misery belts."

The technological advancement in the industrial enterprises and the oversupply of the labor force increased the employers' demands for ever higher levels of education. If ten years ago it had been sufficient to complete primary to attain a good job in a nonskilled occupation, now the same occupation required secondary education. This prompted many youths, particularly in the cities, to demand secondary education. This undoubtedly limited the creation of secondary schools in the countryside, because the urban areas were given priority in the allocation of resources.

THE CRISIS IN EDUCATIONAL COSTS

In parallel with the preceding events, the educational system began to feel a crisis in costs, produced mainly by the higher level of technology of educational services, as well as by an increase in the level of bureaucratization in the Secretariat for Public Education (*Secretaría de Educación Pública*; SEP), which was strongly centralized and characterized by a large number of workers and employees. In consequence, it seemed urgent to find alternative methods of education capable of expanding the supply and lowering costs. All of the preceding conditions were particularly serious among the rural populations. There, the numbers of students without access to secondary education were significantly higher than the national average. In addition to the strategy of neglect toward peasants, there were real obstacles such as the high geographical dispersion of the rural students, the difficulties of access to many communities, and the limited appeal among teachers to work in the rural areas. Against this background, the growth of television in the country presented an alternative worth exploring.

CHARACTERISTICS AND EVOLUTION OF TELEVISION IN MEXICO

The high economic dependency of the development model in Mexico carried with it an ideological penetration, of which the electronic mass media became a vital component. In 1950, through an agreement with the government, Channel 4, and a year and a half later, Channels 2 and 5, started broadcasting. Their interests at that time were strictly economic.

The monopolistic character of the TV broadcasts was obvious since the beginning, and it grew with the support of the good will of the government bureaucracy and its interest in economic development. The government supported these efforts so that the diffusion apparatus would become part of the economic process. The cultural and educational content of commercial TV today is determined by the economic interests of the buyers of transmission time; that is to say, the large transnational corporations—almost all U.S.— have turned the medium into a nondemocratic vehicle from the perspective of the sender and into a confusing stimulus for a large number of receivers.

Commercial TV, as a means of communication linked to the transnational model of culture, fulfills two functions determined by big capital. On the one hand, it influences consumption through advertising, thus speeding the last phase in the accumulation of capital and the achievement of value through material goods production. On the other hand, it performs the process of reproduction of social conditions for dependent capitalism.

Not surprisingly, the state TV did not start functioning until 1959, with Channel 11. This channel seeks to be "cultural," as it is totally financed by the government and free of commercial advertising. It offers programs developed mainly by government agencies. Channel 11 has a limited coverage and reaches a small audience, a consequence of the stultified programs and the distance between these programs and the interests of the majority of the public. Its formal educational broadcasts are limited to language and math classes, and to reinforcing and supporting the programs of intensive adult primary education.

The state subsequently created another channel, Channel 13, and in 1985 created Channel 7. The administration of Channel 13 has been erratic, directors have changed every eighteen months on the average, and the channel resembles more a commercial than an alternative channel. In 1993, as part of the privatization process started by the government of Carlos Salinas de Gortari, Channel 13 was sold to a private enterprise group.

The preceding information is significant, particularly if we consider that in Mexico, according to its federal laws regulating radio and TV, these media are defined as being an activity of public interest and it is asserted that only the state can allot national space for broadcasting. In addition, the law claims 12 percent of the emission time as a form of tax payment, which in turn means that thirty minutes daily are to be given free to the diffusion of educational, cultural, and advisory programs. The entire legal corpus regarding TV is full of noble statements and purposes regarding the objectives of TV programs, such as "to avoid nefarious influences on children and youth," "to strengthen national integration," and "to raise the cultural level of the people." However, the multiple studies conducted thus far, reveal two consistent findings: the lack of interest on the part of the private monopolies regarding national interests, and their conservative, manipulating, and consumer-oriented character; and the technical and material impotence of the state TV.

THE TELESECONDARY IMPLEMENTATION PROCESS

The Telesecondary Model

The training manual for the new Telesecondary teachers defines the program as:

> a formal approach to the national education system, in conjunction with primary schools, providing general education, designed to give the students a complete education and to train them to participate actively in society. Its emphasis is on the population seeking secondary education in communities with at least 15 to 20 primary school graduates per year. (SEP, 1995)

The objectives of Telesecondary were stated as follows:

l.   To satisfy the demand for basic secondary education in rural areas, which because of special circumstances do not allow the construction of regular high schools

2. To supplement the demand for secondary education in urban and semiurban areas

3. To provide didactic support to high school personnel who use the broadcasts and the educational materials of Telesecondary in their function as teacher aides

4. To bring families, in proper pedagogical dosage and sequence, useful knowledge regarding secondary education

5. To promote cultural diffusion

6. To foster community development

When Telesecondary started its broadcasts in 1968, the number of enrolled students was 6,569, from seven states: Morelos, Tlaxcala, Mexico, Hidalgo, Puebla, Veracruz, and Oaxaca. Also included was a group from Mexico, D.F.

The Mexican Telesecondary followed primarily the model of the Italian Telesecondary. This model (see Figure 6.1), in addition to the students and the program itself, comprises three elements: (1) the tele-teacher, who was to present the lesson from the TV studio; (2) the teacher-monitor, later called the coordinator, who was to conduct the class following the TV broadcast, thus personalizing the work of the tele-teacher as well as making the necessary adjustments to the presentation to meet the comprehension abilities of the students, and helping them to do their exercises;[3] and (3) the tele-classroom or a room with a TV.

The curriculum program conducted by Telesecondary has been basically the same as provided by the regular junior high school in terms of objectives as well as topics treated under each course: Spanish, math, physics, chemistry, civics, and so on.

Production

The program has been broadcast live. The tele-teacher is helped by an assistant in the development of the script. Once the teacher is in front of the cameras, she/he acts out the classroom situation. Devices inherent to TV or radio presentations have scarcely been used.

The weekly programming consists of six morning sessions of one hour each, from Monday to Friday. Saturday is assigned to meet the needs of the coordinators. From Monday to Friday, each broadcasting hour is divided into three parts: during the first twenty minutes, programs for the first year are transmitted; in the next twenty minutes, programs for the second year; and in the last twenty minutes, programs for the third year of high school. Thus, for instance, after having watched the twenty-minute program, the

Figure 6.1 Elements in the Mexican Telesecondary System

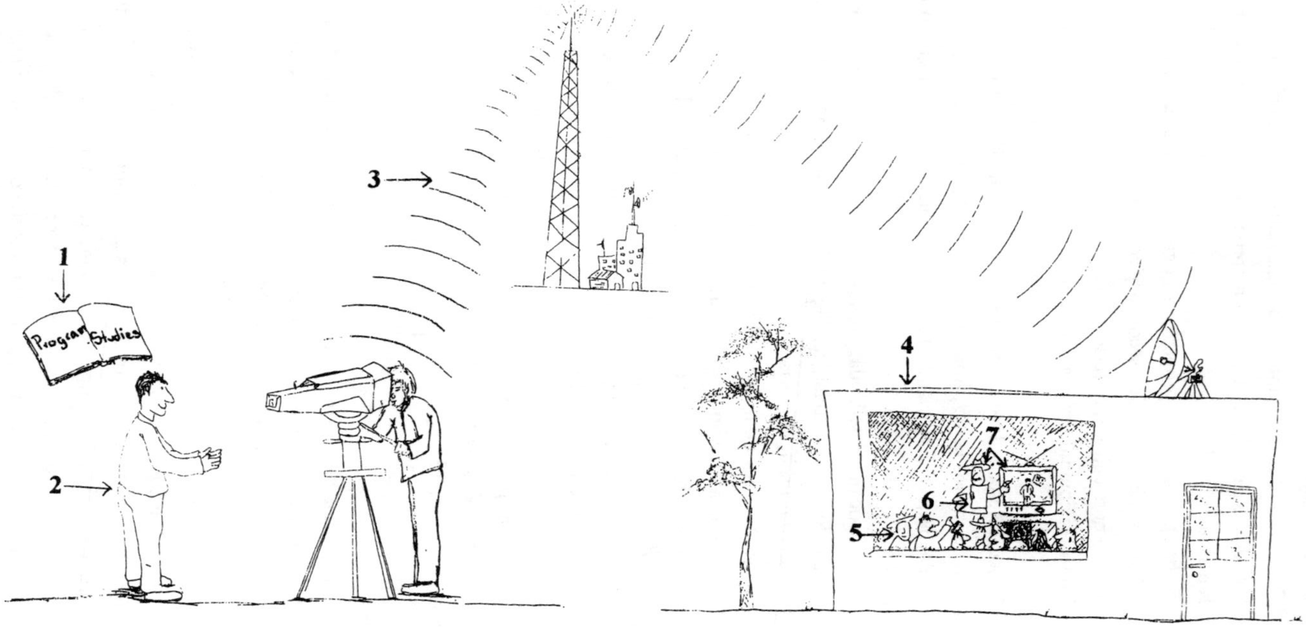

1. Program of Studies
2. Tele-Teacher
3. Broadcasting Station

4. Tele-Classroom
5. Students
6. Study Guide

7. Teacher-Monitor

first-year students turn off the TV and go to another room to carry out the corresponding exercises. To facilitate the carrying out of exercises and the expansion of themes presented during the TV broadcasts study guides are given to the students.

Each group should have more than fifteen and fewer than thirty students. There are two types of students: regular and "free." The main difference is that the free students can watch the program and do the exercises on their own at home; almost always the free students are adults who had dropped out from regular schooling.

Follow-Up and Evaluation

To undertake these functions, various mechanisms were put into place: On the one hand the coordinators were to send a monthly report to the Directorate of Telesecondary. There were also traveling supervisors who made visits to verify the program's functioning and to detect problems. These were complemented by regional meetings between coordinators and tele-teachers to analyze problems and develop joint criteria. On the other hand, there was a bimonthly newsletter, the *Telesecondary Post,* which reached all classrooms with information to support the work of the coordinators.

As stated earlier, there was also a Saturday session to amplify and clarify the contents to be presented the following week in order to facilitate teaching. During school vacations diverse courses were held to improve the coordinators and bring them up to date, also using closed-circuit TV.

Community Participation

The model considered some degree of community participation in the functioning of Telesecondary. In consequence, the model fostered the creation of school-level committees composed of parents and representatives of local nonprofit organizations. Their main responsibilities were to contribute funds and to maintain the building. However, in many communities these school-level committees performed an important role in assuring continuity of service in cases of emergency. They were also very important to many coordinators, generally committed to helping the students, when the coordinators were attacked by the bureaucracy of the official teachers' union, given the situation of constant conflict that emerged between the two.

Accreditation

Since the program of studies of Telesecondary was the same as that of the regular high school, the accreditation was also carried out through final written exams. Free students, following studies at home, were authorized to take pass or fail exams and thus to obtain their certificate.

Institutional Location

The national system of Telesecondary was placed within the General Division of Audiovisual Education, which had implemented a literacy program using TV several years earlier.

THE TELESECONDARY STUDENT

As mentioned above, telesecondary initially considered two types of students: regular and free. The latter students were serviced in an open modality and were generally young adults. Below is a description of the main features of the regular students, based on a study conducted for the academic year 1978–1979 by the Telesecondary Unit of the Secretariat for Public Education.

Their ages ranged from twelve to eighteen years, with 77 percent being between fourteen and seventeen years old. About 36 percent lived in houses inhabited by seven to nine persons. Eighty-two percent owned their houses, and approximately 74 percent had water, sewage, and electricity services. In terms of education, 85 percent of the students had not repeated a grade before, 81 percent studied about two hours after school, and 31 percent read in their spare time. Regarding their family environment, 68 percent of their mothers and 80 percent of their fathers knew how to read and write although their maximum level of education was grade 4. About 37 percent of the families had monthly incomes lower than 1,000 pesos (about US$40 at that time); only 9 percent of the families had incomes greater than 4,500 pesos (more than $200 at the time). Sixty-five percent of the students were not working for wages, even though they performed domestic and agricultural tasks. The average Telesecondary student has maintained those features over time, so she/he can be characterized as predominantly a member of rural and low-income social classes.

HISTORICAL EVOLUTION OF THE PROCESS OF IMPLEMENTATION AND ADOPTION

In the historical evolution of Telesecondary six phases can be distinguished: experimentation, expansion to the rest of the country, evaluation and validation, educational reform of 1970–1976, the teachers' labor crisis, and current status.[4]

Experimentation

In 1965, facing the problems discussed in the preceding section, the secretary for public education decided to use TV to augment the provision of secondary education. A source of confidence was the relatively successful experience with the literacy program using TV carried out by the General Directorate for Audiovisual Education. Within this general directorate the Telesecondary Directorate was created and its staff went on study tours to the United States, Japan, Italy, France, England, and Germany, among other countries.

On their return, they designed a model inspired primarily by the Italian experience. From September 1966 the innovation began implementation using an experimental group and closed-circuit TV. The best high school teachers were selected and consultants on TV production were hired. A total of eighty students were invited to participate, divided into four groups in the following manner:

Group 1—students from eleven to twelve years of age, coordinated by a primary school teacher

Group 2—students from eleven to twelve years, coordinated by a high school teacher

Group 3—students from fifteen to eighteen years, coordinated by a high school teacher

Group 4—students older than twenty years of age, without teachers

Group 1 obtained the best results. Group 4 functioned satisfactorily, from which it was deemed feasible to have free students. The pilot experience showed that primary school teachers, who deal with all grades up to grade six, were the most competent to provide the assistance that Telesecondary required. In contrast, this was not the case for high school teachers, whose expertise was limited to a single discipline. Moreover, it was evident that the supply of primary school teachers was greater than that of secondary teachers. The evaluation of the pilot project was extremely careful, including the videotaping of the pilot sessions. Regarding the students, 75 percent were able to pass the test equivalent to the first year of high school, which was the initial year covered in the experimentation phase.

Expansion to the National Level

The favorable results obtained during the experimentation phases prompted the government to expand the program nationwide for the 1968 academic year, a period in which work was conducted more with enthusiasm and inspiration than with sufficient economic and material resources. In 1968, 6,569 persons enrolled as regular students and another 6,000 as free students. Two years later there were 23,763 regular and 30,000 free students.

The number of graduates was 5,437, which represented a percentage higher than the national average for regular high school students.

Evaluation and Validation

Starting in 1970 several significant modifications were introduced in the program. Among the most important was the improvement in the production process, since the tele-teacher now had the support of a professional TV producer in the preparation of the script, and more resources were allocated during this phase, which allowed it to be produced in color. On the other hand, the possibility of having free students was eliminated, despite the acceptance it had received among the population at large.

It was at that time that some journalists in newspapers having national coverage started to criticize the approach. They claimed that Telesecondary was a second-rate service, that it did not have trained teachers, that the tele-classes were of low quality, and the requirements for student admission were not flexible. This prompted the SEP to commission Stanford University in California to conduct a general evaluation of Telesecondary. This was done in 1973. Four Mexican states were selected for the sample, and were subsequently compared with a control group from the regular high school system, both groups chosen randomly. The evaluation centered on the third year of high school.

The evaluation findings showed that the Telesecondary was cheaper than the regular school, costing US$115 against US$200 per student per year. The levels of achievement were more or less equal for the two groups. The evaluation found that 44 percent of the sample students continued studies in some form of tertiary education. It concluded that there were no substantial differences in the teachers' qualities between the two approaches. This did not mean that the teachers were very effective, since a persistent recommendation from the evaluation was the provision of in-service training programs for the teachers. The result of this evaluation, together with the increased demand from new students, led the government to retain and even expand Telesecondary.

THE EDUCATION REFORM OF 1970–1976

The educational sector, as well as other sectors of the country, was affected by efforts by President Echeverriá to renew the structure of a political system that had been strongly questioned in 1968. An educational reform was implemented, which, regarding the secondary level, sought to "attack two features of the traditional high school: first, the strong emphasis on the transmission of information to the detriment of the acquisition of fundamental scientific training, of logical reasoning, and of the strengthening of basic abilities in reading, writing, and math; second, the consequent academic approach that had multiplied the number of courses, generally taught isolated from each other and with different methods.

Following a plenary meeting of the National Assembly on Basic Secondary Education, held in August 1974, the curriculum content was modified. One of the most important results of this reform was that the traditional division of courses was modified and more integration emerged. Thus, biology, physics, and chemistry were united under the natural sciences. History, civics, and geography were combined under the social sciences. In general, interdisciplinarity and the learning of methods were favored. Telesecondary was one of the approaches that most quickly introduced the new features.

These features were easily introduced at the level of production of the TV programming. At the level of training of the coordinators and the preparation of study guides there were serious deficiencies. In fact, some new guides were not properly developed and the use of texts developed by private consultants, though authorized, produced a certain degree of inconsistency and even anarchy. One of the manifestations of the secretary for public education's lack of competency to implement the reform was that a hybrid program of studies was approved. This contains two different programmatic structures, one focusing on disciplines and the other on areas— a system that continues untouched today.

Another consequence of the educational reform was that under the strengthening of the administrative decentralization process, the new tele-classrooms were placed under the responsibility of the state educational agencies. The SEP continued to produce and broadcast programs and to administer the tele-classrooms that had been created before 1976.

The Teachers' Labor Crisis

The device of using primary school teachers for the Telesecondary placed the monitors in a difficult situation. On the one hand, as primary school teachers, they were conducting a more complex task than the regular primary teachers; on the other hand, these teachers did not have the training that in general the traditional high school teachers possessed.

On several occasions, the tele-teachers had requested the bureaucratic and conservative National Union of Educational Workers *(Sindicato Nacional de Trabajadores de la Educación;* SNTE) to allow them the right to create a union. This request was denied repeatedly. Initially, the coordinators mobilized themselves into the National Commission of Coordinating Teachers (*Comisión Nacional de Maestros Coordinadores;* CNMC). From 1975, this commission succeeded in creating a *licenciatura* (B.A. degree) in the field of coordinating teachers for Telesecondary. This degree permitted them to rebut the criticism about their lack of technical preparation and simultaneously gave them greater right to demand an improvement in their salaries. Once these studies were recognized with a degree, the CNMC continued to press the demands of the coordinators. By 1977 it had attained a large membership, mainly in the states neighboring the capital. That year the CNMC attained an important triumph by having the position of "coordinating teacher of the tele-classroom" formally recognized and thus able to be transferred from the General Directorate of Primary Education to the General Directorate of Secondary Education.

Much of the strength of this mobilization was due both to the acceptance that this effort had gained among the coordinating teachers and to the support given to them by the communities in which the Telesecondary teachers worked. This is a fact that merits special attention because the school-level committees became deeply committed to the effective functioning of Telesecondary. In many cases, in the face of official indifference, the community itself paid the salaries of the teachers, who often had no specific training as coordinators. In fact, having the same production personnel and the same infrastructure as in 1972, the TV system had tripled its enrollment.

The union bureaucracy of the SNTE received the support of secretariat authorities and the conflict was resolved using the principle of "divide and conquer." Relying on the argument that the coordinators were of low quality, the SEP decided that the Telesecondary should be an open modality and that it should benefit both youths and adults. This meant a transfer of the coordinators to another part of the institutional structure. The General Directorate for Audiovisual Educational Materials, which manages the broadcast and most of the tele-classrooms was transformed into the General Directorate of Didactic and Cultural Materials. Thus, this directorate was charged only with the development of pedagogical lessons and the TV scripts. Another general directorate, the General Directorate for Adult Education was charged with the technical-administrative tasks: to coordinate the teaching staff, to administer the Telesecondary, and to evaluate the performance of the students.

Regarding the tele-teachers, several modifications were introduced into their work. There would be: (1) a group of high school teachers with experience in different disciplines who would develop the texts and the lessons according to the recommended program of studies using the books approved by the SNTE and the intensity of presentation required by the academic calendar, (2) a group of scriptwriters who would adapt the content of the lessons to the TV medium, (3) a team of professional producers of educational TV who would supervise the editing of the scripts, and (4) a team of presenters that would appear on the screen to explain the lesson.

In addition to this restructuring, there were also changes in the employment contract of the tele-teachers. From then on they would be hired as free lances, which eliminated the condition of dependent work, thus preempting the possibility of belonging to a labor union.

CURRENT STATUS

The objectives of Telesecondary continue to be the same as the original:

1. *The Study Plan.* As already noted, the study plan for Telesecondary has been the same as in the regular high school and has undergone all the changes that have been introduced to the latter. Table 6.1 shows the topics of study and the number of sessions per week.

TABLE 6.1 Topics of Study and Sessions per Week

Topic of Study	Number of Sessions per Week
Spanish	4
Math	4
Foreign Languages (English)	3
Natural Sciences	7
Social Sciences	5
Physical Education	1
Technical Education	5
Art Education	1

Source: SEP, 1982

At present the production and broadcasting of the TV materials are done by the Cultural and Educational Television Unit (UTEC) of the Directorate for Didactic and Cultural Materials. The first step consists of translating the technical scripts produced by the Telesecondary Unit into TV scripts. Later, an interdisciplinary team analyzes them at a preproduction meeting, where the audiovisuals considered most adequate are then suggested.

The editing of the scripts is the responsibility of the professional TV staff, working as free lances. Even though the presenter of the lessons is a high school teacher, he/she is required to have theatrical abilities and is often supported by professional actors or *guignol* teachers. Today, thanks to the presence of satellites and the expansion of retransmitting stations of the Mexican Republic Television (*Televisión de la República Mexicana;* TRM), the broadcasts cover all the national territory, allowing Telesecondary to reach over 90 percent of the country.

2. *Performance of the Work within the Tele-Classroom.* At present eighteen lessons are transmitted daily from Monday to Friday, from 8 A.M. to 2 P.M. The length of each lesson has been reduced from twenty to seventeen minutes, but the most important change is that the students depend less on the TV lesson. In consequence, new guides to reinforce the lesson content promote self-learning and the acquisition of supplementary knowledge derived from reading. During the subsequent thirty-three minutes, the coordinator promotes the use of the guides and clarifies any doubts. Within the daily programming there are two cultural blocks: one of thirty-six minutes and the other of eighteen.

3. *Study Guides.* To decrease the dependence on the broadcasting, the guides are structured in the following manner:

    a. Name of unit and lesson
    b. Objective
    c. Introduction
    d. Synopsis of the content
    e. Development of the content
    f. Learning activities
    g. Self-evaluation exercises
    h. Key to answers and rating scale
    i. Bibliography

    These guides are developed by a team of teachers graduated from the Higher Normal School, who are also advised by specialists. Each month the materials for the next thirty days are produced and sold at a reduced price, about US$0.40.

4. *Follow-up and Evaluation.* There are several mechanisms in place to ensure the improvement of the system: The lessons are recorded on videotape and thus can be revised each cycle. Opinions from students and coordinators are regularly collected; these opinions are submitted in writing. There is an annual meeting of the Academic National Junta, which comprises inspectors, directorate heads, administrative leaders, and the leaders of the Telesecondary Unit. There are periodic surveys using random samples. The results of the performance tests

for the cycle are examined. Finally, the authors of the texts and the program producers receive copies of the proceedings of the Junta.

5. *The Coordinating Teachers.* At present the newly hired teachers must be graduates of superior normal schools or their equivalent. In addition, they must pass an intensive training program that lasts fifty hours. Six months later the participants must conduct an evaluation workshop so that on the basis of their experience they may consolidate their new knowledge.

6. *Community Participation.* Although in previous years the state conducted all the improvements needed in communities having Telesecondary, the recent drastic reductions in the national budget, imposed by the economic crisis and the IMF, made it necessary to consider a wider participation of the community in the work of the Telesecondary.

7. *Accreditation.* According to the reforms introduced in the national educational system, the evaluation for accreditation will take place throughout the school year. The final exams and the procurement of diplomas are the same as for the regular high school.

8. *Organizational Placement.* The Unit of Telesecondary is now located in the Undersecretariat for Basic and Normal Education. It continues to be separated from the process of production, which remains in the hands of the General Directorate for Didactic and Cultural Materials.

In early times, the tele-classrooms were informally set in various places of the community. Later, the department within the SEP charged with the construction of schools, designed a prototype for Telesecondary and offered technical assistance to the various community-level associations regarding buildings and maintaining them. Today, that department builds the majority of the new tele-classrooms. Figure 6.1 illustrates the various components of Telesecondary.

CONTRIBUTIONS OF TELESECONDARY TO THE NATIONAL EDUCATION SYSTEM

In this chapter, by way of conclusion and final reflection, we will address the main contributions of Telesecondary to the objectives and logic of the national educational system, functions that in my opinion include the reproduction of the technical and ideological traits of the social forces. The points to be discussed are the following: contribution to satisfying the social demand, quality of the teaching approach and evaluation of student achievement, retention and internal efficiency, and contribution to the acceptance and expansion of the use of TV in education.

As observed earlier, the demand for secondary education was the main reason for the adoption of Telesecondary. In view of its performance after thirty-one years of existence, it can be affirmed that Telesecondary has made a positive contribution in this respect. Today, it would be difficult to provide a different alternative to the graduates of primary school in dispersed small communities. In 1982 approximately five hundred such communities with more than fifteen and less than one hundred primary graduates were identified. Telesecondary provides for over 87 percent of this potential demand, which parallels the percentage not covered by the regular high school. Telesecondary has been characterized by continuous expansion of the system and has become an alternative to education provided by federal and state agencies through conventional forms of high schools.

QUALITY OF TEACHING AND STUDENT ACHIEVEMENT

The quality of Telesecondary's teaching has been one of the most controversial points of the innovation. We saw earlier that in response to the constant criticism of its low quality, the secretary of education requested an external evaluation. This evaluation, carried out by Stanford University, concluded that the differences in performance between the Telesecondary and the regular high school students were not statistically significant. This is very important if we consider that, even though the program of studies is the same for both approaches, educational services in the rural areas, after the exciting but brief period of the "rural Mexican school," are deficient because of the inexperience of teachers working in rural areas, the majority of whom show little commitment to work there, which becomes reflected in both lack of care and acute absenteeism.

In 1981 an intersecretariat commission that requested various studies evaluating and prescribing improvements for several modalities of the educational system requested one such study on student achievement. This study, which included Telecondary, was rigorous. A sample of students and coordinators from the three grades, distributed among the different federal states, was used. Three types of data—cognitive, attitudinal, and ethnographic—were collected through interviews and student tests. The main conclusions were that the levels of performance attained by Telesecondary students taking the tests were quite high, except for first and second grade math. It was also found that Telesecondary students with parents having higher levels of schooling and better economic conditions and under teachers who reinforced and adapted the materials tended to obtain better results. This was no different from that reported by evaluations of other forms of the education system, except for two findings: (1) despite contextual differences faced by students in Mexico City compared to those in small communities, there were no large differences in performance, (2) after the third grade of high school, differences in socioeconomic origins and levels of parental schooling did not affect individual performance.

Teleseondary coordinators and students shared similar opinions regarding the convenience and utility of the didactic materials. However, another study, carried out at the same time but focusing on the study guides, concluded that more than half of these guides presented ill-stated objectives, had badly structured self-evaluation activities, and in general made scant use of problem solving or syntheses and reinforcing activities. This study questioned the emphasis on the transmission of information, the lack of linkage between the topic and reality, and the absence of reference to values. Even though we consider that this second study was well made and that some materials for Telesecondary seem to have limited appeal at first sight, it should be stated that these characteristics also apply to many texts used in the regular high school.

RETENTION AND INTERNAL EFFICIENCY

Another finding of interest regarding Telesecondary is its relatively high level of retention and terminal efficiency. Dropping out between the first and third years does not show statistically significant differences when compared to other forms of secondary education. However, there has been a slight decrease in retention, from 95 percent in 1976–1977 to 80 percent in 1980–1981.

Regarding the terminal efficiency, (i.e., the ability to complete the program), the rate has been gradually improving. The rates for terminal efficiency by type of educational service has evolved in the following manner: during 1970–1971 and 1972–1973, the highest rate was for Telesecondary with 60.9 percent, workers' secondary reported 59.4 percent, general secondary 57 percent, and technical secondary 51.5 percent. During the period 1975–1976 and 1977–1978 the highest rate was also shown by Telesecondary, with 73.2 percent, followed by general secondary with 67.8 percent, and technical secondary with 63.9 percent. For the 1978–1979 and 1980–1981 periods the highest rates were also for Telesecondary with 94.5 percent, followed by general secondary with 76.8 percent, technical secondary with 7.8 percent, and then workers' secondary with 63.7 percent. The increases during these three periods were 19.8 percent for general secondary, 20.3 percent for technical secondary, 4.3 percent for the workers' secondary, and 33.6 percent for Telesecondary. In 1995 the terminal efficiency for Telesecondary was about 90 percent.

Another statistic of interest comes from a study based on a sample of 777 students who completed Telesecondary showing that 44 percent of them in some way continued their higher education studies, which is a high proportion given the social origin of the Telesecondary student and the limitations that exist to satisfy the demand for senior high school. It should also be remembered that fewer than 5 percent of the students that receive their bachelor's degree at the National Autonomous University of Mexico are of peasant origin.

CONTRIBUTION TO THE ACCEPTANCE AND EXPANSION OF THE USE OF TV IN EDUCATION

Educational authorities consider that Telesecondary as an alternative approach has become fully accepted, at least for the first cycle of secondary education. Evidence of this is the continued existence of the program in a country that was characterized by the lack of continuity in its innovative programs, particularly from changes in government every six years.

In recent years some programs have been established to support the Intensive Adult Primary Education and the bachelor's degree. The National Autonomous University of Mexico (UNAM) signed an agreement in 1981 by which, in addition to its university extension course, it would broadcast programs related to curriculum. However, the antiunion position of the TV monopolies has weakened this relationship. When the workers' union of UNAM declared itself on strike, the private TV company promised and broadcast TV programming to enable nonunionized TV teachers to provide lessons.

THE ROLE OF TELESECONDARY IN THE SOCIAL REPRODUCTION OF TECHNICAL AND IDEOLOGICAL FORCES

Taking the central thesis of Baudelot and Establet (1976) regarding the division of education into two networks:[5] professional primary for the leading classes of the bourgeoisie and workers' primary for the semiskilled proletariat, we can pose the following questions. Given the function of social reproduction that schools fulfill under capitalistic conditions, we can ask, What impact does Telesecondary have on the formation of social classes? What is the role of Telesecondary in the social, technological, and ideological reproduction? Are the Telesecondary students served within only one network of the educational system and encouraged to train and be placed as workers with low qualifications and probably working under conditions of subordination?

The first reaction is to respond yes to this last question. In fact, the most constant criticism of Telesecondary is that it is a "second-rate education." In addition, it is addressed almost exclusively to the most marginal peasants in the current period of urban-industrial growth. The Mexican educational system seems to support Baudelot and Establet's notion of the two branches that have been found to exist in the French educational system. However, in our judgment this question deserves a negative response, not only in the particular case of Telesecondary but also in the case of the entire national educational system.

Three arguments can be offered to support this negative reply:

1. *The Need to Consolidate the Nation-State.* To understand many of the differences between educational systems of countries such as France and those in Latin America—which has been characterized by large territorial expansion and low population density—we must remember than in Latin America, as the new ruling class began to sever the colonial ties in the political sphere, it needed urgently to create a real nationhood within the territory that used to belong to the Spanish Crown. Failing to do so immediately meant running the risk of losing those territories, whether to the hunger of the emerging United States—which appropriated over half of the new Mexican state and sponsored the separation of part of Colombian territory to set up Panama and build the canal, or because of the internal division among incipient power groups that always leaned toward autonomy and secession for the region each controlled.

    This reality imposed upon the school the need to contribute to the process of unification, not only in language but also in terms of the concept of nationality that was to become a biding element for the diverse ethnic groups remaining within the new states. To be sure, the leading social classes required additional training for themselves to fulfill their functions, but at the same time, this was accomplished mainly through "extracurricular" (informal) education strategies, such as the analysis of certain authors in literary and political circles, and visits to Europe and the United States. Since the capacity to attend to the demands of the new nations was very limited, this need to satisfy the social demand for education was still unmet by the twentieth century.

2. *The Populist Ideology.* In countries such as Mexico it became imperative for the ruling classes to adopt a populist line to attain the consensus every hegemony requires. As a result, the text of Article 3 of

the constitution offers individual and social guarantees. In the case of Mexico, democratization referred not only to the mass expansion of schooling but also to the role of education in fostering the concept of democracy. Democracy was to be, according to the Mexican constitution, "not only a judicial structure and a political regime but also a way of life founded on the constant economic, social, and cultural improvement of the people." In addition, democracy was to:

> contribute to better human coexistence because of the elements it provides to strengthen in the students—together with the appreciation of the dignity of the person and the integrity of the family—the conviction in the general interest of society as well as the care in strengthening the ideals of fraternity and equality of all men, avoiding the privileges attached to race, sect, affiliation, and sex of individuals. (Article 3)

Based on this, even though the school programs became increasingly influenced by the French and U.S. education systems, various school textbooks and particularly teachers' guides incorporated many of the social demands that the government inherited from the 1910 revolutionary movement and which it had not yet been able to fulfill.

In this sense, it is of significance that the most important signs of rebellion that have become translated into guerrilla actions in the last thirty years have been led by rural teachers: Genaro Váquez, Lucio Cabanas, Rubén Jaramillo, among others. Moreover, the notion that the teaching force is merely a consumer, repeater, and disseminator of intentions in study plans created by leaders of the SEP is to ignore the social composition of the teachers at the basic and secondary levels of education.

3. *Social Mobility and the Expansion of the Middle Class.* A characteristic of Mexico during the current century has been the substantial growth of the middle class. This can be explained by the very small middle class at the beginning of the century, by the partial replacement of the bourgeoisie that lost political power in 1910–1917, and by the expansion of the industrial sector, which have demanded and facilitated an intense social mobility.

It is one thing to take as a point of departure the assertion—which we consider correct—that our societies are divided into classes with antagonistic interests and are consequently struggling with each other. It is another thing to maintain that the process of social reproduction of their classes is marked by the imperatives of divided production, offering thus a very mechanical interpretation of the process of reproduction of the classes, and to state the problem as taking place along two parallel networks that have in common only the perspective of an ideology that reinforces the class division.

This latter position ignores what occurs dialectically between the classes, particularly within the ideological arena. Here, the culture of resistance is produced by the popular sectors, in part because of the stability that some of the pre-Hispanic civilizations showed in their past, and in part because of the daily and passive strategy of resistance that the lower classes have adopted to survive the diverse structures of domination.

In this regard, Adriana Puiggrós (1980) makes a detailed critique and asserts that:

> To consider that bourgeois pedagogy has as its only function the maintenance of the division of classes is to take as a point of departure that capitalist society is a caste-like society (even though the authors of books having this perspective may deny this). Bourgeois hegemony implies the articulation of multiple forces in the particular expressions of the national reality. (p. 294)

As does Puiggrós, we question the category "schooling networks" because (1) it assumes a dualistic conception, not a Marxist one. It implies a relation between opposing terms that maintain a linear rather than a dialectic relationship; and (2) it assumes the existence of two mutually exclusive cultures inside the capitalist society. Their unity is only apparent. This appearance of cultural and political unity takes us back to the notion of colonialism. In this sense, we will express as hypotheses interpretations for colonial society offered by Frantz Fanon and Paul Nizan. However, Fanon never forgot that the unity of the French nation was one of the factors that made possible the colonization of Algeria and characterized Algerian culture as an internal duality that reflected the antagonism between two different peoples and cultures, one oppressing the other, and that within this process of colonial domination the class struggle grew. This model of political and social organization is very different from the French model. Colonial struggle is explained through a model that is not transferable to the class struggle within advanced capitalism.

After all this, we should ask, what then is the role of Telesecondary in the social reproduction of technology and ideology within Mexican society?

We believe that its contribution occurs along three dimensions:

1.   *Reinforcement of the Value of "Hope."* To maintain social peace among a traditionally violent people that have shown three times in less than a century that they are capable of altering the established social order[6] and whose basic welfare conditions are far from being satisfied, requires something that not only constrains their vindicative capability but also incorporates the most dangerous sectors: the peasantry and the urban-industrial proletariat.

It would appear that in the case of Mexico the manipulation of the "hope" factor—in combination with other factors—has been critical for the political elite. Through a number of measures addressed to the popular sectors, the political elite has sought to convince the lower classes that their personal situation will have a solution thanks to two key processes: agrarian reform and social mobility based on schooling. Today, even though there are more peasants without land than when the revolution began, there are three million peasants who do have land. This, however, does not mean that the peasants are no longer poor and subordinated.

In 1920, less than 7 percent of the population lived in urban areas having access to minimal social services and infrastructure. In 1980 at least 40 percent of this population had these services. From 1934 to 1964, thanks to the expansion of the economy and the administrative apparatus of the state, a portion of the population that had attained schooling was able to become absorbed into jobs that allowed them to become a middle class.

Despite the structural limitations that both processes have reached, the "hope" factor has been effective. In consequence, parents of peasant families still consider it a priority to demand that their children have schooling and the state seeks to widen, free of costs, the service that give it legitimacy in many respects.

2.   *The Strengthening of Nationalism.* The objective of attaining a stronger national identity has become important again in recent years, mainly in border towns and in small rural communities. In the latter the cultural identity is often being affected due to the impact of radio and the work of several Protestant groups, promoted in part by U.S. political groups, to encourage individualism and demobilization. But, perhaps the most impacting element of all is the heavy migra-

tion of youths who go to work in the United States. Many of these do not return to their communities, but those who do have frequently acquired consumption habits or expectations based on the American way of life. Within the current geopolitics it is clear to the ruling classes that one way to ensure their survival is to strengthen nationalism and to attain legitimacy through the mass media. All of this imposes an important role for schooling at both primary and secondary levels.

3. *Modernity and the Expansion of the Internal Market.* Within the dialectical tension described above, the state also promotes the modernization of agricultural practices and the expansion of the internal market, given the difficulties it faces attempting to export to its advantage something that is neither oil nor precious metals. The possibility of introducing a new technology carries with it the need for increased mastery of basic skills and receptive attitudes that the school seeks to promote to ensure that these attributes will be present in the reproduction of the labor force. These are, in our judgment, the main functions fulfilled by Telesecondary and which explain both its continuity and expansion.

NOTES

1. Emphasis is placed on "relative" food sufficiency because, while Mexico does not import staple foods, its population is not able to consume the required minimum intake of calories and protein.

2. According to the National Plan of Development 1983–1988, Mexico had at that time 6 million illiterates and 15 million adults with incomplete primary education (Presidencia de la RepΣublica, 1982, p. 224).

3. On the basis of the televised class, the teacher-monitor uses the study guide to go over the lesson objectives and content. Later, he/she sets up small groups to review the material. The teacher-monitor also conducts ongoing evaluations.

4. SEP, 1981.

5. We use here the central theses of Baudelot and Establet (1976) regarding the segmentation of education in two different networks: "professional primary," designed for the children of the leading strata of the bourgeoisie, and "workers' primary" for the children of the semiskilled proletariat.

6. This comprises the struggles to achieve independence from Spain between 1880–1821; the overthrow of Maximilian of the Hapsburg monarchy, imposed by Napoleon II in 1863–1867; and the Mexican revolution of 1910–1917.

REFERENCES

Baudelot, C., and R. Establet. *L'école capitaliste en France.* Madrid: Editorial Siglo XXI, 1976.

Presidencia de la República. *Plan Nacional de Desarrollo* 1983–88. México: Presidencia de la República, Gobierno de Mexico, 1982.

Puiggrós, A. *Imperialismo y educación en América.* Mexico, D.F.: Nueva Imagen, c. 1980.

SEP. *Documento Básico del Curso de Capacitación de Telesecundaria.* México: Secretaría de Educación Pública, 1981.

———. *Primera Reunión Nacional de Telesecundaria.* México: Secretaría de Educación Publica, 1982.

———. *Manual de Capacitación de la Unidad de Telesecundaria.* México: Secretaría de Educación Pública, 1995.

7 TRAINING TEACHERS AT A DISTANCE

THE CASE OF LOGOS II IN BRAZIL

João Batista Araujo e Oliveira and François Orivel

BACKGROUND

Brazil has been named "Belindia" by economist Edmar Bacha. By that he meant a country similar in some aspects to the development level of Belgium coupled with the widespread poverty of India. A country of contrasts, with excessive concentration or richness on one side and, on the other, vast areas containing the poorest pockets of poverty of Latin America.

Education and educational policies follow the same pattern. Rich minorities send their children to elite, private schools, and, later on, to the free public universities. The majority of the population send their offspring to the mass government-run schools. Over seven million out of thirty-two million school-age children are out of school. In rural areas, where over 30 percent of the population remains, the typical arrangement is the one-teacher school taught by an unprepared teacher. The poorer the situation, the worse the quality of educational services delivered.

EDUCATIONAL STRUCTURE

Being a federation, the country divided educational tasks in a very peculiar way. The central government is in charge of overall regulation and primarily concerned with higher education. States are the bodies in charge of secondary schools. Municipalities are responsible for primary education. Under a highly concentrated fiscal policy, the periphery has been increasingly unable to cope with its tasks. The results—which are part of a long history of a country which has never adequately faced its educational problems—is a chaotic educational system for the majority, topped by first-class schooling, including graduate level schools, for the minority.

An evaluation of a World-Bank-funded project in northeastern Brazil (EDRURAL, 1982) confirmed what was already known: over 50 percent of the students either flunk or abandon school before their second year; less than 15 percent reach the fourth grade; in all cases tested, no student was able to satisfactorily pass a minimum competence exam. Textbooks are rare, the national average in public schools being less than one book per student; school lunch programs for a starving population are directly proportional to the quality of schools: the worse get the worst. Teachers are typically unprepared and unlicensed: the majority of teachers in the rural areas, in the northeast in particular, have only four years of scholing. Their salaries are generally well below the already insufficient minimum wage. In fact, most teachers receive less than one-fifth of that minimum, which is not even enough for a person to buy food.

Overall, the country has more than 800,000 acting teachers for a population of more than twenty-five million pupils enrolled in primary schools. Project Logos II was geared toward the 300,000 teachers lacking minimum qualifications who are part of this group. Even though the states and the central government have been experimenting with various kinds of teacher training activities for many years, the new project represented a dramatic departure from these earlier attempts.

Logos

Logos II was preceded by Logos I, which was an articulated attempt to answer simultaneously a series of problems related to teacher training in the actual conditions of the country. Logos I was conceived from a very narrow and systemic perspective, incorporating most of the knowledge then (1972) available about educational technology and distance teaching. But the project was realistic enough to submit itself to the test of reality. The results of this pretest, implemented in the most difficult regions and under adverse conditions, provided the basis for setting up the final features of Logos II. The new project was structured in its following form:

Scope

Logos II was aimed at offering in-service training for unqualified and nonlicensed teachers. Initial plans called for partial implementation in five states, enrolling up to 49,000 teachers, under a carefully controlled system. If successful, the project would then be extended to other interested states. The five states initially participating decided to implement the project progressively in the majority of their territories, thus providing opportunities for many of their teachers (Oliveira, 1983).

Shortly after the first groups finished the program successfully, initial resistance was overcome, and tremendous pressure was exerted by many states toward the Ministry of Education and Culture (MEC), forcing the project to be expanded quickly without waiting for the results of the evaluation. Under this pressure, the Ministry decided to expand the project and CETEB (Centro de Educação Tecnológica de Brasilia), the agency in charge of implementation, had to adapt itself to meet the new challenges.

In the following paragraphs, there is a brief presentation of the main characteristics of the project Logos II.

IN-SERVICE TRAINING

To succeed, the new project had to meet teachers where they lived. Previous attempts failed, in part, because most teachers could not leave their homes,or classrooms to go to project classes. Logos II's answer was an in-service training program that teachers could follow without leaving their posts. Moreover, curriculum and guidelines were made relevant to their daily activities in the classroom.

A few requirements were set up. First, only working teachers could enroll; second, their administrative superiors (generally the municipalities) formally agreed to increase the teacher's salaries and/or give them a more stable position after successful completion of the program. Teachers would study mostly by themselves, under the supervision of learning centers set up in a few places.

CURRICULUM CONTENT

Most teachers had not even completed primary school (four years of education). Logos II had to make up for both basic schooling and specialized teacher training. The curriculum, in fact, corresponded to the upper part (last four years) of basic school plus three years of secondary education, including the pedagogical disciplines. Thus, the overall content was split into two major parts, general studies and educational studies. Table 7.1 illustrates this division and presents information on the number of learning modules required for each subject.

Every module had its own pretests and posttests (in three forms). Participants could go on from module to module and from discipline to discipline to the extent that they succeeded in the competence-based exams. To pass an exam, participants had to correctly respond to over 80 percent of the questions. There were no final exams.

SELF-PACING

Individualized instruction was coupled with self-pacing. Participants could move on as they saw fit. To accommodate this, the curriculum was divided into subject matters, and each discipline into specially prepared learning

TABLE 7.1 Distribution of Instructional Modules

General Studies	No. of Modules	Educational Studies	No. of Modules
Introductory modules	7	History of Education	6
Study Techniques	10	Didactics	8
Language	20	Educational Sociology	6
Social Studies	4	Educational Psychology	6
Civics	4	School Legislation	6
Sciences	13	Supervision	3
Mathematics	15	Language Teaching	8
Literature	8	Mathematics Teaching	8
History	8	Social Studies Teaching	8
Arts	8	Science Teaching	8
Geography	8	Physical Ed. Teaching	2
Health	6	Arts Teaching	8
Physical Education	3	Recreational Activities	6
English	6		
Subtotal	120	Sub-total	85

Total: 205 modules

modules for individualized instruction. These came in various sizes, forms, and levels of complexity, but obeying the general pedagogical principles of Logos II. Participants could choose to follow one or more discipline at a time, according to their own background, motivation, available time, and ability to pass the exams. The only sequencing was within a given discipline, where modules had to be taken in order. Most of the study was done at home.

LEARNING CENTERS

Logos II was designed for teachers working in rural areas. A central city with minimum conditions was chosen whenever a certain number of teachers—fifty or more—was enrolled. Each learning center was led by a "monitor," recruited locally within the regular school system.

At the center, the participating teachers would engage in several activities: registration, pretests, posttests, solving specific problems, obtaining additional modules, meeting with other colleagues, participating in in-group activities, and so on. The center was located in a room provided by the municipality, and its size was generally comparable to that of a classroom. A typical center had a few chairs and tables, shelves for stocking the modules and tests, a very small library, and the administrative materials necessary for record keeping.

MICRO-TEACHING

Micro-teaching was a substitute for direct supervision. Distances, shortage of resources, lack of qualified personnel, among others, were the reasons for dropping initial attempts at direct supervision of teachers in their own classrooms. Five abilities were considered essential for the teachers to master: providing diverse stimuli to students, increasing verbal communication, using reinforcements, illustrating with examples, and increasing pupils' responses in the classroom. Every participant was required to prepare and present an actual lecture, after which he would receive feedback from his peers and the monitor. Special modules were prepared to introduce the teachers into the technique and help them to plan their classes better according to predefined teaching strategies.

In short, Logos II was conceived as a distance-learning in-service training combining basic and technical education, allowing student-teachers to apply recently acquired learning directly in their classrooms. The project has attempted to give teachers the maximum flexibility to choose specific disciplines, the amount of time spent on each module, and when to study. Following graduation, it was expected that the teachers would get a pay increase or a more stable contract.

THE PROCESS OF IMPLEMENTATION

The Participants

The participating teachers were required to complete modules and pass the corresponding exams. For each module there were specified objectives. Participants could choose to take a pretest if they thought they had the knowledge. Otherwise, they could take home as many modules as they wished to study. After a few weeks they would return to the center in order to take tests, to look for specific information or orientation, and to obtain new modules.

Other activities include the micro-teaching sessions, a once-a-month group meeting for socialization purposes, special tutoring in the most difficult topics, expressive activities (music, arts, etc.), and civic celebrations. In a few cases, teachers met in small groups to study together or to profit from a colleague who was further ahead in some series, discipline, or content.

Distances and isolation complicated these interactions. The average distance between teachers' homes and the learning center varied from two or three to twenty or more kilometers. In many cases, there was no regular transportation, and distances sometimes required a few hours of walking, usually at night.

Studying was a major challenge. Enrollees typically worked in their schools in two shifts and some of them also taught adult literacy courses by night. The majority were also housewives and mothers. In rural areas, this meant not only the usual domestic chores but, while the man did farming, the wife had to feed the animals, take care of the water supply, dispose of the garbage, and undertake a myriad of other tasks. Being a community leader, the teacher was frequently involved in meetings, vaccinations, other health campaigns, family counseling, and so forth. Husbands were not always tolerant and competed fiercely for the wives' time. Logos II took from thirty to fifty months of their "spare" time. Study rooms were house tables; a dictionary was a valuable rarity; a library, a dream. On the average, teachers studied from nine to ten hours a week, generally after the children went to bed.

The Logos System

The "system" can be divided into three segments: local, state, and central. The *first level* was the learning center, where the key figure was the monitor. Monitors were recruited locally under a screening process which combined minimum technical prerequisites in schooling with political appointment. Monitors had to have at least the secondary-school diploma—not always available—and, preferably, some managerial experience in education (as librarian, supervisor, school lunch director, etc.). Monitors did almost everything from sweeping the floor to convincing the mayor to support the project to getting someone to fix a broken desk. Monitors taught students individually and in groups. They worked six days a week, including weekends, when teachers had more spare time. They also managed the microteaching sessions; they organized the monthly meetings; they got support from the community in the form of food for the teachers, preparation of civic or religious celebrations, recruitment of specially skilled teachers to volunteer for tutoring in mathematics, English, or social studies; they kept detailed records on each student, using an elaborate system of data-gathering and reporting, in addition to their own personal notebooks; they gave emotional support for students and families; they acted as counselors of students or for their noncollaborative husbands; they received visitors from state and central authorities who came for supervisory activities; they filled a variety of forms and reports; and they participated in training sessions and project review meetings from time to time. For those tasks, experience has shown that the most successful monitors established and kept very good relations with the local community and had good managerial abilities. More than those qualifications, a key to success was the degree of commitment to the project and to the students, for beyond salaries they received no extra pay for extra work.

The *second level* was state coordination. Every state set up a group which varied in size from five to twenty. This group was in charge of implementing the project locally. That meant establishing priorities for setting up centers, establishing contacts with the mayors and educational authorities, recruiting and selecting students and monitors, training their personnel as well as the monitors, supervising the operations of the system, channeling information to the central headquarters, and making sure that every center maintained an adequate stock of modules, tests, and all forms and supplies necessary for the smooth operation of the project. State coordinators played ed an important mediating role between local political pressures and technical requirements. Since Logos II accepted only acting teachers as students, when a teacher was fired she was also disconnected from the project. Avoiding such situations was a major activity of middle-level management. At the state level, this coordinating group had to interface with the State Secretariat of Education and the local Education Board on matters related to project financing and accreditation.

The *third level* was split into two segments. Overall monitoring, financing, and final decision making was the responsibility of the MEC. A small staff of three was in charge of the project. Their activity consisted mostly of reading the reports, passing on recommendations, suggesting modifications, and deciding on which states would get what amount of money. They were also responsible for funding CETEB's activities, which are explained below. Finally, this group was in charge of the computerized information system, which never managed to produce reliable data throughout the project's life.

Under the ministry's coordination was CETEB, the private educational organization hired to coordinate and implement Logos II. Its functions included: overall implementation; setting up of learning centers; structuring state coordination and training their personnel; training for coordination, supervision, and monitoring of the learning centers; supervision, implementation, and data gathering in the field; writing reports; evaluating ongoing activities; proposing expansion, changes, or other measures; and solving problems as they arose. An important task of CETEB was the production and constant revision of printed materials. For that purpose, a team composed of subject-matter specialists, distance-teaching experts, and educational technologists was gathered for the task of writing the modules for the various disciplines. As the project progressed, feedback from the field was integrated into the revision of the materials. Producing, printing, and distributing modules throughout the country was, in itself, a major logistical accomplishment. Delays were avoided, since they would have compromised the best efforts of monitors to get participants moving along the modules.

Costs, Results, and Effectiveness

Costs

It is currently common practice to make a distinction, in distance education projects, between two major categories of costs: fixed and variable. Variable costs are so-called because they vary with the number of students. The fixed costs include the cost of preparation of the study units (booklets) and the administrative costs incurred by the MEC and CETEB. The variable costs are of two types: the printing of the booklets and the operation of the project offices in the states (in addition to the basic center in each state, which we have treated as a fixed administrative cost).

Fixed Costs

Production of Booklets

The first edition of the booklets prepared in 1976–1977 was written by teachers who were paid about Cr$2,000 per booklet, making it a total of Cr$400,000. The second edition, in 1978–1979, used the same booklets, which were simply revised to a limited extent by CETEB itself. For the third edition in 1980–1981, some substantial revisions were done and were paid for at the rate of Cr$1,000 per booklet, together with a complete rewriting of some booklets and the addition of new ones, at a cost of Cr$6,000 each. The total cost of these changes and additions is estimated at Cr$80,000. The Cr$400,000 spent in 1976–1977 is equivalent to Cr$2.48 million in 1980 cruzeiros.[1] If we add to this figure the Cr$80,000 for the third edition, the total production cost of the three editions amounts to Cr$2.56 million. The number of copies printed was 12,000 for the first edition, 17,000 for the second, and 22,000 for the third, making a total of 51,000 for a unit production cost of Cr$50 per booklet.

Central Administration Costs

About ten CETEB staff members worked with Logos II. The annual payroll cost amounted to Cr$10.5 million, including the institution's overhead.[2] There were also expenses of Cr$1.5 million for travel to the United States.

A substantial part of the worktime of the CETEB team, when the project was started, was devoted to preparation of the booklets. This became a progressively smaller burden, as far as time is concerned; over the whole period it is estimated at 40 percent. For the six years of work to produce six editions, a cost of 24/60 of the remuneration of the team can be assigned, that is, Cr$25.2 million (1980 cruzeiros). This gives a figure of about Cr$500 per series of booklets to be added to the Cr$50 mentioned above. The costs of administration and supervision, properly speaking, incurred by CETEB are:

$$10,500,000 - .40 \times 10,500,000 + 1,400,000 = 7,700,000$$

ADMINISTRATIVE COSTS OF THE REGIONAL OFFICES

The size and composition of the offices varied from state to state, particularly with regard to the teaching centers. The number of persons working in the offices varied from one to twenty-five. These were usually staff working in the State Secretariats of Education and there were, therefore, no additional costs for office space. In some cases, however, they had premises of their own for which the rental costs must be included. From the data obtained from seven of the ten regional offices, we can extrapolate the total costs, which, for 1980, amount to Cr$7.525 million. (See Table 7.2 for chart of fixed costs.)

TABLE 7.2 Fixed Costs of Logos II Project

Booklets (3 editions	Author's copyright	2,560,000
over six years)	CETEB contribution	25,200,000
Subtotal A		27,760,000
Administration/Supervision	CETEB	7,700,000
cost per year	Regional offices	7,525,000
Subtotal B		15,225,000
Production of booklets,		
cost per year		
Subtotal C		4,625,000
Subtotal D (B+C)		19,850,000
Unit of value: 1980 cruzeiros		

Variable Costs

PRINTING OF BOOKLETS

Each student received 205 booklets averaging 30 pages each, that is, a total of 6,090 pages. Printing was contracted through competitive bidding. For the first edition the average cost per booklet printed was Cr$5, Cr$8 for the second, and Cr$12 for the third. These figures include the cost of distribution of the booklets to the Logos II office in each state. It should be emphasized that inflation outpaced the cost of printing and that a cost of Cr$12 was very low.[3] The total cost of printing a complete series was Cr$2,500, representing a cost per page of Cr$0.4 (1980).

OPERATION OF THE TEACHING CENTER

The pay received by the monitor of the teaching center (OSD) varied from one State to another. The States that joined the project most recently tended to pay higher rates than those involved in the pilot phase. Toward the end of the project, in the mid-1980s, the rates varied between Cr$6,000 and Cr$20,000 per month (including social security). In addition, the average number of participants at each center varied from thirty to seventy, depending on the state. It is not possible, therefore, to calculate a uniform variable cost, for which reason Table 7.3 gives different costs, varying in relation to the number of participants and the salary of the OSD.

TABLE 7.3 Variable Cost per Participant per Year

	No. of Participants		
Monthly pay	30	50	75
6,000	2,400	1,440	960
10,000	4,000	2,400	1,600
15,000	6,000	3,600	2,400
20,000	8,000	4,800	3,200

The cost per participant is thus very sensitive to variations in these two parameters (it can vary by Cr$1,000 to Cr$8,000), but the most frequent cases were those where there are about fifty teachers participating in the center and the salary of the OSD was Cr$10,000, giving an average cost per teacher of Cr$2,400.

OTHER OPERATING COSTS OF THE CENTER

These were are follows:

1.   *Premises.* The arrangements made were extremely varied and we have no precise data from which the local costs could be estimated.

Logos II frequently occupied offices in public premises on a temporary basis so it is difficult to work out the real cost.

2. *Running expenses of the centers.* We were not able to obtain usable data from the offices on this point. The main expense was transportation for the OSD and, as far as we were able to estimate, the annual cost was equivalent to one month's salary.

3. *Student transportation.* The means of transportation varied The most frequent answers to a questionnaire we sent out to the regional project managers were: on foot, horseback, a vehicle belonging to the local authority, personal means of transport (e.g., bicycle), bus, or other means. Unfortunately, the answer given in 75–90 percent of the cases was "other means," which seems somewhat strange; any estimate based on this information would be suspect and we have therefore thought it better to omit this cost entirely.

COST ANALYSIS (IN 1980 CRUZEIROS)

1. *Annual Costs*

   Total cost = fixed costs + variable costs x number of participants

   Total cost = 19,850,000 + VC x N

   Total cost = 19,850,000 + 4,900 (based on a variable cost of 2,400 per teaching center)[4]

2. *Unit Costs*

   Cost of one student completing the course in thirty months (2.5 years)

   Cost of booklets:

production	550
printing	2,500
Administrative costs (for 24,400 students during length of course) 625 x 2.5 years	1,560
Teaching center costs (2,400 x 2.5)	6,000
Total	10,610

   Cost of one student completing the course in forty-eight months (4 years)

   Cost of booklets:

production	550
printing	2,500
Administration	3,125
OSD	9,000
Total	15,125

RESULTS

Each regional office, at the state level, collected a certain amount of information on the participants (sex, age, initial schooling, teaching experience, type of school, salary before enrollment in Logos II, and—about every six months—the cumulative number of modules achieved approximately every six months) and on their monitor (sex, age, schooling, teaching experience, class size).

For the purpose of the present study, we had access to the data collected by two States: Rio de Janeiro, rather better off in many respects, and more representative of the South half of Brazil, and Piaui, one of the poorest states in the northeast part of the country. We took the cohort which entered into the system in early 1980, most of whom had either completed the 205 modules or dropped out.

BASIC CHARACTERISTICS OF THE PARTICIPATING TEACHERS

SEX

The sample contains 1,561 participants of whom 90 were male (5.7 percent). When the state of Rio de Janeiro is considered separately, the proportion of males is only 1.2 percent. It must be remembered that the social status of primary teachers in Brazil is extremely modest and, as elsewhere, this pattern leads to a high rate of feminization. Of the sample, 326 participating teachers belonged to the state of Rio and 1,291 to Piaui.

AGE

The age profile (see Table 7.4) is quite different in both states. Seventy-five percent of Rio's teacher participants were above thirty-five, while 70 percent of Piaui participants were below this threshold. This reflects the fact that in Rio teachers hired during the past two decades were reasonably well qualified and only older ones needed significant retraining. This improvement is not yet visible in Piaui, where schooling is not universally distributed, and where new teachers are quite often poorly qualified.

TABLE 7.4 Participants' Ages by State

		< 20	20–24	25–29	30–34	35–39	40–49	50+	Total
Rio	No.	13	27	27	20	46	109	83	325
	%	4.0	8.3	8.3	6.2	14.1	33.5	25.5	100
Piaui	No.	58	449	337	177	97	97	21	1,236
	%	4.7	36.3	27.3	14.3	7.8	7.8	1.7	100
Both	No.	71	476	362	197	143	206	104	1,561
States	%	4.5	30.5	23.2	12.6	9.2	13.2	6.7	100

INITIAL SCHOOLING

Theoretically, requirements for primary teachers are achieved after eleven years of schooling (see Table 7.5), and Logos II provided an equivalency corresponding to the seven final years, which means that in principle Logos II participants should have finished at least the first four years. Actually, 56 percent of the participants had fewer than 4 years of schooling. In Rio, however, three-fourths of students have received more than four years of initial schooling which again illustrates the relatively better situation there.

TABLE 7.5 Participants' Years of Schooling

		N.A.	1–4	5	6	7	8	9	Total
Rio	No.	9	81	76	17	18	103	26	325
	%	2.8	24.9	23.4	5.2	5.5	31.7	8.0	100
Piaui	No.	59	793	90	60	37	240	14	1,236
	%	4.8	64.2	7.3	4.9	3.0	19.4	1.1	100
Both	No.	68	874	166	77	55	343	40	1,561
States	%	4.4	56.0	10.6	4.9	3.5	22.0	2.6	100

TEACHING EXPERIENCE

The teaching experience structure (see Table 7.6) is close to the age structure. Logos II participants were more experienced in the state of Rio, where they were older (almost 40 percent have taught for more than twenty years). On the other hand, in Piaui, two-thirds had only between one and four years of teaching experience and 1 percent have more than twenty years.

TABLE 7.6 Participants' Years of Teaching Experience

		N.A.	1–4	5–9	10–14	15–19	20+	Total
Rio	No.	7	54	35	29	73	127	325
	%	2.2	16.6	10.8	8.9	22.4	39.1	100
Piaui	No.	143	837	175	47	18	16	1,236
	%	11.6	67.7	14.2	3.8	1.5	1.3	100
Both	No.	150	891	210	76	91	143	1,561
States	%	9.5	57.1	13.5	4.9	5.8	9.2	100

If one wants to compare the characteristics of Logos II teachers with those of other primary school teachers, one would find the same extremes illustrated by the cases of Rio and Piaui. Even though age and years of experience are fairly similar, years of schooling is the major difference: the richer states in the south and the state capitals will have a majority of teachers with secondary school level plus teacher training. However, even in the rural areas of states like Sao Paulo (the richest one) one would find a considerable number of practically illiterate school teachers. The more backward the state, the lower the salary, and, consequently, the less qualified the teachers.

Table 7.7 gives a rather dramatic perspective of the salary structure of primary teachers in Brazil, as reflected in the Logos II participants. In Rio de Janeiro, the modal salary was about 5,000 cruzeiros, which represents, at the 1980 exchange rate with the U.S. dollar of 52.5 Cruzeiros per U.S. dollar, about US$100/per month, or $1,200 a year, near the average GNP per capita in the country, but much below the GNP per capita in Rio state. In Piaui, the overwhelming majority of teachers received less than 2,000 cruzeiros, or US$38 per month, for an average of about 1,000 cruzeiros (US$19), and here again, it is less than the average GNP per capita in this state. Such low earnings are partly due to the insufficient qualification of the teachers and may explain the motivation of candidates for Logos II, which would place the teachers on a higher salary scale, although a modest one by international standards.

TABLE 7.7 Distribution of Monthly Salaries by Participants (in 1980 Cruzeiros)

		<2000	2000–3999	4000–5999	6000–7999	8000–9999	>10,000	Total
Rio	No.	72	52	122	39	33	2	320
	%	22.5	16.2	38.1	12.2	10.3	0.6	100
Piaui	No.	1,190	12	—	—	—	—	1,202
	%	99.0	1.0	—	—	—	—	100
Both	No.	1,261	64	122	39	93	2	1,522
States	%	82.9	4.2	8.0	2.6	2.2	0.1	100

PARTICIPANT RESULTS

PASSING RATES

Passing rates are surprisingly high. As shown in Table 7.8, almost 80 percent have graduated from Logos II. The passing rate is better in Piaui, where teachers are younger, and therefore probably more motivated, since the benefits of the retraining will last for a longer period.

TABLE 7.8 Participants' Rates by State

		Did Not Pass	Passed	Total
Rio	No.	110	216	326
	%	33.7	66.3	100
Piaui	No.	239	1,052	1,291
	%	18.4	81.6	100
Both States	No.	349	1,268	1,617
	%	21.6	78.4	100

RHYTHM OF LEARNING

The rhythm of learning being determined individually, one observes a rather large range of paces. The average number of modules completed for program graduates is 6.78 modules per month, which is near the average expected by the initiators of the system. It must be recognized that a significant proportion of participants, about 40 percent, had already completed more than four years of schooling, which means that they had previously learned part of the curriculum they were being taught in Logos II.

The pace observed since 1980 was better than that found by earlier evaluations (see, for instance, Oliveira and Orivel, 1981), which noted that half of the participants had a pace requiring sixty months instead of the anticipated thirty. (See Table 7.9). This had a strong impact on costs, since the monitor had to be paid for twice the time, even if only a few late teachers remained in the system. Apparently, regional offices dealt with this problem successfully.

TABLE 7.9 Number of Modules per Month Completed by Graduating Students

		4*	5	6	7	8	9	10+	Total
Rio	No.	0	1	101	112	0	1	1	216
	%	0	0.5	46.8	51.9		0.5	0.5	100
Piaui	No.	1	529	265	80	13	28	136	1,052
	%	0.1	50.3	25.2	7.6	1.2	2.7	12.9	100
Both	No.	1	530	366	192	13	29	137	1,268
States	%	0.1	41.8	28.8	15.1	1.0	2.3	10.8	100

*Modules rounded off to nearest whole number.

PACE OVER TIME

The pace was far from stable throughout the life of the project. For those who graduated, the average number of modules per month was between one and two for the first six months, between three and four for the next six months, between five and six for the third six-month period, and above seven for the remainder, which lasted from twelve to twenty-four months (an average of eighteen).

Those who dropped out often began at the same pace, but completed only two to three modules during the second six-month period and slightly more than three during the third. After eighteen months they had finished an average of forty modules, one-fifth of the requirement and, with only eighteen months remaining, completion was simply not achievable. Consequently, the slow pace at the beginning was not a problem, as long as the acceleration rate was good enough to lead to a rhythm of six to eight modules monthly after eighteen months.

SOME FACTORS INFLUENCING PARTICIPANT SUCCESS
Using success (or failure) as a dependent variable, we ran some logistic functions, with independent variables put under the form of dummies. The main conclusions of this exercise are the following:

- The likelihood of success was significantly higher in the state of Piaui than in the state of Rio de Janeiro.
- Participants with five or more years of schooling had a greater chance of completing Logos II.
- The sex of the monitor had no significant impact, but teaching experience had a highly significant positive influence.
- The teaching experience of the participants was positively related to success, but only after six years.
- The optimal age for participants was about twenty-one to twenty-two, and the worst was just below that age.
- Participants with the lowest or the highest salaries had poorer results than those near the average. It may be that motivation was too low for those with the highest salaries, and the lowest salaries may have seemed to offer little future.

EFFECTIVENESS
With a passing rate close to 80 percent, after some four years of running a center with its monitor, the actual cost per graduate remained slightly below 20,000 cruzeiros, or US$380. How can we compare this figure with some alternative?

COMPARISON WITH A SIMILAR PROJECT
In the Brazilian context, Logos II used to have a close competitor with the

Hapront project, very similar in its format, but implemented on a much smaller scale.[5] Its costs were as follows (1980 cruzeiros):

1. *Fixed Costs*

Production (250 units x Cr$2,500	
in 1975–1976, i.e., Cr$625,000	
in 1976 cruzeiros)	3,875,000 (1980 cruzeiros)
Administration	1,440,000 (1980 cruzeiros)
Total	5,315,000 (1980 cruzeiros)

2. *Variable Costs*

Printing of Booklets. Each participant received 250 booklets over a period of three years, with an average of thirty-five pages per booklet; the unit cost was: Cr$45 (1980 cruzeiros) making the total cost for the 8,750 pages Cr$11,250. Since the distribution costs are negligible, the cost per page was Cr$1.30.

Operating Costs of the Centers. There was one tutor for fifty participants, with a monthly salary of about Cr$50,000, paid by the state, and a supplement of Cr$3,000 out of project funds. The total cost amounted to Cr$216,000, giving a cost per student of Cr$4,320. The project used premises in schools or public buildings, the opportunity cost of which may be regarded as nil.

Although the fixed costs of the Hapront project (see Table 7.10) are significantly less than those of Logos II, the fixed costs per participant are higher because of the limited number of participants compared with the Logos II project.

TABLE 7.10 Total Cost of Hapront Project

Variable Cost	Per participant one year	Per participant three years	Per participant earning diploma (70%)
Booklets	3,750	11,250	16,000
Teachers	4,320	12,960	18,600
Subtotal	8,070	24,210	34,600
Fixed Costs			
Booklets	710	2,130	3,050
Administration	1,600	4,800	6,850
Subtotal	2,310	6,930	9,900
Total	10,380	31,140	44,500

Similarly, the costs of reproducing the booklets are much higher since, because of the limited number of copies, there can be no economies of scale with the methods of reproduction used.

In spite of these disadvantages, the total cost per Hapront-trained student was not impossibly high, thanks to the relatively rapid rate of progress imposed on the students and also to the high success rate, which made it possible to limit the variable costs of the OSDs. With a cost per student trained of Cr$44,500, the Hapront project comes in at about twice the estimated cost per student trained by Logos II.

Comparison with the Traditional Education System

Here we make the comparison with the regular secondary school, since it is the equivalent level of the teacher training program.

1. *Cost of Books.* In secondary school (*ginásio*), the estimated cost of the books needed for the four years of the second cycle of the first level was Cr$4,000–6,000 (1980) and of those for the second level was Cr$3,750–10,500 (five to ten books at an average price of Cr$300).

    The total cost of the books varied between Cr$7,750 and Cr$16,150. For the Hapront project the cost was Cr$11,250 and for Logos II Cr$3,050.

2. *Teachers and Operating Expenses.* In the traditional school system there is typically a wide variety of costs among institutions, as well as notorious differences in quality. Although in the public schools the costs may not be much more than Cr$10,000 per student, it is not unusual for a private school to charge more than Cr$40,000 per student per year (1980 costs). We may compare the Logos II student with a student in a medium-cost school, assuming a cost of about Cr$20,000 a year, for a total of Cr$140,000 over seven years. Allowing for repeaters and dropouts, the cost for a student trained in the traditional school system can easily be as much as Cr$200,000, which is ten times the cost per participant obtaining a diploma from Logos II.

    Last but not least, Logos II had the advantage of being an in-service teacher training system, which avoided, for the individual, the loss of an income. To conclude, Logos II was clearly, from an economic perspective, a highly cost-effective system to qualify Brazilian primary teachers.

Implementation of Innovations: Success and Failure

Most of Logos II's features were innovative, at least in Brazil. Its major innovative feature was the structuring of the project itself, as an in-service teacher training model coupled with individual learning while accommodating the individual's teaching. For the purposes of this chapter we shall comment upon a few innovative characteristics which might suggest examples and lessons for other similar projects.

The Management of Motivation

Most educational technology innovations fail because they do not adequately take motivation into consideration. Logos II has learned that important lesson. First of all, the monitors must be constantly motivated. The process starts with recruitment and selection, which cannot be done in a very formalized and bureaucratic manner. Training was a major instrument for the tasks of initial socialization and indoctrination. But permanent supervision was the key. Yet in spite of being tightly controlled by reports, files, memos, and direct supervision, the monitor enjoyed a considerable degree of freedom and had a very peculiar job as far as teaching is concerned. Being in contact with outsiders, including people from the federal capital, gave them high visibility and prestige. It remains a question whether one would keep such motivation and involvement when the project becomes more institutionalized and bureaucratized. So far, experience shows that monitors either prefer to continue as such or to move into administrative tasks. They seemed no longer to fit back into the traditional classroom after Logos II came to an end. Apparently there are two major reasons. One is that monitors got additional salary incentives, and would hardly accept to return to a lower-paid situation after a few years out of the classroom. The other reason is that, having acquired new skills, they might think of themselves as better equipped to get involved in other areas, particularly administration, planning, and community-relation activities.

A second aspect is the motivation of participants. Motivation was crucial to keeping them in the project, not to mention having them learn something. Curriculum relevance and immediate applicability of knowledge and skill may also have helped. One important feature of Logos II seems to be the freedom to choose modules and disciplines. Apparently, this gave teachers the opportunity to see success in the very first steps, raising their feelings of self-reliance which are important for an undertaking of this nature. It seems that control by success and external reinforcement to maintain rhythm is a better strategy than forcing all students to follow a more structured program.

Two other motivational tools deserve comment, and both are related to group phenomena. Typically in distance-learning projects, students complain about the lack of group instruction and opportunities for socialization. In the present case, in addition to the contacts that participants could have with the monitors at the learning center, they did manage to establish small study groups with their neighbors. One manifestation of such groups consisted of peer tutoring, and it was supposed that, besides contributing to their colleagues' studies, tutors would also gain in terms of motivation, prestige, and self-image thus increasing their own performance in the course.

Another important tool was the socialization activities developed during the monthly meetings. The songs, poems, speeches, and personal statements reveal the strong emotional attachment of students to each other and to the project. Spontaneous bonding was carefully channeled by the monitors in order to maximize motivation and enthusiasm toward the project.

The Management of Time

Time is a matter of great concern in a project in which teachers can proceed at their own pace. Spending thirty to fifty months of an adult's life in any activity is a terribly long time. The economists keep worrying about shortening training time, and so do educational administrators. The teachers would rather finish their course more quickly.

Logos II was very demanding in terms of time. Theoretically it expected students, proceeding at their own pace, to complete 205 modules in thirty months, which means an average of 6.8 modules a month. A more realistic expectation—which is also closer to empirical data—would have set fifty months as a good average, given that students can rarely put more than ten hours a week into the project.

Given the pedagogical flexibility, Logos II devised strategies to keep teachers at a good pace without taking away their freedom to choose, which is important for motivation and for enhancing the sense of responsibility and control of one's fate. Emulation, competition, prizes, peer tutoring, individual counseling, among others, were a few such devices to keep teachers in the expected track. In one case, the mayor gave a financial bonus for every seven modules completed in a given month, and the response was very positive.

Time could also be saved in other ways: The curriculum had been split in three parts, corresponding to the primary school, secondary school, and specialized teacher training levels. By showing their diplomas or submitting to entry tests, students could enter directly into an upper level.

Logos II seemed to demonstrate that one can manage flexibility while obtaining satisfactory performance in terms of learning, motivation, rhythm, and completion rates.

The Management of the Environment

Teacher training is part of a context. Teachers need to be trained in Brazil because most have never had a chance to attend secondary school, let alone a teacher-training institution. They belong to a low-paid, low prestige profession working under extremely bad conditions.

Logos II, within this context, was a very strong candidate for being a victim of its own success. Most of the participants who managed to graduate have refused to remain in their previous situation as rural school teachers. They either have gone to the university or have looked into better positions within the educational system. Unable to manage the environment, which is structurally hostile in this regard, the best one can hope for is to wait for the market to saturate. In the future, the surplus might supply teachers with no alternative except to teach in such schools—which will hopefully present better teaching conditions to a more professionalized class.

The Mastery of Distance-learning Technologies

THE HUMAN FACTOR

Favorable structures, political conditions, funding, timing, and luck are a few important ingredients for project success. People are another. However, it is very difficult to evaluate people's effectiveness and the amount of their direct contribution to overall results. A well-connected politician may be more crucial, at some times, than the best of the experts. A dedicated supervisor can be more efficient than a powerful manager.

Two aspects of Logos II managerial personnel, including the staff, deserve some comments. First, Logos II suffered neither from excess personnel nor from overmanagement, both characteristic of large-scale projects. As observed in the descriptive section, headquarters were kept to a minimum. Project directors, at the central ministry, were relatively low-key people, not important enough to be in evidence and challenging on an everyday basis.

Second, besides having a small staff at headquarters and state-based centers, the project managed through training to develop a fairly competent team. The quality of local leadership, which varied from state to state, contributed to make the difference in those cases in which the project was more effective.

Beyond personal characteristics, the exercise of managerial and technical skills and talents was made possible within an organizational framework which evolved from a highly centralized operation to one with a fair amount of decentralization and considerable room for discretion.

Logos II is a good example of competent implementation. CETEB was already familiar with the technology of adult distance education. It did know about printing educational materials. Professional management made it possible to run the project with a fixed staff of fewer than twenty people. Before implementing Logos II, CETEB already knew about individualized instruction, distance learning, competence-based education, training, micro-teaching, and a few other technologies. Such previous knowledge contributed to the successes obtained: while setting up Logos II undoubtedly presented new challenges, not everything was entirely new.

CENTRALIZATION, DECENTRALIZATION, AND THE GRASS ROOTS

The issues of center-periphery relationships are magnified in a country like Brazil. Several factors militate in favor of centralization. The federal government was very powerful, both politically and economically, when Logos II was conceived. Teacher training was a natural mission to be undertaken by the center. Talents were in the center, the best people were concentrated around the federal ministry. Top quality, high-level authority, and reduced local deficiencies were synonymous with "federal." Getting money depended on the will of the federal people. The country, in spite of the tremendous differences in social conditions, climate, geography, and the ethnic and cultural backgrounds of the population, possesses two shared characteristics: a unique and rather uniform language (Portuguese) and a fairly strong sense of national identity. Educational legislation and curricula have differences in emphasis, but not strong enough to discourage centralized educational efforts.

From such a background emerged the systematically designed and well-planned Logos II project. Everything was planned in advance: curricula, activities, operational guidelines, training, setting up of the project, negotiations with local authorities, evaluation schedules, and so forth, including the institution building of local capacities to implement and manage the project at the local level.

The main actors of centralization, however, were not at the center: the ministry did not involve itself in the planning and implementation phase. A private institution with a background in the field was in charge of making things happen. A familiarity with grass-roots problems and experience with the importance of local involvement in order to get things done might have contributed to sow the seeds of decentralization.

As the project progressed into the implementation phase, reactions started to emerge. State authorities wanted more say in the curriculum in order to adapt it to what were perceived as local needs and peculiarities. Forms were found to be too cumbersome to be filled. Centrally prepared distribution and logistics schemes did not always meet the anticipated results. In their daily practice, monitors started adapting general guidelines and even specific instructions into feasible and more realistic activities.

A few examples illustrate the dialectics of decentralization. The use of micro-teaching and the social sciences curricula are two cases in point. In the earlier phases of the project, it was planned that a supervisor would visit classrooms from time to time in order to help student-teachers to improve their practical skills and make sure that the project's contents and teaching skills were being introduced in actual classroom practice. When this alternative became impossible due to financial constraints and lack of adequate personnel, the headquarters decided to replace the field-based supervision by micro-teaching sessions. The micro-teaching, however, was too much a novelty, and the rigidity with which it was introduced and the perceived difficulty of meeting its requirements caused very strong reaction from the "base." At first the center did not accept any changes, but as time passed and pressure augmented, it started accepting adaptations and changes.

Social studies made a good case for decentralization. Even though it was planned beforehand, the actual preparation of content required a much stronger dose of interface with each state. This process made the introduction of several other modifications in the project possible through the dialogue that was opened around the discussion of the local social studies activities. Moreover, states tried to leave additional room for adaptations at the municipal/rural level, which became increasingly acceptable by an initially reluctant center.

At the macro level, political changes contributed to make Logos II a less centralized project. Decentralization became a big word in every sphere of political and economical activity, including in the education sector. States fought for more discretionary resources and more autonomy. It became chic to criticize the center and centrally conceived larger-scale projects and interventions—most of which, indeed, were big mistakes with fairly poor results and high costs.

Responding to pressures and also as a consequence of the institution-building process at the state and local level, it was possible to progressively decentralize Logos II. The first step consisted of transforming CETEB into an advisory agency, with two main tasks: produce the contents and give technical assistance to the states, on request. The Ministry of Education gave up the idea of evaluation and centralization of the accreditation process, as states became legally empowered to do these functions.

Not much is known about the results of the ongoing decentralization of the project, in part because of the lack of interest and the difficulties of gathering data in each of the states. Verbal information collected by CETEB's technical staff seem to indicate that a few states have replaced not only the actual contents, but the whole operational structure of the project. Since there are no means to impose quality controls, it remains a challenge to evaluate the advantages and the shortcomings of the project, in terms of operational efficiency and learning. Nothing is known, also, about the cost implications of the new arrangements. Under the existing political circumstances, CETEB apparently did the most it could in order to build up local capacities, but there is no way to ensure that political winds do not come by and destroy entire groups, as has already been the case in a few states. In another known case, the decentralization of Logos II made it possible to incorporate some of the project's ideas and materials into other teacher-training activities of the educational sector.

ORGANIZATIONAL LEARNING AND TECHNOLOGY TRANSFER
A fair analysis of Logos II implementation has to distinguish at least two phases: In the first, implementation was very rigid and departures from prescription were severely punished. Mayors would receive strong letters from state authorities, if they were not abiding by the contract; states would receive notes from the ministry, asking them to take specific actions in order to correct any disturbances in the system as planned. Monitors would have to keep detailed records of their activities and present accurate reports. Reactions, complaints, disagreements, local adaptations, and even small innovations were very hard to get through.

In the second phase, modifications and changes were adopted only after much discussion in regional meetings. Sometimes, they were implemented without knowledge of or consent from central authorities, but this was a risk that few monitors were willing to run. From CETEB's standpoint, the reason was very simple: the experiment had to be implemented as planned, as the commitment to the details was total. The idea was that modifications could be implemented only after the pilot project, and until then orders were orders.

The new external realities already commented upon forced the ministry and CETEB to adopt a new strategy of decentralization without being prepared for it. Moreover, an intended evaluation was never quite implemented, for two main reasons: first, evaluation is a rare art, not commonly used in Brazil, and it is not surprising that the ministry or the states have never seriously concerned themselves about it; and second, because the data base upon which the planned evaluation should proceed has never been placed under operational conditions, except for peripheral matters.

Thus, one can see two models for organizational learning and technology transfer. Under the centralized phase, the system was prepared to receive only negative feedback, that is, information about deviances. Once notified, actions were taken to reduce the disturbances. Local adaptations and innovations could not be processed. Transfer of experiences between states were limited to exemplary cases of strictly following the rules. All "right" changes had to be implemented underground, at some risk.

As the project started to be decentralized, the center assumed other tasks, and its main function, besides producing materials, consisted of exchanging experiences from one state to the other. CETEB was acting mainly as a clearinghouse which used training and technical assistance as its main strategies to implement innovations. States were also free to design their own innovative strategies as well as to copy from others.

The Mismanagement of Information Systems

Sophisticated information management systems can become instruments for mismanagement and Logos II is a good case in point. The overall evaluation and information processing framework set up for the project by the ministry to monitor Logos II was formidable. It required the project to coordinate and fill out dozens of reports every month on every single aspect of the project's operation—an impossible task. Organizational schizophrenia and incompetence were instrumental in allowing reality to play their role.

Locally, monitors devised their own control mechanisms in order to cope with their daily needs; the other reports were filled out as possible, with no major concern for accuracy; states acted upon instincts, insights, common sense, and firsthand knowledge. They did play the game, they ran after the data, they filled out their own reports, but daily management and strategic decisions were based on simpler data bases. Even CETEB has never replaced firsthand knowledge and supervision with written reports. A preliminary evaluation of Logos II undertaken by Oliveira and Orivel in 1981 revealed and confirmed the absolute irrelevance of the gigantic mass of data which was accumulated for nothing, at a very high cost. The situation did not change, but data continued to be accumulated, until decentralization came in.

For all practical matters, the project was generally well informed, including on cost matters. However, a systematic information system never developed.

In-service or On-the-Job?

In-service training means that teachers study without leaving their own duties. Logos II attempts to make the curriculum and practical activities as useful as possible. However, the project was neither conceived nor implemented within the context of their regular activities. In fact, this was a federal project implemented under state supervision in the villages. The villages did agree and participate, but none was able to fully integrate the project.

Under this situation, practical problems arose. Curricula were not always relevant, both in terms of content as well as in terms of methodologies and techniques suggested. Lack of realism was the major criticism of the teachers teaching in rural areas.

In some cases, there were conflicts of orientation. One instance is the case of literacy methods. Teachers, in many villages, were instructed to follow a given method. Logos II taught them three new methods. Most teachers thought that a new method could be better for their pupils, but they could not use it without raising strong arguments from their supervisors. In the cases where supervision was absent or inoperative, the teachers managed to introduce new methods on their own.

A third type of integration was at the practical level. Teachers were supposed to come to the village from time to time in order to solve their personal problems, get their salaries, obtain materials or lunch for the students, meet with supervisors or local authorities at the municipality, receive orientation for health campaigns, and so forth. In many cases the activities related to Logos II were not related to those other responsibilities, and teachers had to come on specific days just to meet such obligations, instead of accomplishing several things at once, and in the same direction.

This type of problem can be overcome only to the extent that a better integration is intentionally sought and carefully managed. In most cases, however, teacher training, even in-service training, remains as a separate activity. It is thus not surprising that so many teachers leave the educational system once they receive a better education.

There has been no systematic data collected about the turnover of teachers and Logos II-trained teachers out of the educational system. Typical turnover rates exceed 25 percent a year. Traditionally the teachers who leave the system are the best trained ones, and it is not surprising that Logos II would produce better qualified teachers who would seek employment in higher-status levels of the educational system—such as secondary schools, educational administration, or as college students—or in the regular job market. Only a surplus of trained teachers would be able to circumvent such a structural characteristic of the labor force under a reasonably competitive market. A few attempts have been made by local mayors to set up a career plan for Logos II graduates, but those remain partial solutions with limited application.

Logos II seems to have been a valid effort to use distance education as an instrument for training teachers in remote areas. It is certainly also adequate for better-equipped regions. However, critics could quickly raise several doubts about the project's conception, process, and results.

From a structural point of view, the project can be seen as reinforcing inequality: regular schools for the teachers in the best cities, and distance education for the rural areas. Moreover, as most of the teachers leave the system upon graduation, Logos II can be seen as a big failure, if the intended objectives are taken seriously. From a pedagogical viewpoint, the project is vulnerable on many counts: provisions for entry requirements and remedial studies are very deficient and responsible for a significant proportion of drop-outs; curricula are not always relevant, adequate, or interesting. Teaching English in such areas—which is formally required by the state curricula—seems a total waste of time, energy, and resources, and it is never well learned. The quality of materials could be significantly improved, given that unit costs of a large scale project could easily justify the recruitment of excellent personnel for this kind of activity. The pedagogical approach of Logos II is also a matter of criticism: too many behavioral objectives, too much guidance, excessive reliance on a single source of information, and so on. Some of these criticisms cannot be answered; others can be useful to improve the project or redirect it.

On the positive side, there are many lessons which might be useful for other similar undertakings. First, results are not poor, and they can be dramatically improved within the presented models even with small changes. Management seems to be the strongest point. Different from many other governmental attempts, Logos II was professionally managed. CETEB was not only professional, but was fairly competent. Overhead costs are minimal, both at the central and at the state levels. The impact of light-handed management is not only on costs; the periphery becomes more important, more active, and more responsible if the center leaves room for local activities and initiatives.

Other specific lessons from Logos II have already been commented upon, such as the modularized format, the social control of rhythm, the socialization activities designed to overcome the feeling of loneliness, and the management of the student's motivation. This seems to be a rare case of a reasonable combination of centralized planning with decentralized implementation, and in which technological constraints (tests, modules, etc.) can be used to give individuals more freedom to learn and to manage learning.

Domestically, Logos II also offers an important contribution: monitors become active in promoting nonformal education activities in their villages. They also contributed to the exploration in the field of the potential of distance learning, self-study, and many other innovations associated with teacher training. There are indications that regular schools were already benefiting directly and indirectly from this interaction. As for the children in the local schools, there is not much hope under present circumstances. If one takes a more realistic view, Logos II perhaps contributed to a slight improvement in the fate of those condemned to be taught by the rural teachers who lack so many alternatives that they are not able even to improve their own lot and look for a better job. In the long run, as previously stated, projects like Logos II can saturate the market and may contribute to improving the general quality of education in the rural areas.

Epilogue

This study on Logos II was initially written in the mid-1980s. Since that time, education in Brazil has changed a great deal, showing evidence that it has begun to improve. More than 90 percent of the current teachers have formal degrees; the remaining 10 percent is concentrated in the rural areas of northeast Brazil. The persistence of the problem is attributed to hiring and political factors, rather than to the lack of training facilities. There is also some evidence based on student evaluation tests that primary school students perform better with teacher with eleven to twelve years of education than with the typical Logos II teacher, who normally has fewer than nine years of formal education.

As the economy has improved, education has also improved, more than 95 percent of school-age children are enrolled in primary school (grades 1–8) , according to official statistics. Teachers' salaries have also improved—they are still not very attractive, but in the majority of the country, teachers' salaries have increased relative to the early 1980s. As of 1988, the average monthly teacher salary, including salaries in the northeast, was about US$300 for twenty hours of work per week.

Logos II is no longer in existence, even though a few states still use Logos II materials in association with teacher-training activities. There are no records or central controls of any kind. If implemented or updated today, Logos II would have several different characteristics. Changes in technologies, communication, and delivery systems would certainly have an impact on the design of the project. Logos II has made a definite contribution to the thousands of participating teachers, to teacher training, and to training design. It remains as an outstanding example of a well-conceived, well-designed, and given the circumstances, a well-implemented teacher-training system. And, as we have shown, one that is cost-effective.

1. Relative values to the cruzeiro: 1976=100; 1977=143; 1978=197; 1979=304; 1980=620.

2. General administrative costs. In fact, according to CETEB officials, the real costs are much above the amounts transferred by MEC.

3. About US$0.2.

4. The variable cost is equal to the sum of variable costs per students in each teaching center (2,400 cruzeiros); see text above, "*Operation of the Teaching Center;*" and the printing costs of a series of booklets (2,500 cruzeiros); see text above, "*Printing of Booklets.*"

5. About 2,300 students at the same time in Hapront, versus 20,000 to 30,000 students at the same time in Logos II.

REFERENCES

EDRURAL. *Avaliação de Edução Rural Básica no Nordeste Brasileiro. Relatório Técnico*. Vol. 7. Fortaleza: UFCE, Fundação Cearense de Pesquisa e Cultura, 1982.

Oliveira, J.B., and F. Orivel. *Cost-effectiveness Analysis of an In-service Teacher Training System: Logos II in Brazil*. Washington D.C.: World Bank, Discussion Paper No. 81–40, 1981.

Oliveira, J.B. *Logos II: Registro de uma Experiência*. Brasilia: CETEB, 1983.

8 EDUCATION FOR DEVELOPMENT IN A CONTEXT OF DEPENDENCY

AN HISTORICAL REVIEW OF INNOVATIONS AT THE LESOTHO DISTANCE TEACHING CENTRE

Michael L. Basile

INTRODUCTION

Distance education earned its place among the options available to a variety of learners throughout the world a long time ago. Correspondence education, for example, has been a fact of life for generations of certification- and degree-seekers in industrialized countries since the turn of this century and in many countries of the Third World at least since the early 1960s. In recent years, distance education has been adapted to play a broader role in supporting programs that extend beyond the traditional correspondence-schooling model to include community outreach components, such as literacy, skills training for jobs in the trades, preparatory courses for advancing within the education mainstream, radio and other hard technologies as aids to formal education, and citizen/entrepreneurial support activities of great variety. The evolution from its origins as a compensatory option toward a more complex and development-oriented mission, however, has proved to be problematic for distance education.

This chapter takes a look at one case in point, the Lesotho Distance Teaching Centre (LDTC), whose mission has been to extend educational opportunities and support to primarily rural populations located throughout Lesotho.[1] The first part of the chapter discusses the recent historical context of Lesotho, concentrating on its political, geographic, and economic position in both the southern Africa region and internationally; on the capacities and limitations of its government and other social institutions to address the educational needs that are conditioned by this position and to manage appropriate programmatic responses; and on the current state of education and its potential to play an effective role in this context. The second part examines relevant aspects of diffusionist versions of innovation theory and their role in expanding the mission of distance-education programs to include development. The final part of the chapter focuses on the

problematic history of building LDTC's institutional capacity to accommodate this expanded mission over the long term.

THE GEOGRAPHIC AND SOCIAL CONTEXT

Physical and Historical Setting

The mountain Kingdom of Lesotho, a constitutional monarchy about the
size of Belgium, is situated entirely within the confines of the Republic of
South Africa. Traditionally rural, its sharply contoured average elevation lies
above 1,500 meters, severely constraining the agricultural pursuits that had
occupied over two-thirds of its people until the middle of the twentieth century. Of a total population estimated to have reached about 1,700,000 in
1988, about 80 percent remain classified as rural, though a shift from rural
to urban has gained momentum over the course of the past thirty years, with
a significant increase in density in the lowlands and the capital of Maseru.
Over the past two decades Maseru's population has grown to exceed 60,000,
resulting in overtaxed municipal services and problems (such as crime) common to urban centers of much greater size. This shift is underscored by a
sharp relative decline in the production of agricultural goods and almost
equally sharp increases in commercial and industrial activity (World Bank,
1990).

Given the fact less than 15 percent of Lesotho's land is suitable for
cultivation, pressure for wage employment remains well beyond the current
absorptive capacity of the country's still modest but expanding commercial
and manufacturing sectors, which, as of the early 1980s, in their aggregate
still accounted for less than 20 percent of GDP levels (Bardill and Cobbe,
1985, pp. 56 and 61–68). Both soil erosion and severity of climate continue
to constrain recent but largely unsuccessful efforts to increase crop and livestock production for internal market consumption.

The domestic unemployment problem is not new. For generations prior
to gaining independence from British protectorate status in 1966, a significant
percentage of young male Basotho had been remitting a portion of wages
earned as gold mine laborers in the Republic of South Africa to their relatives
in Lesotho. While up to three-fourths of all Basotho wage earners had been
so employed, remitting over 70 percent of Lesotho's average annual income
by 1975 (Bardill and Cobbe, 1985, p. 93), since that time South Africa has
restricted employment of foreign workers due to the automation of its mines
and other internal factors. Possible further shifts in migrant labor policy by
South Africa's post-apartheid government are as yet unclear.

Bardill and Cobbe (1985, pp. 59–62) observe that Lesotho's overall economy became even more dependent on the remittances of its migrant labor force by a factor of three during the early 1980s. The extreme need to generate disposable income at home, however, has not been matched by sufficient growth of any domestic sector. While they appear to show significant growth relative to past performance in the early 1980s, the domestic manufacturing and handicrafts industries, for example, began from such a tiny base that their relative earnings actually fell compared to remittances from abroad (Bardill and Cobbe, 1985, pp. 58–60). Significant expansion of the larger retail trade sector over the same period should also be understood in light of the fact that most trade-related expenditures have gone toward payment for goods imported from and through South Africa.

Modern History

The people of Lesotho emerged as a nation under the leadership of Moshoeshoe, chief of a small tribe who, through years of open conflict, unified with various other tribes of Basotho by the early nineteenth century. Struggling to remain free of Boer, British, and Orange Free State Burgher influence, Moshoeshoe was finally granted British Government protection in 1868. But competing Orange Free State interests in the fertile western wheatlands remained strong enough to win their cession from Basutoland in 1869. The remainder of the country was annexed by the Cape Colony in 1871. Although its administration was officially transferred to London's control in 1884, Basutoland was still administered as a colony by Britain's High Commissioner to Pretoria until its independence in 1966 (Lundahl and Petersson, 1971, pp. 20–29).

Traditionally, that is, prior to and during the early colonization period, the Basotho used grazing land communally, this practice being basic to cultural patterns of family welfare, production, and distribution (Patrick, 1978), individual property ownership being less important than usage (Lundahl and Petersson, 1991, pp. 23–24). While some efforts to reform the land tenure system have been initiated periodically since political independence in 1966, long-standing trends toward agricultural decline have not been reversed by efforts to spur agricultural production for cash, even considering substantial increases in international aid to agriculture.[2]

From the viewpoint of its modern history, Lesotho's gradual though profound shift from a pastoral and agricultural, semimigratory people without sharply delineated boundaries to a nation whose income is derived principally from its migratory proletariat has had severe social and cultural ramifications. Generally speaking, the pastoral and agricultural domestic way of life has been all but totally replaced by internationally regulated wage employment. In spite of the fact that individual ownership of land has become national policy, wage earnings from abroad have, for the most part, not been devoted to investment in private village modernization and agricultural mechanization schemes. For example, even though some remittance earnings not spent on imported durable and consumable goods (such as food) have been invested in livestock, these investments are not regarded as immediately convertible to cash income (Ferguson, 1990, pp. 154–157). By long-standing custom, livestock ownership instead represents "stored" surplus as a form of social security. The rural Basotho family of today is thus left with acute needs for cash. Though some products of the land, including women-owned and managed—usually noncattle—livestock, are now traded, such income has been insufficient to reverse trends away from both subsistence and cash agricultural production. Bardill and Cobbe (1985) remark on the "inevitable consequences [of land tenure reforms of] more landless people and greater inequality of income and wealth in rural areas" (pp. 79–80).[3]

Furthermore, the long-standing drain of migrant workers to the Republic of South Africa has had profound social consequences. Generation after generation, the rural family has lost males in their physically most productive years. Women have had to compensate by assuming tasks and responsibilities traditionally reserved to men, with deleterious consequences for the family's capacity to sustain a subsistence-based livelihood (Droegkamp, 1982). Children, particularly boys, have had to assume a variety of family support tasks in addition to traditional herding that have sharply increased the opportunity costs of school attendance. Such long-term trends toward urban migration and pressures for wage employment and income generation have had irreversible detrimental consequences for the learning of skills suitable for sustaining rural life. To aggravate matters, Cobbe (1985, pp. 265–266) observes a period of "alienation from community" that attaches to "women of business," which she imputes as a social cost incurred for their non-traditional—namely, commercial—endeavors to provide for immediate family needs (pp. 265–266). Malahleha (1984) adds that such "economic, technological and social changes have greatly increased women's dependence upon men and decreased their autonomy, without decreasing their domestic and managerial tasks" (p. 9).

GOVERNMENT, DEPENDENCY, AND AN IMPOVERISHMENT THESIS

This chapter argues that study of Lesotho's modern educational predicament should begin from an alternative perspective, what I call an "impoverishment thesis," with due attention to the contextual complexities peculiar to Lesotho's history. Briefly, this thesis bucks the linear and progressive assumptions built into development and growth theories advanced since the 1960s, whose point of departure is a backward state of underdevelopment. Instead, the thesis of impoverishment begins from the position that poverty—namely underdevelopment—is a consequence of economic, political, and cultural penetration that distorts, co-opts, and perverts local systems of endogenous relations. Amin's (1976) analysis is useful in setting out the theoretical parameters for examining the complexes of international and national relations that factor into processes that result in cultural and historical disintegration.

Prior to the age of colonization and modernization, pastoral, communal, and quasi-feudal societies like that of the Basotho were characterized by mutually supportive systems of reciprocal relations of production and reproduction between classes, particularly around the subsistence mode of social organization. As the colonial era took hold, imbalances of power and privilege that inhered in these traditional systems were transmuted and reified into economic and social formations. Initially, Lesotho may have experienced some modest prosperity during the early colonial period as access to nontraditional economic activity was opened to commoners. As the colonial period introduced new economic activity and relations, the traditional power base of the ruling class gradually eroded. The significance of its traditional functions was superseded by commercially active lower classes, the migrant proletariat included. As a result, the reciprocal bonds between the ruling and the lower classes steadily attenuated. The rise of a trading class was fueled by incomes remitted from a new class of laborers, whose dependence on local chiefs declined.

This development had direct social consequences. The metaphor of the traditional ties that bound herdsman to livestock to land to chief was replaced by new practices and authority relations. As the nineteenth century passed disparities of livelihood emerged between the rural and urban/commercial ways of life. The growth of new import enterprises spurred the development of new institutional forms to protect and support their commercial interests, interests that developed apart from the traditional political power structure. The development of new administrative functions of government, for example, was spurred in part by commercial enterprises that required not just regulatory oversight, but also other government-supported services such as property protection and an educated labor pool to draw on. The incremental growth in and authorities of these services took the form of bureaucratic regulation that progressed along class lines. Murray's (1981) account of class formation in Lesotho stresses the confluence of both internal and external factors that accentuated the social divisions that ensued. Eldridge (1993), tracing the incidence of material scarcity from precolonial times into the modern period, finds the severity and prevalence of basic security needs of the majority of the population to be an unprecedented feature of modern life (pp. 28–41).

Government Development Policy Today

Since political independence in 1966, the government has turned its attention toward development policymaking in several economic sectors. Such attention, however, has been highly politicized and sporadic in result. The government's power to deploy consistent policy since independence has been subject to both severe external economic and political fluxes and extremes of internal partisan conflict. Irrespective of these last thirty years of turbulence, however, the government's need for more revenues to support its various development initiatives has thoroughly outpaced the rate of overall domestic economic expansion (Patrick, 1978; Ferguson, 1990). To secure case reserves, it has: (1) instituted heavy import and local commercial taxation policies to partially support its recurrent operations; and (2) accepted massive amounts of foreign assistance from European, American, and multi-lateral agencies to support the activities set out in its five year development plans.[4]

What has emerged in this era of government-backed development programming is an interventionist state bureaucracy heavily, albeit often unpredictably and inconsistently, involved in virtually all sectors of Lesotho's society: namely health, physical infrastructure, commerce, tourism, handicrafts, agriculture, manufacturing, and education. While such governmental social activism in a mixed capitalist context may not be unusual, Lesotho's unique condition of almost total geographic and economic dependency has spawned a plethora of state-sponsored development activities unparalleled on the entire continent. When considered in light of low overall population of widely dispersed settlement (with the possible exception of Maseru), dependency on government and international aid to lead the way out of poverty is felt as hope long frustrated in every corner of the land. The national fixation on the undelivered promise of development pervades official discourse at all levels, provides rationales for continued government expansion into civil society, and frames the discussion of national economic policy for all sectors under one predominant ideology: development as the solution to poverty. The state of economic dependency is absent from this discourse.

Ferguson (1990) takes a critical view of this grim state of affairs when he concludes:

> The "development" apparatus in Lesotho is not a machine for eliminating poverty that is incidentally involved with the state bureaucracy;

it is a machine for reinforcing and expanding the exercise of bureaucratic state power, which incidentally takes "poverty" as the point of entry—launching an intervention that may have no effect on the poverty but does in fact have other effects. Such a result may be not part of the planners' intentions—indeed, it almost never is—but resultant systems have an intelligibility of their own. (pp. 255–256)

When development is considered, the options available within the present economic and political order are few. The International Labour Office (ILO) report issued fifteen years ago is perhaps a more prophetic, if not understated, description of both the current economic situation and accelerating social and cultural dissolution. The report, *Options for a Dependent Economy* (1979), foresaw the system of political and economic relationships that form the basis of Lesotho's present realities this way:

> For over a hundred years, it has exported something like half of its male labour force across the Caledon River to the mines, collieries and farms of the RSA and the remittances of these migrant workers have doubled, tripled, and in recent years sextupled rural household income, directly and indirectly financed one-third of the Government budget, and generated two-fifths of the national income. Wages and prices, interest rates and customs receipts, even the exchange rate of its monetary unit, are all determined by RSA which in addition controls every trade and communication link of the country to the rest of the world. There never was a country so dependent for its development on another—in this case one with which it has the most profound political differences. (pp. 1–2)

While evidence to date does not point to a single catastrophic economic and social crisis that looms on the immediate horizon, given present trends, the kingdom of Lesotho is in for more periods of disaffection and confrontation, the causes of which relate very much to its profound and evolving state of dependency. So far, the forms that evolution has taken extend not just to the economic sphere, but also to the functions of government development policy and administration, which have become the site of intense international involvement.

EDUCATION AND SOCIETY

In furtherance of its ideological commitment to development, the government has tried numerous innovative programs to modernize the education sector over the past three decades. The programs span such an array of formal and nonformal interventions that it would be useful to reflect on the historical evolution of education as a way to set the stage for these modernization efforts.

On the African continent especially, the history of education has been reified into institutionalized forms of schooling associated with colonial and mission presence. Indigenous educational practices have been relegated to the realm of cultural and historical artifact. If today's educational development focus is to be understood in context, some reflection on the traditional and diverse socialization practices that once animated rural social life should be taken into account first.

The Basotho obviously engaged in educational and socialization practices long before the advent of European influences. Though the practices may seem to have been informal, they were nonetheless integral parts of social and productive processes where children learned the skills and attitudes that would insure their active participation in family and community life (Government of Lesotho, 1982). Learning and living in the community were not dichotomous activities. The curriculum of the past, present, and future was in the hands of kinfolk, elders, and local religious and other community leaders. While this may indeed be reminiscent of an old story repeated throughout African history, it is instructive to recall how the locus of control over the socialization of the young shifted exogenously during and after colonization. The shift outward corresponds temporally to the increased state of dependency characteristic of the modernization process.

Even though indigenous education practices are in a state of utter decline, it can still be argued that the arcadian image of precolonial Basotho society is relevant to the historical context in which the modern educational scholar/developer now works. A pastoral people free of external domination, once fully responsible for their own cultural and economic reproduction, stands in marked contrast to the externally conditioned educational system of today. The European schooling model was established over the relatively brief period which also saw the degeneration of pastoral economic and social life (Eldridge, 1993). The initiation schooling process was only one of its many casualties. The modern school was introduced into colonial Basutoland by the Christian missions. The impact of mission education prior to 1850, however, was negligible. The missions themselves began modestly, with low conversion rates throughout the nineteenth century (Eldridge, 1993, pp. 94–96). While their direct social impact may have been minimal, however, they still captured the attention of the local chiefdom enough to initiate open resistance to the Christian ideology and the "Europeanized" lifestyle by 1850.

More penetrating than Christian ideology, according to Eldridge (1993, pp. 95–96), were the social effects of trade practices that increased the purchasing costs of locally produced goods. The rise of a commercial trading sector simply made it less costly to procure needed items through retail markets. The development of the commercial import industry, however, was not necessarily accompanied by the development of local manufactures industries. It arguably curtailed them as part of an international economic "decentering" process that had other irreversible economic implications, foremost among them increasing the need for convertible cash income. The early seeds of Lesotho's continuing dependency on its migrant labor were thus sown from the very start of the colonial period. The need for the right kinds of training to fill new institutional roles also spread. Literacy became necessary for employment at home and in the Republic of South Africa.

Although the proliferation of Christian missions may have been spurred as much by commercial necessity as it was by ideological appeal, modern education brought new values, habits, clothing, and behavior (GOL, 1982, p. 20). Mission schools established education as a technological process with facilities, teachers, and students (see, for example, McGinn, 1994). At the same time, schools represented eventual access to other Western technologies, gadgets, weapons, clothing, information, and, occasionally, the commoner's route to status within an urbanizing social context. Their spread thus coincided with the emergence of needs for a host of institutionally related developmental skills. In relatively short time, the missions went on to establish their respective networks of primary schools, with uniforms, examinations, and their own curricula. Basotho children privileged enough to attend school soon learned there was a life and future that existed beyond the confines of their individual communities; a world apart, but newly emergent; within reach, but dependent on access to and performance in a meritocracy that represented a new order.

During the century prior to independence, the colonial administration first took a supportive role in providing education. Originally in the form of finance, by the 1930s the support extended to standardized curricula (emphasizing facility in English and literacy) and external examinations. By the middle of the twentieth century the established, overwhelmingly religious system of schooling came into conflict with the government's attempts to escalate secular authority over education. The last several development plans provide for more explicit government control over the management of primary, secondary, and nonformal/adult education. Frequently, this initiative has been confrontative, particularly at the postsecondary level (GOL, 1982).

The relative powers of church, community, and state in the provision of education at all levels remain a point of contention to this day.

Since the 1970s there have been sporadic efforts to redress the problem of the lack of commercial and technical skills taught in the schools, as well as to increase overall enrollment. While primary classroom enrollments have risen to include about 80 percent of eligible school-age children, other problems have surfaced. At the secondary level the enrollment percentage of eligible children falls to fewer than 20 percent, with even greater needs for qualified teachers, space, and equipment. Due to the still pressing need for boys to tend to cattle herds, for example, girls continue to outnumber boys in school attendance by a ratio of almost three to two (Rihani, 1993, p. 3). Though innovative programs to introduce practical subject matter into the curriculum have been initiated with outside donor support (e.g., at the National Teacher Training College and other ministerial units), the gap in providing adequate formal educational opportunities persists. Realizing the limitations of such reforms, the government embarked on alternative approaches to solving the problem of increasing access to education more than two decades ago.

DISTANCE EDUCATION AND THE FOUNDING OF LDTC[5]

The context for introducing curricular and institutional reforms into all facets of education, including distance education, was politically charged from its inception. Traditionally, authority over curricula, staffs, teacher training, and operations had been exercised more by the churches than by government. The government's struggle to assert more control over education was furthered by international attention to unmet needs in rural areas. The rationale for the government's new thrust into education was based on the private formal system's current overemphasis on academic subject matter. The government saw the opportunity to offset it by mounting programs to meet the immediate practical needs of a rurally settled society dependent on wage labor. Even though Lesotho's Distance Teaching Center began as a quasi-independent body, it represented the government's agenda to extend its role in the provision of education to outlying areas. The opportunity presented to government by the international donor community to extend itself through externally provided new financial resources proved irresistible.

Almost since their beginning, then, Lesotho's distance education programs have been introduced in the context of political struggle for the loyalties of a populace sharply divided by religion, political affiliation, and social standing. The government's struggle to introduce credible programs in distance education has been waged under the development banner: alternative opportunities for study and certification in diverse fields and supplemental job-related training to civil servants, managers of private and parastatal organizations, and members of credit unions, cooperatives, church and women's groups, and community development groups (GOL, 1982). Collectively, the initiatives have been deployed through a strategy of strengthening central institutional capacity to organize programs that compensate for the shortcomings and failures of the formal system. Motivation to reshape and take full charge of LDTC's originally more modest mission is thus complexly intertwined with the government's overall endeavor to assert itself vis-à-vis rival institutions.

In the past ten years, the total of LDTC's efforts is estimated to have reached well over 300,000 individuals, young and old. Founded by the International Extension College (IEC) of Great Britain in 1974, LDTC's original purpose was to explore distance-teaching methods for the majority of the population which had disadvantaged access to the formal system (Cain and Method, 1979). Early LDTC activities concentrated on the production of booklets and radio broadcasts primarily for extension to rural areas (Cain and Method, 1979; Selbin, 1984a)[6] The degree of external advice, financing, and education model-building adequate to mount a distance-education program of this scale was evident in the establishment of presses, a radio recording facility, and a staff of about thirty members, 20 percent of whom were expatriates occupying senior positions (Krueger et al., 1983). Literacy and numeracy programs, basic and rural education, and service to other educational organizations became part of a new emphasis on using nonformal educational techniques for development-related needs (Selbin, 1984a; Cain and Method, 1979). Radio broadcasting and the production of booklets on a variety of topics related to practical skills in rural areas were also added (Morolong, 1983). At this time several objectives in addition to the dissemination of information to rural areas became part of the LDTC mission:

- Helping correspondents to study for equivalency examinations
- Investigating needs for and ways to provide literacy and numeracy instruction
- Serving other educational organizations (Cain and Method, 1979)[7]

Since IEC's charter was specifically restricted to distance-teaching methods and the government of Lesotho was unable to undertake projects solely on its own, infusions of foreign assistance were necessary. The expansion of LDTC's mission in the late 1970s and early 1980s was facilitated by the U.S.

Agency for International Development (USAID) and European donors. From 1977 onward the relative emphasis placed on enhancing LDTC's mission toward supporting development activities is pronounced. By 1983 the staff had increased to seventy, with a significant proportion of the increase going to one outreach section, the Service Agency (SA). This relative increase corresponded roughly to the level of USAID project commitments to LDTC. While other sections of LDTC (e.g., literacy, radio, course writing, and formal correspondence courses) maintained their original levels of staff activity, the Service Agency went on to administer a diverse range of programs, including a revolving developmental fund for rural and community groups (Krueger et al., 1983). Up to the mid-1980s, plans to continue this trend formed a basic part of future commitments of USAID assistance to LDTC (Selbin, 1984b).[8] These plans were made in the context of larger projections of USAID assistance to the education sector in general (USAID/Lesotho, 1983; USAID, 1984).

The decade of the 1980s, however, was less than prosperous or auspicious for the LDTC. Radical personnel changes begun shortly after its full appropriation into the Civil Service in 1982 depleted the organization of many of its most skilled and highly trained staff. On the one hand, becoming a full-fledged agency of the Ministry of Education provided a sense of security for personnel, long subject to the uncertainties of external funding commitments. On the other hand, LDTC's distinguished tradition as an independent provider of services to needy populations and as an innovator in extending practical and appropriate educational opportunities, for many years a model for other countries, was severely compromised (Dodds and Mayo, 1992).

THE FUSION OF INNOVATION AND DEVELOPMENT THEORIES AT LDTC: DEPENDENT HYBRID WITHOUT OFFSPRING

Ferguson's (1990) analysis of the function of development policy in the Lesotho of the 1980s makes a strong case for a dependency-informed perspective on government-sponsored innovation activity. The development rationales advanced by government provide the rhetorical context in which innovations were introduced at LDTC over the decade. Development is presented as government's rational response to economic and political realities that obliged educational policymakers to overhaul the weaknesses of the education system. For instance, the rationale to introduce practical subject matter like gardening, food preparation, construction skills, health and nutrition, and other market-oriented craft activities into the formal curriculum is based on external efficiency. Reinforced with regular and significant doses of donor assistance, the rationale has served as an effective mobilizer for initiating new programs at LDTC specifically and other units of the ministry generally. The rationale and its program initiatives are indicative of two basic assumptions about the supposed causal relationship between education and deliberate social and economic change:

1. The main purpose of education is to fuel the transition to a modern economy.

2. Innovations and changes of emphasis introduced into the education system will result in more trained cohorts of graduates who will more effectively engage in productive activities. This engagement will infuse itself into all sectors of the economy, eventually lifting the society as a whole toward development and modernization.[9]

These assumptions are based on an ideological orientation that takes a teleological view of the purpose of education: to reinforce social organization, economic growth, and institutional relations toward some preconceived, overarching vision of modernity.[10]

Adopting and Implementing Innovations

Fullan's (1989) brief on the evolution of innovation theory is useful in examining the institutionally based logic applied toward strengthening LDTC. Fullan notes that early variations of innovation theory paid slight regard to social and historical context. The earlier institutional development approach to innovation relied on by donor agencies involved with LDTC distinguishes two major chronological stages of innovation practice: adoption and implementation. The former refers to the decision-making and policy-setting function required to undertake a particular innovation; the latter refers to the longer-term work and commitments necessary to sustain its operation. Only after 1970, considering evaluative information made available on the widespread failure of the adoption approach alone, was attention systematically paid to issues of implementation. This heralded the present phase of search for (universal) "factors of success." The currently operational phase Fullan calls "managing change," a period in which educational outcomes are becoming the primary focus.

Fullan (1989) proceeds to recommend a longer-term approach that allows for consistent support from initiation through implementation to institutionalization stages. Several characteristics that take some account of the context he identifies are: "clarity/complexity, consensus/conflict, and quality/practicality." Each characteristic provides a conceptual means for designers and implementers to raise and confront issues along their respective continua as the implementation process unfolds. The outcomes achieved through this participatory process provide discrete opportunities for what Fullan calls "progressive mastery over the innovation" process while it "builds commitment" (pp. 23–24).

This said, the scale of operation implied by such a process is relatively modest. Fullan concludes his analysis with a comparative list of salient characteristics of educational change projects in North America and World Bank reforms typically promoted throughout the Third World:

> Projects with the characteristics noted for World Bank projects tend to be complex, vague (exactly what is the innovation?), hard to coordinate, slow moving, and notoriously difficult to evaluate or assess in progress. (p. 29)

While the classification "conflict/consensus" is broached in Fullan's analytical scheme, it is done so from "the inside looking out," so to speak. The historical and political situation of the targeted client population is approached exclusively through putative institutional relations directed from the administrative center—the "inside"—looking out at the client located on the "outside." Though the need for innovation is recognized, such recognition falls totally within the ideological context of the development policy discourses authored by government. LDTC's innovation history is no exception.

The innovations implemented at LDTC in the 1980s had several features in common:

- An extensive amount of their support came from foreign sources
- Their basic purpose was to enhance LDTC's institutional capacity to provide outreach services
- The ultimate target of these services was the rural and urban poor Basotho
- They required extensive staff training and facility improvement at LDTC to deliver
- They were coordinated centrally. While user input was often sought, programming decisions and responses were reserved exclusively to LDTC staff.

As LDTC's original mission was converted, its organizational form was also changed. The new emphasis on its role as innovative conduit for the diffusion of nonformal methods in needs assessment, learner-centered training, program development, impact evaluation, and a range of other outreach initiatives necessitated significant internal changes which, in turn, required extensive external support. LDTC staff members were trained to undertake and manage these services with on-site long-term technical experts.[11]

Collectively, the changes meant that the momentum for generating educational innovation was institutionally similar to that used in formal education. New programs derived from a centralized source, supported by significant inputs of donor support. While the educational message stressed nonformal values of empowerment and self-reliance, the delivery system was virtually identical to that used by other agencies and organizations with outreach responsibilities. From the point of view of the consumer, though the package may have changed color, the way to access it was little different. The basic rules of the structural relationship, namely that between provider and consumer, were the same.

Vargas-Adams and Bastian's (1983) study of nonformal education in Lesotho observes that:

> Evolution may appear to be more difficult than creation, but in the long run an educational process which evolves from its traditional roots to meet the newer challenges may strike a more responsive chord from the society it is to serve. (p. 31)

They further conclude that most NFE programs in Lesotho, are "mainly formal in nature," especially with respect to their "program development process, structure, decision-making patterns and constituency of the programs. These tend to be either colonial or, secondarily, traditional in form" (pp. 305–306).

THE SERVICE AGENCY

In 1982, Barnett and Engle prepared a document for USAID on the subject of institution-building. It was designed as a practical guide for project managers who were to make use of its recommendations and findings in the process of identifying and supporting institutional development opportunities in a variety of Third World settings. The principal rationale for institution building in AID's estimation is stated in the introduction:

> Self-sustaining growth in the developing nations depends on the ability of countries to introduce changes, through their public and private

sectors that lead to improvements in productivity and higher standards of living for large numbers of people. At times, important changes can be affected [sic] through a single action, such as a shift in pricing policies. More often, however, a series of actions can best be fostered and maintained when an organizational infrastructure is set in place to efficiently and effectively introduce conditions that lead to desired results. Whether these changes are instituted through a nation's public health service or by private medical practitioners, through government marketing boards or private corporations, institutional capacity lies at the heart of long-term improvement efforts. (p. v.)

The document proceeds to outline a series of factors, inputs, and precautions necessary for development project managers to consider in their efforts to augment institutional capacity. Their central focus is on the institution as an entity to be established presumably before meaningful development initiatives can be sustained in the field.

Several LDTC project documents prepared under USAID auspices accepted this concept of institution building as an indispensable prerequisite for increasing LDTC's *development-oriented* service capabilities (see, for example, Krueger et al., 1983; Cain and Method, 1979; Hoxeng, 1980). The overall purpose for augmentation involved the enhancement of technical capacity in NFE materials development, training, communications, and finance (Hoxeng, 1980, pp. 8–9). Project evaluations done at the time focused on the degree of success in achieving enhanced capacity in this manner. The evaluations also assumed capacity building as a necessary precondition for development.

The paradox in all this is striking. LDTC's continued dependency on external support to carry out its expanded development-oriented programs violates Fullan's later focus (Fuller and Stiegelbauer, 1991)on those factors deemed necessary to support institutionalization in the long run: more attention to the politics of educational change, the formation of alliances, the production of alternative discourses on change, and the sustenance of "critical masses" of supporters and stakeholders (pp. 345–354). Such a focus would have striven to consolidate technical know-how with political action, all locally, of course. Insofar as the political economy of Lesotho precluded such an activist strategy toward self-reliance, however, such a decontextualized institutional development strategy was contradictory. A technicist approach was only half the story.

While Hoxeng (1980) raises several issues that address both the political and the technical halves of the institutionalization equation, his argument remains circumscribed by the development-oriented context of governmental policy, stuck in the dependency predicament. He argues the technical merits of increasing service capacity through nonformal education outreach advanced by the LDTC this way:

> *NFE practitioners maintain their independence and initiative, take responsibility for their activities and are flexible in their programming* . . . . This paper proposes that governments allow those programs to maintain their autonomy, while at the same time cataloging and mapping their activities, responding to their requests for technical/financial assistance, and supporting their expansion into areas (both subject and geographical) where people have not had access to FE or NFE opportunities. *The product of such an approach would be an NFE support organization which builds on NFE's strengths and addresses its historical weaknesses.* (p. 6, emphasis added)

The practical problem, specifically unaddressed, was the unavoidable fallacy of exchanging one form of dependency for another. Freedom from government control did not equal autonomy. About the time the surge of foreign assistance to expand its mission came at the end of the seventies, LDTC became an attractive alternative for absorption into the government service. The successful international and domestic reputation it had earned under its previous quasi-autonomous status made it ripe as a lead organization to substantiate the government's push to reinforce the education-development linkage. The GOL's decision to incorporate LDTC as a body into the government, and to cite it in the 1980–1985 Five Year Plan as the "country's major institution for nonformal education" (Selbin, 1984a, p. 7), made it a convenient experimental hybrid for the fusion of development and educational innovation theories into visible programs of state action. LDTC's international reputation as principal center for innovative educational development initiatives (Cain and Method, 1979, pp. 48–49; Krueger et al., 1983) made it too attractive—at the price of continued outside assistance— to leave alone.

As expected, donor assistance from European and U.S. assistance agencies amounted to about 40 percent of LDTC's total operating budget (Krueger et al., 1983, pp, 7–14). Further growth was planned as several options for expanding the coordinating responsibilities of the Service Agency were considered for the mid- to late 1980s (Selbin, 1984b). Institutionalization of outreach capacity was thus an ongoing process which could sustain momentum to the extent external support was made available. The primary aim of the Service Agency's expansion had been to support existing programs and organizations in their grassroots development initiatives (Selbin, 1984b). To this end Selbin recommended several tasks be undertaken by representatives of government and the private sector on behalf of LDTC in the mid-1980s:

- Formation of a design group from the ranks of government and the private sector to analyze beneficiary and client populations to determine the kinds of services that were being offered currently and to assess needs for additional development-related services
- Prioritization of tasks for the Service Agency based on the above results
- Assessment of "centralization-decentralization requirements" to provide specific services, the relative merits of using currently available services and expanding them, and the kind of agency structure suitable to deliver the above services
- Establishment of an interinstitutional planning process for accomplishing the above.

Selbin contrasted the intent and modus operandi of the new Service Agency approach to development by describing it as a "support" rather than as a "lead agency," the primary characteristic of the latter being the delivery of its own services directly rather than the enhancement of the service capabilities of other agencies and organizations (1984b). A major consideration in the restructuring process was therefore the institutional form the Service Agency would assume in its role as support service provider. The extent of centralization/decentralization of important innovative educational functions such as materials production and delivery, advice giving, evaluation, credit facilitation, staff development, and many others was of primary consideration in this institutional development strategy.

As the decade of the 1980s advanced, however, this support diminished sharply, with adverse consequences for the programmatic capabilities of LDTC as a whole, the Service Agency included. User- or consumer-generated fees for LDTC's services, for example, have been on the increase. Predictably, as the level of foreign technical assistance dropped in the latter 1980s, there was reason to doubt LDTC's capacity to fulfill even its more modest, original mission. This current state of affairs contrasted markedly, if not sadly, with the period of great promise at the dawn of the 1980s (see, for example, Betz, 1984, pp. 165–167; Tsekoa, 1983; Vargas-Adams and Bastian, 1983; Hoxeng and Murphy, 1983; Krueger et al., 1983; and Selbin, 1984b).[12]

INNOVATION AND DEPENDENCY: THE DILEMMAS OF DEVELOPMENT-BASED INNOVATION

Considering this history of dependency, one would have to ask whether Fullan's (1991) context-responsive and strategic mobilization perspective has any possible relevance to the conditions of Lesotho. In hindsight, such recent advances in innovation and organization theory would suggest that the Service Agency should have been structured to respond to locally felt and articulated needs as flexibly as possible. The organizational choice to be made was whether LDTC should offer its services directly from a centralized facility, or whether LDTC should play more of an advisory, coordinating role. Technically, this choice should have been informed by the kind of organizational networking and outreach services needed. As it turns out, political and historical factors determined that the Service Agency retain a centrally organized structure for all its services. Absorption of the LDTC as a unit into the Ministry of Education doubtless was one of the decisive factors that constrained its authority to alter its organizational form to more closely align with its client groups.

Aware of the change in LDTC's autonomy status, Selbin (1984b, pp. 27–28) suggested a three-stage growth process for the Service Agency, beginning with initial discussions among decision and policymakers about its revised form, role, and purpose. The next stage proposed was the consolidation of initial activities, a vigorous staff development program, expansion of outreach services, assessment of current programs and activities, and the initiation of network building. This stage would be completed with the establishment of a basic services structure and capacity. The final stage would involve expansion of the support system and full integration with other service delivery and grassroots development organizations.

In effect, what Selbin (1984b, p. 29) had proposed was a conceptual shift, namely, from "expansion of the organization" as such to the more flexible idea of "organizational expansion." The intent of the shift was to position the LDTC, through the Service Agency, to promote the concept of "organizing as participatory activity" to other groups, institutions, and developmental programs. Under this approach, the role of the Service Agency would be one of intermediate service to other service providers. The reasoning behind this strategy anticipated the problem of expanding the staff, budget, and facilities of LDTC proper in direct competition with other agencies of government. The new strategy depended on closer ties among education and other government and nongovernment agencies through a combination of new policy directives and networking arrangements. The possibility these organizations would have a local service agency like LDTC to call on for assistance in developing their own capacities to deliver services was expected to be a persuasive selling point. Although many organizations that had been providing services no doubt had received the help of outside consultants before, the prospect they would actually be able to network together to give and receive help reciprocally was argued to offer the best opportunity to exercise local control over the service delivery system over the long term.

In retrospect, this proposal to restructure LDTC's outreach strategy addressed one of Fullan's (1989) major concerns about implementation. The approach embodied in the proposal appeared to be a progressive step along the continuum from imposing an innovation by adoption toward the participatory development, placement, and support of locally controlled change projects. The approach recommended would in effect configure the Service Agency as a mechanism for reinforcing and supporting educational change through flexible institutional responses in training, technical assistance, and credit. It would therefore enhance the outreach efforts of other agencies involved in rural development without rivaling or duplicating their approaches, methods, or purposes. In sum, it offered ways to increase and improve communication and collaboration among development agencies, rural-based organizations, and their respective clients.

The failure of this strategy to take hold is reflected in a bureaucratic shift away from rural and nongovernmental participation in the restructuring process toward the establishment of LDTC as an agency of government rather than as an evolving, manipulable intermediary to help others bridge the gap between government, city, and the rural areas. According to the original proposal, the Service Agency was intended to encourage other agencies to increase their respective access to marginal populations and nongovernmental local organizations. What the decade of the eighties turned into, however, was a struggle for bureaucratic survival under great pressure to demonstrate progress in numbers of constituents served for development purposes. In the struggle, LDTC's capacity to diversify its offerings and to decentralize appropriately was severely curtailed.

DISTANCE EDUCATION AND DEPENDENT DEVELOPMENT

This study of the history of development aspirations projected onto LDTC's mission by the GOL and by international development agencies in the early

1980s has thus stirred up several contradictory issues. On the one hand, early conventional wisdom about diffusing innovations presupposed an instrumental relationship between the institutionalization of innovation and development; the former was conceived to be an indispensable prerequisite for the latter. The instrumental logic behind innovation theory would seem to support direct efforts to substantiate the resource base and status of any agency of government charged with the task of investigation and dissemination of innovations.

On the other hand, the LDTC experience challenges the linear, abstract thinking lodged in the instrumentality perspective. Recognition of the challenge arises from the context in which the attempt was made to radically change LDTC's mission. Before LDTC was restructured to accommodate development objectives into its portfolio, its identity turned on educational programs designed to partially compensate for the inadequacies and imbalances embedded in the formal education system. Its offerings were designed, accordingly, as alternative means to enhance education missed. Once development was granted priority status by government, LDTC's external mission was expanded concomitantly. At the same time, however, its autonomous status was revoked. The Service Agency was tasked with and supported for income generation, cooperative development, staff training, and other nonformal education services while its capacity (admittedly undeveloped at this critical stage of history) to reconfigure its organizational form according to client need was abrogated. What the Service Agency did in this predicament was to offer limited services in the same mode as its traditional educational offerings: as provider to client.

In this scheme the clients of the Service Agency's nonformal education programs remained as much pupils as the students of the formal system. While the new client in the expansion was now more clearly the development technician located somewhere within the service delivery system, the ultimate rural client was still to be treated as a consumer of services presumably more efficiently tailored to meet his or her needs for productivity and marketability in the drive toward modernization. That client was still a receptor of new knowledge, a beneficiary, so to speak, who, given a "fair chance," would potentially make the most of his or her own ambition, "God-given" talent, and new skills to advance up the social and economic development ladder.

In concluding his recent study of LDTC's role in helping rural groups to generate income, former USAID contract adviser Richard Betz in his doctoral dissertation questions the end result of educating for increased production as a purely technical problem:

Ultimately the issue comes down to increased production/income and control over production. The question becomes one of who benefits from the increased production. Where do increased income and resulting profits accumulate? If the beneficiary are the elites in the modern sector, then the approach presented here is of no more benefit to the millions of rural poor than previous development efforts. Such questions are ultimately settled in the political arena. (1984, p. 166.)

In the context of Lesotho's political economy, insofar as basic questions about the limited options of dependency, the beneficiaries of capital accumulation, and the social and cultural effects of increasing market productivity as an end of education go unaddressed, the rural client remained a pawn to advice and educational programs devised centrally. The educational programs were still managed from an increasingly rigid administrative structure, which itself was a creature of political realities interpreted by certain national and international powers. The impetus to reproduce the complex of dependency-conditioned institutional relations in Lesotho's rural areas thus remained overwhelming.

The fact LDTC had adopted technical innovations to modify its programs by soliciting the input of its clients through nonformal education did not alter the basic conditions under which its services were (and still are) offered. As with any service outreach program, programmatic responses are dependent on the resources available to deliver them. The allocation of those resources is a complex process involving not only the contributions and priorities of international assistance agencies, but also the dynamics of international and national political economics. The direct political involvement of the ultimate consumers of these programs in making even basic decisions about curriculum remains circumscribed totally by bureaucratically contrived organizational forms.

If the government's real intention at the time was to strengthen LDTC's capacity to service other organizations to respond to local needs, then the function of the variegated development discourses it had produced had the effect of containing the expression of such needs within certain ideological, technical, and apolitical parameters. The development discourses deployed under such parameters had the effect of delimiting the sociopolitical space in which only certain kinds of questions could be asked to implement innovations in nonformal education. Such innovations were limited to development-specific measures as increased numbers of clients reached, higher program participation rates, and maybe, somewhere down the line, indicators of better and more linkages between the economy and the educational system. The result intended was a reproduction of the basic social and economic patterns that prevailed already, only with more widespread participation. Notions of critical thinking, culture, and power (e.g., Giroux, 1983, pp. 215–216)—essential elements of recent innovation discourse (Fullan, 1991)—disappear at last under the imperatives of the overarching institutional relations in force.

Insofar as the goals of the nonformal education offerings of the Service Agency had become directed toward developmental ends in the absence of critical reflection by the rural client, the client remained an object rather than a subject of education. The function of the educational process then is to absorb nonparticipating, marginal citizens by extending duplicates of centralized organizational forms to the local level.

In Lesotho this structural duplication has evolved into a variety of institutional forms. Development-derived discourses about capital accumulation, profit maximization, growth as a self-justifying end, efficiency, productivity, labor, management, and other prerequisites to a modern capital economy are analogs to institutional forms whose function is to regulate the transition from one kind of dependency to another within a preexisting and evolving spectrum of administrative, political, economic, and social relations. The attempt to restructure LDTC can be understood as contradictory only in this light. Complicating its traditional compensatory mission with development logic, LDTC took on more than could be managed within the constraints of the government's capacities to sustain in the face of flagging international commitments.

Furthering the cause of development through the administrative apparatus of government-supported education innovation may well be an untenable process. The complexities involved in realizing the multifaceted role of education, when considered in the harsh light of Lesotho's evolving state of dependency, seem to expose the contradictions of centrally initiated programs more starkly, tending to weaken support. The expansion of LDTC's mission was undertaken at least in part to consolidate the preeminent position of government and other organizations involved in the promotion of development only by avoiding contextual issues of dependency. By so doing, rural Basotho have once again been relegated to the status of consumers within a system over which they can assert no real control.

NOTES

1. The Lesotho Distance Teaching Centre today undertakes a variety of activities which go beyond what has traditionally been regarded as "distance" or "correspondence" education. For a review of programs and activities commonly referred to as distance teaching, the following works can be consulted: Neil, 1981; Daniel and

Stroud, 1981; Erdos, 1967; Kabwasa and Raunda, 1973; UNESCO, 1978; Young, Perraton, Jenkins, and Dodds, 1991; Perraton, 1991; Dodds and Mayo, 1992; Murphy and Zhiri, 1992.

2. Since the early 1980s ultimate responsibility for plot allocations has resided legally with the Ministry of the Interior, with actual allocations made by village-based land committees (Ferguson, 1990, pp. 142–143), the principal criterion for eligibility being marriage and a family.

3. This observation, incidentally, contrasts rather starkly with the sanguine assessment made by the World Bank of the relative economic equality characteristic of rural areas (Bardill and Cobbe, 1985).

4. The five-year planning process instituted more than twenty years ago has consistently counted on the infusion of foreign assistance to cover the development activities of government. Recurrent costs for the most part have been covered by domestic taxation. The International Monetary Fund, however, has implemented a structural adjustment loan in the past ten years that has stressed domestic productivity and the domestic tax base further.

In an early effort to curb its consequential increasing dependency on external resources, the government embarked on an austerity program, imposing restrictions on new hiring and adopting other measures to reduce the rate of increase of its expenditures (USAID/Lesotho, 1983). Trends toward bureaucratic expansion and requirements for external support of recurrent costs, nonetheless, have not been reversed.

5. An historical account of the development of LDTC as an institution has not been undertaken to date. Several project evaluators, however, reviewing documents, activity chronicles, statistical records, and personal accounts, have drawn inferences mainly from the perspective of donor interest in determining the extent to which specific project development objectives have been accomplished (see, for instance, Krueger, Valdivia, and Wilbur, 1983; Cain and Method, 1979).

6. The World-Bank-supported comparative study (Murphy and Zhiri, 1992) of the organization of distance-education programs at the secondary level provides useful information on alternative approaches to institutionalizing delivery of distance-education services. See also Perraton's (1991) analysis of administrative structures for distance education done for the Commonwealth Secretariat and The Commonwealth of Learning. A 1980 work by Young, Perraton, Jenkins, and Dodds, updated for the International Extension College in 1991, reviews the utility of different models and approaches implemented in selected countries for rural and village education.

7. An example of the effort put into surveying village needs over one decade of LDTC's operations can be seen in Makheta and Bastian, 1980.

8. Rihani's study (1993) of literacy programs for out-of-school youth found needs for more support for the staffs of ninety outlying centers, an innovation implemented by LDTC to address the protracted and growing problem of low school attendance, especially for boys, in the late 1980s. The conclusion she reached relevant to this study was that the current professional staff and material resource base of LDTC proper was inadequate to address the needs.

9. Rostowian-derived versions of economic progress still underlie the ideology of foreign assistance to education to this day, that of USAID being only one case in point. Education is viewed as one of several indispensable capital factors required to cultivate a critical mass of productive units for economic "take-off" toward self-sustaining growth. While Rostow's approach is seen more suitable for the analysis of industrialization, its fundamental assumptions remain embedded in macro-versions of international development policies aimed to increase the external efficiencies of education.

10. An exegesis on how that orientation in turn is informed by deeply rooted and culturally relative convictions about human progress and social change is

treated in Preston (1985) and others. Development and social change are analyzed as ideologically informed practices applied by agencies of the state and international organizations. Frequently, the interests pushing the diffusion of these practices are not clear, compatible, or straightforward. Nonetheless, the point of departure for the enterprise of development planning *assumes* the validity of these assumptions more or less by default, as they rarely enter the policy-making dialogue in explicit terms.

      11. LDTC staff were trained to pursue policies of maximum consultation with local leaders. Staff development activities, both in the form of on-site training and degree and nondegree study abroad, have stressed techniques for engaging local groups in stating their own needs and objectives with the expectation that appropriate services and programs would be forthcoming from LDTC.

      12. The most recent copy of LDTC's *Annual Report* (Feb. 1992-Feb. 1993) indicates an approved staffing total of ninety. Examples of program initiatives aimed to facilitate the development of rural special interest groups, for example, women's cooperatives and other demand-driven tailored offerings, particularly from diverse village groups concerned with forming cooperatives and generating income, grew significantly during the period (Vargas-Adams and Bastian, 1983).

REFERENCES

Amin, S. *Unequal Development, An Essay on the Social Formations of Peripheral Capitalism.* New York: Monthly Review Press, 1976.

Bardill, J.E., and J.H. Cobbe. 1985. *Lesotho: Dilemmas of Dependence in Southern Africa.* Boulder: Westview Press.

Barnett, S.A., and N. Engle. *Effective Institution Building, A Guide for Project Designers and Project Managers Based on Lessons Learned from the AID Portfolio.* Washington, D.C.: USAID, 1982.

Betz, R.L. "Organizing to Help Rural Groups: Income Generation and Rural Development in the Third World." Unpublished doctoral dissertation, School of Education, University of Massachusetts, Amherst.

Cain, B.J., and F.J. Method. *Nonformal Education Activities at Lesotho Distance Teaching Centre: Evaluation Report.* Washington, D.C.: Creative Associates International, 1979.

Cobbe, L.B. "Women's Income Generation and Informal Learning in Lesotho: A Policy-related Ethnography." Unpublished Doctoral Dissertation, College of Education, Florida State University, Tallahassee.

Daniel, J.S., and M.A. Stroud. *Distance Education: A Reassessment for the 1980s.* Australia: International Press, 1981.

Dodds, T., and J.K. Mayo. *Promise and Performance of Distance Education in Developing Nations.* Paper presented at the International Extension College's Anniversary Conference, Robinson College, England, September, 1992.

Droegkamp, J.M. *Integrating Vocational Guidance into Programs for Out-of-School Youth: A Case Study of Lesotho.* Unpublished doctoral dissertation, School of Education, University of Massachusetts, Amherst.

Eldridge, E.A. *A South African Kingdom: The Pursuit of Security in Nineteenth-century Lesotho.* Cambridge: Cambridge University Press, 1993.

Erdos, R.F. *Teaching by Correspondence.* London: Longmans Green, 1967.

Ferguson, J. *The Anti-politics Machine: "Development," Depoliticization, and Bureaucratic Power in Lesotho.* Cambridge: Cambridge University Press, 1990.

Fullan, M.G. *Implementing Educational Change: What We Know.* PHREE Background Paper Series. Washington, D.C.: World Bank, 1989.

Fullan, M.G., with S. Stiegelbauer. *The New Meaning of Educational Change.* New York: Teachers College Press, 1991.

Giroux, H. *Theory and Resistance in Education.* South Hadley: Bergin and Garvey, 1983.

Government of Lesotho (GOL). *The Education Sector Survey, Report of the Task Force.* Maseru: GOL, 1982.

Hoxeng, J. "A Semi-Systematic Approach to Nonformal Education." Unpublished paper. Washington, D.C.: USAID, 1980.

Hoxeng, J., and P. Murphy. "Third Annual Evaluation of the Lesotho Distance Teaching Centre and the USAID Project 9311054, Structuring Non-Formal Education Resources." Maseru, Lesotho: USAID, 1983.

International Labour Office (ILO). *Options for a Dependent Economy: Development, Employment and Equity Problems in Lesotho.* Addis Ababa: ILO, 1979.

Kabwasa, A., and M.M. Raunda (Eds.). *Correspondence Education in Africa.* London: Routledge Kegan Paul, 1973.

Krueger, C.E., L.A. Valdivia, and J.E. Wilbur. *Lesotho Distance Teaching Centre Annual Evaluation.* Washington, D.C.: Creative Associates International, 1983.

Lesotho Distance Teaching Centre (LDTC). *Annual Report, Feb. 92-Feb. 93.* Maseru, Lesotho: LDTC, 1993.

Lundahl, M., and Petersson, L. *The Dependent Economy: Lesotho and the Southern African Customs Union.* Boulder: Westview Press, 1991.

Makheta, L., and M.J. Bastian. "Basic Needs of Women and Children in Lesotho, Report of the National Survey." Maseru: LDTC, 1980.

Malahletha, G. *Contradictions and Ironies: Women of Lesotho.* London: Change International Reports, 1984.

McGinn, N. "The Impact of Supra-national Organizations on Public Education." In *International Journal of Educational Development.* No. 14/3, pp. 289–298.

Morolong, P. "Project Paper, The Lesotho Distance Teaching Centre (LDTC)." Unpublished paper, School of Education, University of Massachusetts, Amherst.

Murphy, P., and A. Zhiri (Eds.). *Distance Education in Anglophone Africa.* Washington, D.C.: World Bank, 1992.

Murray, C. *Families Divided: The Impact of Migrant Labour in Lesotho.* Cambridge: Cambridge University Press, 1981.

Neil, M.W. (Ed.). *Education of Adults at a Distance.* London: Kogan Page, 1981.

Patrick, D.H. *Economic Condition in Lesotho.* Maseru, Lesotho: Barclays Bank International Limited, 1978.

Perraton, H. *Administrative Structures for Distance Education.* London: Commonwealth Secretariat and The Commonwealth of Learning, 1991.

Preston, P.W. *New Trends in Development Theory.* London: Routledge and Kegan Paul, 1985.

Rihani, M. *Educating Out-of-School Youths: Alternatives to the Formal System.* Washington, D.C.: Creative Associates International, 1993

Selbin, S.M. "Anatomy of an Education Institution-building Project." Washington, D.C.: USAID, 1984a, mimeographed.

——— "The Nonformal Education Service Agency: A Support System for Grassroots Development." Unpublished project paper. Washington, D.C.: USAID, 1984b.

Tsekoa, K.M. "Lesotho Distance Teaching Center's Approach to the Promotion of Non-Formal Education for Development." Paper presented before the 25th Annual Conference of the Comparative and International Education Society, Tallahassee, March 1983.

UNESCO. *Educational Reforms and Innovations in Africa.* Paris: UNESCO, 1978.

USAID. "RFP No. Lesotho 84–001. Basic and Nonformal Education." Nairobi: East Africa Regional Economic Development Services Offices, USAID, 1984.

USAID/Lesotho. "Basic and Non-formal Education Systems." Maseru, Lesotho: USAID/Lesotho, 1983.

Vargas-Adams, E., and J.M. Bastian. *Non-formal Education in Lesotho: National Study for Policy Planning and Program Development.* Boston: World Education, 1983.

World Bank. *World Development Report 1990.* New York: Oxford University Press, 1990.

Young, M., H. Perraton, J. Jenkins, and T. Dodds. *Distance Teaching for the Third World: The Lion and the Clockwork Mouse.* Cambridge: International Extension College, 1991.

9 INNOVATION AND RESEARCH

ISSUES OF KNOWLEDGE AND POWER

Michael L. Basile and Nelly P. Stromquist

Planning and directing social change is an activity imbued with the clash of meanings—the new colliding with the old in a stream where their separate histories converge. The study of meaning is central to the study of social change. If the term "meaning" is defined as an historical construction, then its function is to interpret and guide action within specific social contexts. This contextual view of meaning counters the tendency to resort to some form of absolute truth as the sole basis to justify social change. It frames the pursuit of social studies as an effort to explore how meanings developed in a specific social context represent a momentary consensus on the interpretation of reality. In social research, this consensus is derived from commonly held assumptions about the nature and application of knowledge to the collective task of ordering social affairs at a particular time and place.

Taken in this light, the study of the introduction of innovations from one social context into another to reform institutions is an event highly charged with the conflict of meanings. One culture's working consensus on reality and its representation qualitatively differ from another's. The innovational process is then imbued with conflicting interpretations of reality, knowledge, and value.

For the one who has adopted this more flexible attitude about the derivation of specific meanings, such a conclusion may seem obvious at first, at least in the abstract. However, it strikes us that current attempts to study the diffusion of innovations fail to appreciate the significance of alternative visions of reality and their interpretation as a basis for change. In the case studies on technological educational innovation presented here, it is our intention to study the accommodation of social difference according to local circumstance. In the abstract, the empirical data used in the case studies to describe and support the diffusion of the innovations are framed with this intent to accommodate local circumstance as a necessary condition to facilitate the adoption process. Yet by virtue of its very presence, the abstract intention to make provision for social difference falls short of speaking to deeply held assumptions about supporting one system for the production and application of social knowledge at the expense of others. These assumptions collectively serve to underpin, indeed conceptually frame, the innovation process in common practice today. They have to do with the virtually automatic legitimacy accorded to empirical research and its validity in guiding and supporting the introduction of innovations into educational institutions of the Third World.

In the explicit sense, the four case studies on technological innovations in this volume are concerned with attempts to remedy the practical problems that arise while improving educational institutions (e.g., schools, classroom instruction, teaching, and educational administration). In the implicit sense, however, overemphasis on the practical tends to divert our attention from the acutely important project of analyzing meaning. As a first step in the analytical process, we adopt the view of institutions as collectivities that embody a set of both traditional and evolving social relations. Such a view allows us to surface the assumptions that implicitly undergird deliberate attempts to change institutions on the basis of empirical research alone.

This strategy for the analysis of meaning probes beyond the explicitly evaluative focus employed by the authors of the case studies. For as practitioners/researchers, their primary interest is to examine how specific instances of institutional innovation fared according to the standards of empirical research applied to evaluate the extent of success or failure. "What went right and what went wrong so that we can know how to do better the next time around?" is the question that guides their respective inquiries. It is primarily a *practical* question with an obvious intent: to improve the innovational process to make adoption more effective.

With this explicitly evaluative intent, however, the authors of the studies have provided the opportunity for us as editors to deal with another question that is implicit in the conduct of empirical research and its social application. The process of institutional innovation appears to depend increasingly on a specific approach to applied research for guidance and support. Derived from empirical methodology, the approach serves to generate theories devised to regulate the innovation process. The theories are applied to the practical task of rationalizing and delineating the course of innovation within specific institutional contexts. As such, the organization and implementation of innovations are activities derivative of the research programs in which they are based. As constellations of meanings, innovation theories are "mobilized" to guide social action.

The term "mobilization of meaning" is taken from Thompson's (1984, pp. 3–6) analysis wherein he proposes reexamination of the social role of functionalist (i.e., empiricist) social science with a view to illuminate the relationships of power embedded in its research programs. To a large extent, his invitation is particularly fitting for those of us engaged in the practice of using empirical research to guide the institutional innovation process. For, once the possibility that the bases of meaning vary according to their place in history is accepted, the problem of generating and analyzing empirical data can be approached as a context-bound activity often prone to disavow or ignore its own socioeconomic origins.

The tendency, indeed the need, for empiricist research to discount its historical referents is indicative of an unconscious, structural predilection for generating knowledge in accordance with certain methodological prescription. The structural aspect of the predilection derives from the contingent institutional relations that are deeply embedded within a particular innovation. In the course of reviewing the cases presented here, we tried to be aware of the extent to which the questions raised in each case study were determined by the set of institutional relations in effect at the time. Of particular interest was to explore to what degree the authors were obliged to refer to conventional research standards of validity, generalizability, and adherence to accepted empirical protocol in their efforts to make sense of the data they had available to them.

Consequently, we have prepared this epilogue in order to examine an epistemic predicament. It is a fact that the four cases selected for discussion are drawn from a wide range of socioeconomic contexts. Yet, despite obvious differences in their personal political orientations and the socio-institutional contexts in which they worked, the authors found themselves in the position of having to rely on the results of the empirical research that was done on their respective innovations. The reliance is noteworthy because it is common to all the articles irrespective of personal philosophy, case history, or social situation. Whether they supported or criticized the merits of their respective innovations, the data available to the authors were collected and analyzed according to the dominant mode of empirical research in practice today. It can be said without stretching the point that the epistemic knowledge base provided by the empiricist approach each had to work from determined not only what was seen but how it was interpreted.

The significance of the predicament is that it is very widespread, as it is implicated in the majority of the innovational support extended by virtually all Western bilateral and multilateral donors. Burrell and Morgan's (1979) observation describes the scope of the problem in practical terms:

It is a regrettable fact that a major proportion of work in the social sciences at the present time results in abstracted empiricism. The drive to obtain research funding to sustain teams of research workers tends to favor the collection of large quantities of empirical data. Indeed, the collection and processing of such data is often equated with the total research effort and is regarded as an essential ingredient of any proposal likely to meet the "quality control" requirements of research funding institutions. The demands for pragmatic results from social science research programmes also tends [sic] to favor some form of substantive information output. Under the pressure of such forces, research programmes often become tailored to the requirements and methods of their data base, to the extent that theoretical assumptions with regard to basic ontology, epistemology and human nature are relegated to a background role and are eventually violated by the demands of empiricism. It is no exaggeration to suggest that there is scarcely a theoretical perspective within the context of the functionalist paradigm which has not been translated into abstract empiricism of one form or another. (pp.105–106)

The distinction between empiricist and alternative modes of research is important to consider in the analysis of social change because adherence to one mode at the expense of others can result in too narrow a field of view and the imposition of prescriptions for innovation that may conceal their contextual and ideological origins. The review by Reason and Rowan (1981, pp. 43–51) of Mitroff and Kilmann (1978) draws the distinction between different paradigmaic approaches to the generation of social science data with a view to raise consciousness about the contextual underpinnings of traditional research methods. Recognition of at least the theoretical possibility of paradigmatic alternatives has allowed us to review the articles from outside the constraints of the functionalist perspective.

In this light, our review of the articles on innovation diffusion across cultural settings aims to expand and augment movement toward the adoption of alternative modes of research to guide the innovation process. Noteworthy in the cases we present here is the effort on the part of each of their authors to interpret empirical findings so as to draw conclusions useful for guiding the implementation of innovation elsewhere, irrespective of content and original setting. In some instances, the authors accept implicitly the validity of the research methodology employed to create and analyze the data and to draw conclusions more or less aligned with the data. In others, they take a more critical view of findings, grappling with the constraints of empirical methodology to draw conclusions that in actuality run counter to the data and the methods used to obtain them. Our efforts in this epilogue are thus directed toward examining the contradictions and difficulties that are inherent in the uncritical adoption of empirical research findings for the purposes of innovation.

EPISTEMOLOGICAL ISSUES ACROSS THE CASES

The cases on technological innovation were not prepared by their authors to raise issues of epistemology. In reviewing them, however, it became apparent to us that empirical research conducted in the positivistic tradition of social science was itself an important factor to consider in the analysis and diffusion of innovations. For, in developing countries, decisions to adopt innovations enter the terrain of the state and its institutional role in society. The terrain of the state is foremost a political realm in which decision makers are called on to set policy across a spectrum of social sectors, education being one. The setting of policy is a process through which contesting spheres of influence resolve their differences in the course of implementing different versions of modernization. Contesting for relative control over the innovation process is, inescapably, an activity characterized by competition among alignments of institutional and individual coalitions seeking to justify the validity of their respective positions to each other and to the public at large.

The effort to win support for the structure the innovation has, therefore, usually been grounded in some generally acceptable paradigm of scientific research, one that can carry weight sufficient to overcome institutionalized resistance of all kinds. In the cases of institutional innovation for modernization (i.e., the use of new technologies and procedures) the empirical model of data collection and analysis, conducted and presented ideally in quantitative, ergo "objective," forms is given credence over alternative models whose roots may be more local and traditional—and therefore "unscientific."

Justification for innovations in educational policy is increasingly dependent on such empiricist approaches. Over the course of the past three decades of development, this reliance has developed into a coalition of western academic experts and Third World policymakers, whose common interest is expressed in terminology reminiscent of Brian Fay's (1975) "policy science." The making of public policy, in other words, is a process now viewed as the proper preserve of those acceptably credentialed in its scientific and technological lexicon. The legitimate power accorded to the practitioners of policy science derives from the integration of a system of meritocractic qualifications with administrative rank, the source of the former residing in academic circles of the West while the structure for the latter is spread throughout tertiary sectors of the Third World.

At the present stage in the history of development assistance the positivist mode of empirical research is clearly established and dominant. Characterized foremost by strict universal standards of procedure, the empiricist mode now sets the parameters for knowledge production for the implementation and diffusion of innovations. While efforts to operationalize the empirical research mode might appear to be straightforward, they are susceptible to oversimplification. There is a strong tendency to reduce the conduct of research to a matter of correct procedure alone. The reductionist tendency of empiricism, however, is often concealed by the legitimacy accorded to its compelling logic: the dictates of valid research procedure, if followed faithfully, produce good findings, which, in their turn, should serve as the basis for enlightened policy.

It is, however, an historical fact that the empiricist approach is an adaptation imported from the natural sciences (Preston, 1985). The practice of the natural sciences comprises the historical locus where the isolation of research variables was conceived to be an ideal process that ought to be intrinsically free of the complexities of human intervention. Correctness of empirical procedure calls for the isolation of a set of variables whose interactions are to be observed, recorded, gauged, processed, and analyzed for interpretation free of the biases of the researcher. The results of the investigation are then converted into interpretations for entry into the policy-making dialogue as technically legitimate findings—*usually stated in terms that are politically neutral*—which are taken as possessing full scientific legitimacy.

The neutrality of the researcher's role in this process is carefully prescribed by strict observance of the rules of objectivity. Objectivity is preserved to the extent the researcher maintains distance from the subjects of the research, or, in the case of educational innovation, teachers, administrators, and students. New knowledge is produced and disseminated objectively so that its eventual client/consumer is protected from the bias of its producer. (One standard of objectivity for social research observed more in the abstract than in actuality for practical reasons is the replicability of results. Researchers acting independently, for instance, are supposed to achieve substantially similar results.) Evidence thus gathered results in findings that are indicative of an internal logic irrespective of individual personality and local circumstance.

The ideal model of empirical research, however, becomes troublesome when applied to matters of social inquiry. Since the contributions of Comte and Durkheim, the method of producing legitimate knowledge of society has never been addressed as cleanly as it has been possible to manage in the natural sciences. The "science of society" and its variations have struggled with spheres of inquiry in which the identification and isolation of variables for objective observation and testing are inevitably ambiguous and arbitrary. The confirmation, denial, or modification of hypotheses according to such variables, regrettable and frustrating as it may be to the empirical social researcher, is not an "exact" science. Sources of ambiguity and authority are always issues to be faced in the conduct of social inquiry. Data is gathered for a purpose—either to carry out or to modify social policy. As such, interpretations of findings are made and evaluated in the political context of stakeholder involved in the struggle to administer social (including educational) reform.

A Look at Innovation in Different Countries

The case studies on educational innovation presented in this volume offer the opportunity to examine how real-life instances of empirical research findings were reoriented to fit the radically different social perspectives of their authors. Implicitly, in the effort to extract learning from very different data sources, the authors raised issues about the epistemological and methodological constraints of the functionalist paradigm of empirical research. The issues challenge the assumption that the knowledge-production process can be exempted from the reproductive and ideological forces at work in the implementation of innovations by virtue of its adherence to the empiricist internal procedural code alone. Recourse to purity of method as a way to circumvent the unpredictability of the institutional environment remains the chief instrumental remedy provided by the empiricist approach. If resorted to exclusively as the primary legitimate means to generate policy alternatives, however, it could and does have consequences for the orientation and control of the knowledge-production process for decision making. We look at how this problem surfaces in each of the cases reviewed here. At the conclusion of each case, issues are raised about its implications for the possible exclusion of alternative approaches to social analysis and change.

Impact in Six Countries

H. Dean Nielsen and William K. Cummings contend with the problem of conducting research in highly complex cross-cultural environments by constructing an analytical framework that contains five constellations of investigative variables. The constellations are designed to cope with preexisting environmental complexity and ambiguity by adopting the suggestion of Havelock and Huberman (1977) that each innovational situation represents a unique configuration of elements that deserves special attention. This suggestion, on the one hand, releases the researchers from the tight methodological constraints of designing a research protocol with which total control is assumed possible. The operational context into which each variation of the innovation IMPACT was introduced was radically different. The application of a narrow set of sharply focused variables under such conditions would have been unfeasible. In response to this problem, the authors devised a comparatively loose set of theoretical constructs to use as investigative variables: (1) strength of the innovation's prototype, (2) availability of resources for dissemination, (3) administrative context, (4) project organization, and (5) consistency and skillfulness of leadership. Additional elements of focus were subsumed under each of these comprehensive constellations. The authors then applied the framework to the comparative analysis of five cases of "national level dissemination." The learning derived from the observations were then evaluated for possible application elsewhere.

The conclusions reached by Nielsen and Cummings are offered in the context of what seems to work best under the conditions actually encountered: success seems to be related directly to the degree of flexibility in implementation. The more adept administrators are in modifying the original concept to suit local circumstances, the greater the chances the innovation would take hold. Extending the innovation to marginal areas tends to conflict with its cost-saving objectives as services provided to outlying rural areas require the introduction of additional incentives. The commitment and talent of leadership prove to be more indicative of success than the quality and extent of research documentation available on the innovation itself. Strong advocacy and the reputation of success are instrumental in marshaling necessary support for dissemination. The innovation is more readily spread where "policy space" exists. Competition from current practice makes it more difficult for the innovation to take root. The involvement of foreign advisers produces mixed results. In some cases it helps, while in others it is not of itself a necessary condition for local "penetration."

Now, the question arises as to how such research findings are to be used to guide the innovation process across a spectrum of diverse institutional and cultural settings. The findings were derived as a result of an investigation of past practice in several countries. How are they to be converted into knowledge to guide implementation in other times and places? The conversion process involved is one whereby empirical findings, in this case those that are for the most part qualitative in nature, are abstracted for application to other social contexts. This abstraction activity is an integral part of knowledge-creation and application within the functionalist paradigm. Abstraction follows analysis. Analysis is based on observation. Observation in turn is made on the basis of the hypothesis originally advanced to guide the observation: in this case, the five investigative variables used by the authors to set up the research protocol in the first place.

What we have here are the basic elements of a knowledge-development/action cycle reminiscent of the "experiential learning cycle" so basic to individual change inducement strategies practiced in applied group psychology since the late 1940s. The premise of the cycle is that study of experience through abstraction and generalization provides a useful guide for future behavior modification. In the case of cross-cultural innovation, the idea that experience gained in one context can logically guide action in another is an extension of interpersonal psychology to an international scale. But in this extension the central unifying focus, the individual and his/her deliberate experimentation with new behavior, is lost. In its stead is inserted an ideal model of institutional rationality, where one cultural definition of ideal social behavior relegates alternatives to the level of tradition, that is to irrationality. New knowledge is not used to guide *individual behavior;* it is extracted from its own past, and, through a mirror image of its own making, is transposed as an *institutional program of action in an entirely different social context.*

The spread of knowledge to guide institutional innovation is thus an activity imbued with value and power. It seeks to reproduce itself in places beyond its original genesis. In so doing, it necessarily takes on new forms, depending on how the key actors and decision makers see the innovation implemented in their respective settings. In the effort to mobilize resources sufficient to plan and manage the implementation process, administrators must reach a working consensus on what the innovation means for institutional reform. The search for new meaning and its diffusion is guided by referral to the operant scientific consensus—that is, the one derived empirically from the abstractions of research findings. The research methodology thus serves as the template for justifying, guiding, and planning implementation in other times and places.

However, given the state of the art on functionalist research to guide the implementation of innovations, it is arbitrary, if not authoritarian, for policymakers, practitioners, and their advisers to refer exclusively to the empiricist template for theoretical support. The practice of basing innovations for institutional reform on the products of this template alone is what is rapidly becoming institutionalized in the bureaucracies of the Third World.

The practice is implicit to most innovational research supported by donor nations. It comes with the territory, so to speak. This is what we meant when we referred earlier to an "unconscious, structural predilection" for knowledge legitimation. It is the very casting that molds and shapes today's lexicon of institutional innovation.

Overreliance on its prescriptions for policy reform is representative of a growing trend. But attempts to justify and order institutional reform on the basis of the "scientific logic" inherent in the empiricist research design alone cannot be supported by the rigor, the clarity, or the certainty of the research itself, as the "looseness" of the variables constructed by Nielsen and Cummings reveals. As a matter of fact, a telling point made by the authors themselves midway through their chapter should be taken to heart. The purported linkage between the quality and availability of innovation research documentation and successful implementation is tenuous under any circumstances. According to them, the availability of good research findings is evidently not sufficient practical grounds for successful implementation, regrettable as that conclusion may seem to the applied empirical researcher.

This insight underscores the twice-removed split between knowledge and action, a split corresponding to the need to abstract from the parameters of concrete observation in order to guide intervention elsewhere. A whole string of history inevitably intervenes between the production and the adoption of empirical research knowledge as a guide to policy adjustment.

Bypassing history will not help. Without history, improving the quality of research according to universal standards can itself be diversionary. Better research conducted by better trained personnel does not necessarily address issues of value and power. On the contrary, it often ignores or distorts them. In the breach, lack of good quantitative data merely offers plausible excuse for the further extension of current forms of empiricist methodology without questioning their ideological function. The questions that need to be raised about the diffusion of innovations have to do with the terms on which the supportive research is conducted. Who determines the questions to ask, the methods to be applied, and the use to which the results are to be put—experts alone or a coalition of experts, policymakers, and political leaders? How are research subjects, such as the masses, treated? Whose interests are reflected in the findings and the programs they are to guide? The conduct of the research protocol represents the intersection between "our" science and "their" culture, the point at which alternative knowledge creation and diffusion systems clash. Fundamentally, the rationalization of change is subject to historical position. It is not simply a result of the compelling logic of positivistic objectivity.

This is not to argue against the need for objectivity in the production of social knowledge. It is, however, a plea to recognize the fallacy of adopting empiricist research findings primarily because they claim to be objective or, alternatively, to reject other forms of knowledge production because they are not. The adoption of innovation occurs within a climate where several economic, political, and cultural forces converge. There is no escape through the portal of empiricism. According to Nielsen and Cummings, the process of implementing a particular educational reform that may be conceptually sound depends finally on how individual administrators and policymakers contend with the forces of vested interest by employing a combination of administrative skills, committed leadership, and technical assistance within the context of an accommodating bureaucracy. This conclusion, however, is more a result of experiential insight than of direct inferential logic. We should not fail to take this into account when introducing new knowledge into other places.

In short, an important issue to consider in the IMPACT case is how to go about the business of stimulating change without begging the question of the relations of power in effect at the time. First, as is the case with most innovations, the scope of the evaluation of IMPACT Nielsen and Cummings were directed to undertake was determined by those institutions which had already made direct investments in the project, namely, international donors and national governments through their ministries of education. The immediate question that arises concerns the independence with which the evaluative task could have been approached from the beginning. Considering the fact that program evaluation is usually supported by those most deeply invested, what could have been done to broaden the scope to include questions of value and power?

The multiple instances of social and institutional conflicts uncovered by the authors in the first several pages of their article seem far removed from the neutral tone of the technical scope of the research variables they actually used to guide their research. The five countries involved in the technological innovations—Malaysia, Indonesia, Jamaica, Liberia, and Bangladesh (the original model was developed in the Philippines in the early 1970s)—obviously presented unique and serious obstacles to successful adoption of what was purported to be a highly flexible innovation design. Emergent conflicts between teachers, parents, school administrators, and other involved groups, including donors, which evidently had a negative impact on the actual extent and pacing of adoption, are highly charged with issues of personal and social value and power. The scope of Nielsen and Cummings's analysis, however, reduces such issues of meaning to questions of organizational development and dissemination (pp. 114–120, this volume), the research themes out of which the authors hypothesized their variables. This decision, perhaps more than any other, is what is responsible for circumscribing their empirical research design. It thereby ruled out focus on the nature of the conflicts, their socioeconomic origins, their historical referents, and the societal and institutional context by which the scope and the depth of educational reform were predetermined.

Second, the attempt to investigate the adoption process according to those variables revealed what appeared to be deep conflicts of social value and political power at the level of technical adjustment. For example, the variable, "consistency and skillfulness of leadership," is a term that connotes, in ostensibly neutral tone, a certain configuration of stable, competent political support necessary for successful adoption. However, the variable is far from neutral. Enmeshed in its discourse is a regulatory political orientation that presupposes societal stability, institutional hierarchy, and an implicit model of administrative rationality as essential to the innovational process. Attention is thereby diverted to the technical requisites needed for the control of the essentialist attributes of leadership consistency and personal skill.

The resultant research protocol then channels inquiry into a dialectical relationship. An implicit ideal model of skillful leadership in an ideal institutional environment is juxtaposed against its binary opposite: a potpourri of institutional and personal lacks, gaps, and barriers to progress. The research agenda is set. The knowledge-generation process is safely ensconced within the crucible of a technical problem. Finally, the effect of constricting the inquiry is twofold: the institutional relationships required to organize and conduct the research operation are legitimated and the scope of inquiry is reduced. The research program is controlled at the level of administrative regulation. Whatever conflicts arose in the nature of what was to be taught, the resources needed to teach, and the form of instruction to be applied still remain the prerogative of the coterie of policymakers and expert specialists called on to manage the innovation process. One does not need to direct—indeed, one is precluded from directing—the inquiry to the roots of conflict and how they relate to the distribution of economic and political power.

The extent and depth of participation in the inquiry process is consequently structured by surveys of representative samples of affected citizenry, among them teachers, parents, and students. Their role is thus limited to replying to the questions put before them, and not to structuring those questions, analyzing their replies, or participating actively in the collective task of changing educational or social policy as a result.

The article on Mexico's Telesecondary project also makes use of empirical research. Drawing on several studies of Telesecondary, particularly the one conducted by Stanford University in 1973, Félix Cadena describes the relationship between research findings and the socioeconomic context in terms more reflective of ideological position than those used by Nielsen and Cummings. Tracing the history of secondary education, Cadena undertakes his analysis of the needs of the Mexican state to consolidate its role in unification and modernization. Education at the time of the Mexican revolution fifty years ago became the focus of special attention, with several creative innovations being introduced, only to be supplanted by adoption of U.S. and French models almost exclusively in recent years. Since the 1960s, problems of Mexican education, particularly at the secondary level, had been defined in terms of needs to expand access under conditions of insufficient capacity, needs for better skill-trained employees, and mounting crises of financial scarcity.

Against this backdrop the Mexican state decided to introduce televised instruction at the secondary level in the late 1960s as a way to compensate for deficiencies it faced in trying to expand the traditional model of classroom instruction. Adopted originally in 1968, the Telesecondary model was based initially on elements of an Italian prototype, with the objectives of extending secondary-level subject matter to rural areas which lacked adequate facilities, or where the delivery of present services was deficient. The delivery model was structured using the "tele-classroom." Provisions were made for program production, evaluation and follow-up, community participation, accreditation, selection of students, and institutional coordination and support. The dissemination process went through a series of six progressive stages that included initial experimentation and development of the prototypical model, national expansion, external evaluation, national education reform (1970–1976), resolution of the teacher labor crisis (1975–1977), and the introduction of improvements in the Telesecondary delivery system.

In his analysis, Cadena refers to the conclusions of several empirical studies that explored the contribution made by dissemination of the Telesecondary model to the basic goals the Mexican state had promoted for secondary education: namely, the satisfaction of social demand; recognition of achievement levels comparable with those taught in traditional classroom instruction; improvements in retention and internal efficiency levels; successful expansion of an innovative model for educational television; and the successful reproduction of the ideological and technical forces of economic modernization, including consolidation of the nation-state, spread of the populist ideology, and reinforcement of the dialectical relation between the working and ruling classes.

An issue raised implicitly by Cadena is the role empirical research itself played in legitimating the social reproduction of ideology and technology. That the contribution of educational television had been instrumental in instilling the ideology and technology of "hope, nationalism, and modernity" is indicated by the research. Yet, in addition to that, the methodology used in the research process tended to reproduce the very same ideology and technology. The research he cites assumed that legitimate ways to collect, analyze, and interpret data were empiricist. The fact that Cadena referred to such empirical studies in his analysis has less to do with their availability than with their authority as legitimate sources of new knowledge.

The empiricist research technology thus reproduces the social relations that prevail. The research process does not stand objectively apart from the system of social relations in current force. To the contrary, it is an integral part of them. It legitimates them. Cadena is then left to interpret the existing data reflectively, in ways outside the stream of empiricist procedure. In so doing, however, he makes use of the research available to bring out critical points, thereby allowing us to draw fresh inferences about the penetration of technocratic consciousness into the conventional research process. While his effort in this respect is directed neither toward an invalidation nor toward a critique of his source material itself, his unorthodox approach to the analysis of findings permits alternative interpretations to be made. We are thereby supported in our own effort to see the research material as an instance of the social reproductive process in a critical light, rather than having to accept the validity of its premises and subsequent conclusions prima facie.

The several empirical studies conducted on the efficacy of Telesecondary programming to which Cadena refers stress a comparison of results with its alternative: traditional classroom teaching. Left only with such data and without the benefit of Cadena's interpretive comments, one would be tempted to conclude that, with appropriate adjustment and improvements, the model could serve its intended audience effectively at reduced cost to the state and leave it to the experts, policymakers, and administrators to implement the necessary improvements suggested by the data and be done with it. One would therefore not have to address larger issues of social reproduction and the needs of the state at all.

In spite of these conclusions, Cadena does just that. Into the previously empirical analysis, he interjects a dialectical, critical analysis that could well serve as a forerunner of community discussion. The focus of the discussion could well be on the social function of the state to "strengthen nationalism" to counteract the influence of the United States on cultural expectations, and to inculcate attitudes essential for modernization of the labor force.

The community-level discussion would turn on the role of the school as the primary means to undertake the socialization task at a critical early age. The school, being located in the neighborhood and the community, would thus become the primary fulcrum where the extension of state interest is contested at the local level. It would provide the opportunity for the members of a community to examine together their own system of values and to ascertain their relative collective power vis-à-vis the state. Instead of setting the parameters of that dialogue entirely by the results of the empirical research mandated by administrative fiat, the community could be the point at which systems of knowledge and value are assessed and choices made. In this dialogical research process, the community is not merely *consulted by the state,* as is the case with conventional research methods. Quite the reverse. The state and its agents are *consulted by the community* in the community's efforts to inform its deliberative process. The community is not just the recipient of better televised instruction. It may well develop its own.

Participatory research lends itself to the exercise of community control through the mutual and informed assessment of needs, problems, resources, possibilities, and constraints. The form of participation is consonant with the practice of the local knowledge system. Whatever local belief systems are in effect at a particular moment in history, therefore, need not be wholly consistent. The participatory assessment of conflicting belief systems is what matters. That based on empirical research is only one among many. The choice is really about who generates the choices and who controls the knowledge systems to inform them.

Brazil's Logos II

Citing extensive quantitative evidence, João Batista Araujo e Oliveira and François Orivel focus on the most salient characteristics of Brazil's innovation in teacher education known as Logos II. Previous evaluations of the project's prototype, Logos I, indicated that certain characteristics were important in disseminating the innovation on a wider scale: reach in-service teachers in-situ; deliver a general (subject matter) and educational (pedagogical) curriculum in a competency-based format; provide support materials and staff assistance at nearby learning centers; and introduce micro-teaching as a system of peer supervision.

This instructional format was organized and managed through a three-tiered system of support. The first was concerned with organization of the local level (the Telesecondary centers) around the services provided by the monitor, who served a multifunction role from facilities manager to individual counselor. The second tier involved coordination by a group (committee) at the state (provincial) level. The third was shared by the financial and decision-making authority of the Ministry of Education and Culture, which exercised responsibility for resource distribution and monitoring at the state level. The remaining responsibility for implementation was exercised by a privately commissioned organization (CETEB), whose functions were the overall dissemination effort—establishment of the Telesecondary centers, materials development and distribution, training of staff, supervision, evaluation, and recommendations for expansion and other steps necessary for policy implementation.

Oliveira and Orivel refer to extensive data gathered from a previous study of the innovation they undertook themselves to analyze the results achieved by Logos II in the areas of cost-effectiveness and performance success, including teacher characteristics, student results, and comparative effectiveness (internal efficiency). Stated briefly, overall achievement for Logos II was "better than anticipated originally," when measured in terms of rates of progression through the modular units, costs relative to numbers of students, and completion rates. The authors attribute these successes to the project's structural concern for the management of monitors and teacher motivation through effective, permanent supervision. In addition to salary incentives, the monitors, as key staff, enjoyed an unusual amount of "freedom and prestige." Individual pacing with phased success was important to the teacher participants. A variety of group and individual peer reinforcement and support activities was also structured into the delivery system. During implementation stages, needs for more decentralized management allowed for variation in pacing and local control.

While Logos II was conceived and planned centrally, its implementation process over time provided for local participation in decision-making, modification of concepts, and interaction with other provincial and local centers. The fact that the ministry was unable to monitor implementation rigidly permitted authority over implementation decisions to be exercised at the lower levels.

Oliveira and Orivel cast their analysis in the mold of the structural tension that exists between the "center" and the "periphery." They conclude with the experience-derived advice that program success seems to relate to the extent to which local control over programming can be exercised at the periphery. The immediate message for innovators working from the central administration is to introduce concepts and procedures with sensitivity to the motivational needs of participants and local staff.

The meaning of their conclusion, however, is more far-reaching than the satisfaction of practitioner and client needs alone. Social reproduction in education is an issue of broader and deeper concern than the simple internal manipulation of the delivery mechanism would have it. The issue of the use to which distance-education research ought to be put cannot be relegated to the level of enhancements of incentives and improvements in technique alone. The authors remind us repeatedly that "far too many" of the successful recipients of training as well as the providers of training failed to return to the classrooms from which they came. This is a structural problem that extends beyond the bounds of successful technique and delivery of services. It underscores the power of the penetration of the innovational process as a structural surrogate for the country's center. In the name of rural improvement the implementation of innovation introduces a few of the tangible benefits society has to offer to those previously excluded. In doing so, it extends the institutional relations of the country's center to the far reaches of rural society by making the delivery of services function more effectively. Structurally, however, nothing is changed. The lure of the country's center is made visible by the proximity of its more accessible services.

The implementation of Logos II is an excellent example of the effects of "local realities" on what began as a highly centralized design for a complex and large-scale innovation in teacher education. Local realities usually emerged around issues of the extent to which teachers and local monitors could exercise control over curriculum content, pacing, and data collection and analysis. The need for decentralization increased in response to problems encountered in the course of implementation. What maintained project momentum was not the planning function imposed by the center, but the almost spontaneous development of systems of communication and interpersonal support at the local level. Since centralized mechanisms for the collection and analysis of data proved to be ineffective, state and community-level exchange and support networks were established to compensate for lack of appropriate support from the central level. Moreover, information exchanged at and between the local and provincial levels did not necessarily reach the national level; rather, it became functional to the local and personal needs of teachers and monitors. Decentralization of data produced at the initiative of the periphery grew to the extent that the CETEB central office lost track of much of what was actually going on in the rural areas.

The problem of data collection and analysis in the implementation of a large-scale effort in distance education points to the need for the development of locally based systems for the generation and application of information. After the breakdown of the national system for the collection and application of project experience, nothing was available to enhance or create systems for the direct use of teachers on site. This is a problem that may be endemic to the epistemological requisites of empirical research methods applied to educational innovation. The implementation of data collection procedures usually reduces the periphery to carrying out the tedious tasks of supplying statistical information without immediate reciprocation. Oliveira and Orivel, placed in the same position, surmise that the work of teacher training along the Logos model continued in various forms depending on local need and circumstance. Teachers themselves presumably did what they had to do to get themselves through the programmed instructional system on their own.

It can be inferred from this experience that the empiricist approach at its present state of the art lacks the means to be readily integrated into the local setting. It is highly dependent on survey and analysis techniques that require specialized training, infrastructure, and equipment, with expertise and centralized coordination essential. Prone to resort to empiricist technology, the field of educational innovation has become overly dependent on this approach to support its diffusion throughout the world. At its current state of development, the field lacks alternative methods for inspiring and supporting community-based initiatives for managing formal education in all its aspects, from curriculum development to teacher training, instruction, and the administration of schools.

The problem is not simply one of extending service more effectively outward. It relates, as Oliveira and Orivel alert us repeatedly, to the increasing sway the provision of centralized social services holds over the educational establishment nationally. The local community then has to be assisted in how to regain control over the socialization of its own offspring. It is a contradictory process that begins from an immediate conflict of interest: is it reasonable to expect that the state will not simply relinquish its authority over a range of educational functions to local entities? But can the state be expected to take concrete steps to actually facilitate the process? So far, it has shown itself inept and disinclined to do so.

The more effective extension of services is an issue also addressed by Michael L. Basile in his analysis of innovation at the Lesotho Distance Teaching Centre.

Since the mid-1970s, the concept of nonformal education has served as the guiding point of reference for a number of innovations to strengthen distance education. Some of the most innovative attempts in recent years have directed foreign assistance to the objective of combining training in organization-building for the purpose of generating income. In this instance, the basic problem of the education of disfranchised citizens is defined as one of economics. Rural people, in the case of Lesotho those located in the remote mountains and valleys, lack the infrastructural support to become active participants in the grand scheme of economic development. Distance education is then considered to be one of a variety of compensatory vehicles to redress the imbalance created by disproportionate attention paid by government to the educational needs of those located in the more readily accessible, usually larger urban centers.

During the years 1975–1983 the U.S. Agency for International Development (USAID), along with other donor organizations, vigorously pursued a policy of institutional strengthening of the Lesotho Distance Teaching Centre (LDTC). One of the most experimental initiatives supported by USAID during the period was an innovation devoted entirely to nonformal education service delivery. Known as the Service Agency (SA), the innovation was directed to the purpose of providing client groups with a range of services, such as financial advice, marketing information, short-term loans, management training, and other needs-related assistance to help bridge the gap between local enterprise and regional and national economic activity.

Briefly tracing the history of the period, Basile draws on several evaluations commissioned by USAID to study the extent to which the LDTC was able to strengthen its capacity to carry out selected aspects of its national charter to provide educational opportunity to those unable to avail themselves of conventional forms of schooling. According to the evaluation material available, various branches of the LDTC, including those specializing in correspondence-course offerings, radio education, and skills training for special groups in sewing, making clothing and uniforms, and some trades, were in fact able to expand and improve services during the period. Added to the LDTC's already diverse inventory of offerings, the SA was established to provide a range of many unique services to existing groups and organizations throughout the country. Both financial and advisory assistance to organize and support SA activities became a matter of high priority for USAID.

While the attempt to shape and target the SA was initially successful—indeed the SA continues to function as of this writing, several years after the evaluations were done—Basile questions USAID's strategy of establishing the SA as the principal development arm of what heretofore had been an agency of the state concerned primarily with providing compensatory options to missed opportunities for formal education. Prior to USAID involvement, successful interventions had in fact been made to direct the energies of the SA toward the task of organizational development through extending financial advice, credit, and training to a variety of local groups concerned either with generating income or with the need to improve service delivery systems of their own.

As with the other articles of this volume, the evaluations available for Basile's review were conducted for reasons of efficiency and effectiveness improvement. The overarching focus was on the question, "Did the LDTC in fact get and implement what was paid for?" Evaluators were primarily interested in what was accomplished and what remained to be done so that midcourse corrections could be made on the basis of some relevant empirical data. The problem with this evaluative strategy as a precursor to the creation of institutional policy adjustment options is that it failed to ask questions of greater importance: what kind of development was envisioned, what role did the SA's clients play in determining the kind of assistance they were offered, and what turned out to be the consequences of redirecting the priorities and functions of an educational organ of the state, the LDTC, into a provider of assistance that was oriented toward primarily economic ends?

Basile looks at how these and similar kinds of policy issues remained the prerogative of a coalition of state and international administrators, with the effect of reserving control over curriculum content and resource allocation at the national center. Consisting of experts, specialists, and holders of key government posts, the coalition decided on the policy course the LTDC was expected to adopt, leaving the rural client in the position of consumer in a fashion not dissimilar to the student in school.

The information available to Basile as critical reviewer, however, is notable for *not* addressing these issues at all. The evaluative data he draws from occupy a space already circumscribed as a technical problem, thereby being exempt from direct political analysis. In order to get at questions of policy choice-making, his analysis is angled from the perspective of one concerned with uncovering the reproduction and extension of an implicit developmental ideology through ostensibly neutral, empiricist means. The problem with using such a critical angle is that his attempt suffers from the selfsame predicament of wearing one set of lenses to examine material created through another. It is as if problem identification and analysis in the functionalist world is an operation conducted on one plane, with the researcher's vision circumscribed entirely by his/her location. Extrication from that plane, according to Basile's analysis, is managed by formulating a critical view, one that releases the analyst from the confines of procedure which focuses attention on targets that are flat, that is to say, those lying in the same plane. The problem that remains, however, is how to go about managing the intersection of alternative views with the empiricist plane, so that communication between the functionalist and the critic is facilitated, not bypassed.

On the face of it, such a challenge might seem daunting to the literacy field worker concerned with the practical problem of developing new materials for the training of a women's marketing cooperative in a mountain town, for instance. It may even seem off the track. But when one considers the fact that functional literacy presupposes a certain view of economic and social relations, that view should not remain exempt from the critical analysis of the membership of the cooperative or the community in which it resides. External pressures to remain at the level of the practical, to teach the basics of double-entry accounting, to help organize marketing schemes, and to "give them what they need," may cause the field worker to shy from overtly political discussion and analysis. After all, the parameters of assistance have been set at a higher level and the time available is limited. Entry into matters of value and politics could be gained only on her/his own initiative and at some risk.

Whether or not such analysis is undertaken at some organized level by the membership of the cooperative and the community, certain decisions will be taken that require the commitment of community resources in the form of time, money, and personal stakes in order to help the enterprise succeed. What are the implications for the community not only of failure in the form of its expended resources, but of success? What will it mean, for example, when a regional marketing network controlled by interests based in South Africa offers the cooperative a guaranteed per-pound price for hogs-on-the-hoof so long as the condition of a minimum supply can be met? What mechanism exists for airing this debate fully within the community? What are the means for assessing the impact on previous family and community responsibilities to assure that the community controls the nature and pace of its economic development? Is the role of the literacy field worker *as representative of the state* limited to that of technical advisor only? If so, what does that say about the state's concern for the exercise of social responsibility at the community level? Does the state have an interest in strengthening the capacity of the community to ascertain and carve out its own role in the development process, even to the extent that it may buck national economic policy?

The techniques of providing such assistance, after all, are not new. Sources on action research and participatory methods for decision making are plentiful, all tested in diverse institutional settings. The problem then is not one of a deficiency of technique. The problem is rather one whereby the seat of administrative power is predisposed to exercise policy choices on the basis of what are highly centralized and limited procedures for the production of knowledge. Empirical research, particularly in its quantitative varieties, lends itself grudgingly, and with cumbersome baggage, to the task of local community empowerment. When it is used as the *exclusive,* even preferred, mechanism for the adjustment of educational development policy, it reinforces the now historical trend away from the revival of rural community life and toward accelerated urbanization. Our fear is that in their fervor for managing information according to technically objective standards, ministries may be prone to settle too quickly on the "hard facts" provided by empiricist research programs and thereby dismiss alternatives too precipitously.

The danger is not necessarily one of commission by well-informed key actors. The real danger is subtle, almost imperceptible to those who are otherwise focused on the pragmatic struggle to get things done under difficult circumstances. The danger is that the growing dependency on abstract empiricism as the blueprint for engineering social development schemes is reinforcing the momentum where rural society is depleted of its intellectual vitality. When the state becomes an unwitting accomplice in that process, the obstacles to development faced by local communities are magnified and their leadership is weakened.

FUNCTIONAL INNOVATION AND EMPIRICAL RESEARCH: IS AN ALTERNATIVE COMBINATION POSSIBLE?

In this conclusion our concern has been to explore two things: how the practice of educational innovation is imbued with the language of empirical research and the implications this innovation-empirical research tandem has for knowledge-building to guide educational reform. We see that the tandem permeates the evaluative and research data available to the extent that the act of objective critique must follow a path of resistance. To a significant extent, irrespective of their political and philosophical orientations, the authors had to begin their analyses with material that was produced to answer the questions put to them by the agencies and organizations supporting their research. Thus, it is clear that the information and explanations they provided were not independent of the phenomena they observe. By and large, the process used to produce the material was consistent with empirical research protocol. Having been invited to present material on instances of innovation with which they were closely familiar, if not involved, the authors were caught up in an epistemic predicament: what they could say about the innovation process was circumscribed by the framework in which they worked.

And this is the crux of the matter. We object to the empiricist trend overtaking educational innovation not solely because it is procedurally flawed, but because it is so apt to reproduce the regulatory relations characteristic of the current social order without addressing the basic assumptions that are being used to restructure institutional relations in foreign lands. We are not arguing that the empirical approach to knowledge-building is inferior. To what would it be inferior? If there is a system for knowledge production to guide social change that is superior to that offered by empiricism, we have yet to discover it ourselves.

What the current study of innovational diffusion teaches is a lesson not intended by its foremost practitioners. It is that this business of social development—and it is in our estimation increasingly being conducted as a business—is being practiced within an overarching framework of social and institutional arrangements that the empirical research approach is, by itself, powerless to change. To the contrary, the approach is being used to authenticate the system of incremental international aid as the primary impetus for evolutionary developmentalism. It thereby precludes genuine consideration of the alternatives we alluded to at the conclusion of each case analysis.

Again, our intention is not to argue that participatory and action research methods, as exemplars of more phenomenological approaches to understanding and action, are essentially superior. To argue thus would be to subscribe to the selfsame error of essentialist-inspired approaches to social change which are predisposed to displace focus from the situational constituents of community, family, and local ecology without due reference to the population affected. As we mentioned here before, that reference is simply not satisfied by the administration of the survey technique for sporadic consultation. When we speak of innovation, we do not mean to see it percolated within a crucible cast at the center. The mold for that casing, too, should be subject to the exercise of definition at the community level.

The very fact that we are able to critique these pieces does not release us by any stretch from the empiricist constraints that we saw imposed on the authors. Our own dependency on the results of the empirical research approach is no less compelling. We read the case material collected and analyzed by its authors and, as editors, have to draw conclusions as well. In this sense, our position as editors of these works, as a matter of fact, further reinforces the point that distance from the scene removes one from the reciprocal relations that characterize and define community. While our critical stance may be enhanced by distance, our dependency remains much as it was. We have merely taken advantage of the space that distance from vested interest has afforded us to take a step on the path of resistance.

By virtue of our position as editors, then, we were able to stand apart from such direct historical involvement with the material. We were detached sufficiently to examine how each of the authors approached the task of drawing insights from practice with which they were intimately familiar. Nonetheless, it would be a mistake to conclude from our historical detachment from specific instances of practice that we were able to raise the epistemological questions we did solely as a result of this detached position. Unlike the empirical researcher, we make no claim to political or value-free objectivity.

To the contrary, we believe that this business of educational innovation should itself be made more subject to critical innovation, it not outright reform. To this end, our focus has not been on the client, or target, of innovation, but on the systemic relations that have impinged on the innovation process. The one relation at issue here in this volume is the implicit legitimacy accorded to empirical research and the sway it has gained over the entire innovation diffusion process. The case studies we chose to include are of great value in that they raise important questions about:

The selection and management of research variables to guide the implementation of innovations. For example, who selects and manages the variables, and how do they influence policy decisions?

The need to abstract from experience in one setting to guide practice in another. How is the abstraction-action cycle used to guide future implementation?

The displacement of alternative knowledge-production systems by the introduction of empiricist methodologies. What forms of knowledge to guide educational practice currently exist in the setting? How can they be used to guide innovations in education? What impact does the adoption of empiricist research techniques have on the delegitimation of local knowledge practices?

The importance of historical position in the innovation process. What means are used to spread knowledge about innovations and how are they related to current arrangements among experts and administrators? What vision of development is being used to structure innovations in education?

The locus of initiatives for innovation. What role is played by national and international experts and administrators in the making of policy to guide curriculum and other reforms?

Finally, the path to critique. What can be done to insure that innovation is not reduced to a technical problem? What process can be developed to address issues about mass participation? How can the current practice of and incentives for turning primarily to external sources of funding and advice to guide educational reform be resisted and reversed?

While more questions can be developed around each of the issue areas, these are provided for the reader to bear in mind when reflecting upon the articles read. If you are an expert advisor in a position to make policy choices, or student of social change, you are doubtless engaged in a search for meaning. We hope this piece serves as a reminder that your search should include an exploration of your own personal and institutional history as well.

REFERENCES

Burrell, G., and G. Morgan. *Sociological Paradigms and Organizational Analysis.* London: Heinemann, 1979.

Fay, B. *Social Theory and Political Practice.* London: George Allen & Unwin, 1975.

Havelock, R.G., and M. Huberman. *Solving Educational Problems: The Theory and Reality of Innovation in Developing Countries.* Paris: UNESCO, 1977.

Mitroff, I., and R. Kilmann. *Methodological Approaches to Social Science: Integrating Divergent Concepts and Theories.* San Francisco: Jossey Bass, 1978.

Preston, P.W. *New Trends in Development Theory.* London: Routledge & Kegan Paul, 1985.

Reason, P., and J. Rowan (Eds.). *Human Inquiry. A Sourcebook for New Paradigm Research.* Chichester: John Wiley and Sons, 1981.

Thompson, J.B. *Studies in the Theory of Ideology.* Berkeley: University of California Press, 1984.

CONTRIBUTORS

NELLY P. STROMQUIST is professor of education at the University of Southern California in Los Angeles. She specializes in international development education, which she observes from a sociological perspective. Her research addresses questions of gender, equity policy, and adult education in developing countries, particularly in Latin America and West Africa. Her most recent publications include authoring the books *Literacy for Citizenship: Gender and Grassroots Dynamics in Brazil* (SUNY Press, 1997) and *Increasing Girls' and Women's Participation in Basic Education* (IIEP, 1997), and editing *Women in the Third World: An Encyclopedia of Contemporary Issues* (Garland, 1998).

MICHAEL BASILE is currently the director of the Institute for International Studies at Murray State University in Kentucky. Previously, he served as associate director of the Center for International Studies and assistant professor of the Adult Education and International Development Education programs at Florida State University. His most recent publication on the school, the community, and development appears in *A Handbook of Education in the 21st Century* (William Cummings and Noel McGinn, eds., Elsevier Science 1997). He is currently working on several nonformal educational innovations studies dealing with community participation and development conducted in west Africa. His interest in governance and education innovation in local Tallahassee schools is the subject of a recent study of direct relevance to community participation and involvement.

FÉLIX CADENA did graduate studies in social sciences at University of Louvain. He has worked for many years in popular education programs emphasizing the formation of popular educators, the development of research methodologies to systematize knowledge from emancipatory programs, and the design of microregional development projects. Two of his most recent publications are *Learning to Become Entrepreneurial* (1966) and *Methodological Guidelines for Microregional Development* (1977). He is founder and member of international networks, including the Latin American Council for Adult Education, and the International Council for Adult Education. Currently, he is the general coordinator of the Latin American Foundation to Support Popular Knowledge and Economy.

WILLIAM K. CUMMINGS is professor of comparative education and director of the Center for Comparative and Global Studies of the University at Buffalo. He has sought in his career to combine practice and scholarship in the effort to understand educational reform. He has spent fifteen years in various overseas setting primarily in East and Southeast Asia. Currently he is serving as senior policy advisor to the Ministry of Education in Ethiopia. Author or editor of 18 books, the most recent are *The International Handbook of Education and Development* (Oxford: Pergamon, 1997) with Noel McGinn and *Quality Education for All: A Community Oriented Approach* (New York: Garland, 1997) with Dean Nielsen.

SYDNEY R. GRANT is professor emeritus from Florida State University's College of Education, having served for many years in the Department of Educational Foundations and Policy Studies. He received his M.A. from the National Autonomous University of Mexico and his Ph.D. from Teachers College, Columbia University. He has served in research and consulting positions in the United States, Namibia, Botswana, Peru, Ecuador, Indonesia, Thailand, Nepal, and other countries. His most recent publications have dealt with education in Peru, and education for citizenship in the United States and the world.

H. DEAN NIELSEN worked for several years as senior program officer for education in Asia with the International Development Research Center (Canada). He is interested in teacher training and innovations. He served as an associate professor in international education at the University of Hawaii. He is presently working in the evaluation of community schools in Egypt.

JOÃO BATISTA ARAUJO E OLIVEIRA has written extensively about educational technologies and innovations. He has held various technical and administrative positions in the national ministries of education, planning, and science and technology in Brazil and has worked for the World Bank in Washington, D.C., and the International Labor Organization in Geneva. He is currently working as a consultant and is president of JM-Associados.

FRANÇOIS ORIVEL is professor of economics of education at the Université de Bourgogne, France. He was previously a researcher and professor at the Institute for Economic Research, Universite de Lyon.

MARIA DEL PILAR O'CADIZ is assistant professor of education at Pacific Oaks College, California, where she coordinates an internship program integrating antibias and multicultural curriculum approaches. She obtained her Ph.D. in comparative education from the University of California, Los Angeles. Her areas of interest include: Chicano and Latin American social and cultural history, education and development in Latin America, and bilingual and multicultural education in the United States with a theoretical foundation in critical pedagogy.

ROSA MARÍA TORRES is an educator and linguist with vast experience in teacher-training and literacy programs. She worked in Nicaragua between 1981–1986 in the adult education process that followed the Nicaraguan literacy campaign. Between 1988–1990 she was the pedagogical director of the "Monsignor Leonidas Proaño" National Literacy Campaign in Ecuador. She has worked as senior education adviser for UNICEF-New York and as the Director of Programs for Latin America and the Caribbean of the W.K. Kellogg Foundation. She is currently a researcher at the Latin American regional office of the International Institute for Educational Planning-UNESCO in Buenos Aires.

Index

PAMONG (Indonesia), 112–13, 122, 125, 126, 127, 128, 133, 136
parents, 32, 87, 88, 112, 122, 158
Partido dos Trabalhadores (Brazil), 14, 21–24, 25–55
pedagogical technology, 8, 24, 28, 71
peer-mediated instruction. *See* tutors
Philippines, The, 13, 112, 115–16, 121, 125, 127, 128, 130, 131, 135, 136, 137
planning. *See* innovations, design/planning
policy, 5, 7, 11, 59, 67, 71, 72, 73, 88, 89(n8), 138, 202
political influences (influences of a political nature), 5, 7, 9, 11, 13, 14, 17, 21, 22, 23–24, 25, 43, 45, 47, 48, 94–97, 103–06, 107, 137, 139, 212–13
political awareness (teaching of), 24, 25, 30, 35, 42, 45, 55, 56(n7), 161–62
popular education. *See* nonformal education
poverty, 15, 21, 22, 25, 30, 33–34, 41–42, 60–61, 198, 200–03, 210, 218
primary education, 13, 14, 16, 21, 59, 60, 62, 63, 71, 111, 125, 128, 130, 143–44, 205
PRIMER (Jamaica), 113
principals, 29
private schools, 21

quality, 15, 59, 62 , 64–69, 158–161

radio, 197, 207, 243
repetition, 167
replication of societal norms. *See* social reproduction
research, 5–7, 59, 70, 138
methodology. *See* methodology
resistance (to change/innovation). *See also* innovation, obstacles, 4, 5, 13, 14, 17, 45–50, 94, 103–06, 119–20, 121–22, 127–28, 137, 138
restructuring. *See also* institutionalization of innovation, 7
risk, 4–5,1 3, 130

rural education. *See also* teachers, rural, 12–13, 111–140(ch), 126, 128, 129, 137–38, 142–43, 144, 145, 146–65, 204, 206, 207, 210, 218

Sao Paulo. *See* Brazil
science, 51, 69, 102
secondary education, 12–13, 61, 80, 143, 144, 146–65
self-instructional modules, *See* modules)
Sida. *See* donor agencies
site-based management, 7
social class. *See* socio-economic class
social reproduction, 5, 12, 118, 160–65
socio-economic class, 23, 42, 150, 159, 160, 162–163. *See also* poverty
state, 7, 10–11, 21, 62, 229, 237, 245, 246
students, 3, 12, 31, 32, 35–36, 46, 112, 121, 145, 149, 150, 158–60
studies (to prepare for funding/innovation), 63, 68, 69–70, 80, 83, 88–89(n1)
supervisors, 111, 127, 149
systemic (comprehensive) reform, 6–8, 12, 73, 97. *See also* institutionalization of innovation and organizational change/learning

teachers, 3, 8, 14, 15, 17, 23, 29, 31, 35–36, 38–48, 50, 53, 65, 104, 114, 123, 147, 157, 158, 160, 178
absenteeism, 84
experience, 70, 179
recruitment, 71
rural, 15, 111–14, 121–22
salaries of, 15, 56(n12), 62, 65, 71, 78, 80, 84, 85, 121, 126, 168, 180, 194
tele-teachers (Mexico), 147, 149, 152, 153, 154, 158
training of, 12, 15, 27, 28–29, 32, 35–37, 50–51, 65, 67, 70–71, 78–83, 106, 107, 113, 152
unions, 67, 121, 153–55, 237
teaching centers, 172, 183